BUILDING a PROFESSIONAL LEARNING COMMUNITY at WORK™
A GUIDE TO THE FIRST YEAR

PARRY **GRAHAM** WILLIAM M. **FERRITER**

Foreword by
Richard DuFour
Rebecca DuFour

Solution Tree | Press

a division of
Solution Tree

555 North Morton Street
Bloomington, IN 47404
800.733.6786 (toll free) / 812.336.7700
FAX: 812.336.7790

email: info@solution-tree.com
solution-tree.com

Printed in the United States of America

13 12 11 10 09   1 2 3 4 5

FSC
Mixed Sources
Product group from well-managed forests and other controlled sources
Cert no. SW-COC-002283
www.fsc.org
© 1996 Forest Stewardship Council

Library of Congress Cataloging-in-Publication Data

Graham, Parry.

  Building a professional learning community at work : a guide to the first year / Parry Graham, William Ferriter; foreword by Richard DuFour and Rebecca DuFour.

     p. cm.

  Includes bibliographical references and index.

  ISBN 978-1-934009-59-8 (perfect bound) -- ISBN 978-1-935249-22-1 (library binding) 1. Professional learning communities--United States. I. Ferriter, William. II. Title.

  LB1731.G67 2010

  370.71--dc22

              2009027099

President: Douglas Rife

Publisher: Robert D. Clouse

Director of Production: Gretchen Knapp

Managing Editor of Production: Caroline Wise

Senior Production Editor: Suzanne Kraszewski

Copy Editor: Linda Harrison

Proofreader: Elisabeth Abrams

Editorial Assistant: Sarah Payne-Mills

Cover and Text Designer: Orlando Angel

DEDICATION

To my mom and dad—who have cheered from the sidelines since the day that I was born—and to my Aunt Brenda, who showed me how noble it is to *teach*

—Bill Ferriter, September 2009

To my daughter, who arrived right before the book began; to my son, who arrived right before the book was finished; and to my wife, who has been there every step of the way

—Parry Graham, September 2009

ACKNOWLEDGMENTS

Like all pieces of writing, *Building a Professional Learning Community at Work* is the product of a thousand conversations and shared experiences. For Bill, those conversations began with the Teacher Leaders Network (TLN), an online community of accomplished teachers who have nurtured his thinking since 2003. Sponsored by the Center for Teaching Quality, TLN and its cadre of practitioners—represented by the likes of John Norton, Barnett Berry, Nancy Flanagan, Renee Moore, John Holland, Susan Graham, and Marsha Ratzel—have served as a constant proving ground and sounding board for Bill's ideas and resources around teacher leadership and professional learning communities.

They continued with his friends and colleagues at Salem Middle School in Apex, North Carolina, who have worked together to explore professional learning communities first-hand since the spring of 2005. Wrestling through the inherent challenges of teaming with Mike Hutchinson, Emily Swanson, Marcy Russell, and Corinna Knight has been equal parts exhaustion and inspiration. The steady confidence of colleagues like Chris Baker and Margaret Feldman paired with the camaraderie of colleagues like Karen Beazlie and Tad Sherman justify Bill's never-ending belief in the power of professional learning communities.

For Parry, those conversations began at North Andover High School. He appreciated and relied on the collegial support of Artha Gerland, Mario Giordano, Ed Martin, Susan Nicholson, and many others. At Co-nect, Parry had the opportunity to work with a number of talented people who pushed—and continue to push—his thinking, most notably Adam Garry, Jean Teillon, Cynthia Addison, and Chip Morrison. From the University of North Carolina at Chapel Hill, Parry is indebted to Fenwick English, Jim Veitch, Neil Shipman, Bill Malloy, Thad Urban, Stan Shainker, and Lori Bruce. In his work in Wake County, Parry has grown as a result of the leadership and support of Dan Burch, Kathy Marynak, Julye Mizelle, and the staffs of Salem Middle School, Cedar Fork Elementary, and Lufkin Road Middle.

For both Bill and Parry, the staff of Solution Tree has been a tremendous support. Gretchen Knapp helped shepherd the book from a rough first draft to a much-improved final copy, with kind words at every step of the way. Caroline Wise has helped through the details and process, keeping everything on track.

In the end, though, Bill and Parry both owe the deepest gratitude to Matt Wight, their principal, mentor, and friend. Without his willingness to question, to believe, to challenge, and to support, this book would never have been possible!

Solution Tree Press would like to thank the following reviewers:

Diane Abbas
 Language Arts Teacher
 Dakota Hills Middle School
 Eagan, Minnesota

Rebecca DuFour
 Author and Consultant
 Moneta, Virginia

Richard DuFour
 Author and Consultant
 Moneta, Virginia

Diana Oxley
 Project Director, Recreating Secondary Schools Program
 Northwest Regional Educational Laboratory
 Portland, Oregon

Paul Wiese
 Principal
 LaGrange Elementary School
 Tomah, Wisconsin

Visit **go.solution-tree.com/PLCbooks** to download the reproducibles in this book.

TABLE OF CONTENTS

Italicized entries indicate reproducible forms.

ABOUT THE AUTHORS

A National Board Certified Teacher, **William M. Ferriter** has been honored as a North Carolina Regional Teacher of the Year. Bill has worked as a contractor for Pearson "Learning" (online) Solutions, designing professional development courses that empower educators with twenty-first-century skills. His trainings include the creative use of blogs, wikis, and podcasts in the classroom; the role of iTunes in teaching and learning; and the power of digital moviemaking for learning and expression. Bill has also developed schoolwide technology rubrics and surveys that identify student and staff digital proficiency at the building level. Bill has published articles in the *Journal of Staff Development, Educational Leadership,* and *Threshold.* Starting in September, 2009, he will write a column on technology in the classroom for *Educational Leadership.* His blog, the Tempered Radical, earned Best Teacher Blog of 2008 from Edublogs. He is a contributor to *The Principal as Assessment Leader* and *The Teacher as Assessment Leader* (both Solution Tree Press, 2009).

Parry Graham is a middle school principal in Wake County, North Carolina. He began his career teaching high school German, and then left the classroom to work at Co-nect, a comprehensive school reform provider, where he designed and delivered national professional development programs focused on instructional quality and teacher collaboration. He has worked as an elementary and middle school assistant principal, and he currently holds a position as a clinical assistant professor in the School of Education at the University of North Carolina at Chapel Hill, where he completed his doctorate. Parry has published articles in the *Journal of Staff Development, Research in Middle Level Education Online, Connexions,* and *TechLearning.*

FOREWORD

Throughout history, people in cultures all over the world have used stories to convey important ideas, to describe exemplars, and teach important life lessons. Whether they are called parables, fables, allegories, or myths, stories are a powerful tool for influencing the ideas and behaviors of others because they appeal to both the heart and the head. As Kouzes and Posner (1999) discovered in their study of excellent organizations, "Good stories move us. They touch us, they teach us, and they cause us to remember. They enable the listener to put the behavior in a real context and understand what has to be done in their context to live up to expectations" (p. 25).

When Patterson, Grenny, Maxfield, McMillan, and Switzler (2008) examined world-class "influencers"—people who had been successful in persuading others to change—they found these masters of motivation were particularly skillful in storytelling. As they wrote:

> People change how they view the world through the telling of vibrant and credible stories. . . . Concrete and vivid stories exert extraordinary influence because they transport people out of the role of critic and into the role of participant. (p. 61)

Peter Block (2003) agreed that "data and measures are not half as persuasive as anecdotes. Anecdotes, stories and personal reminiscences, like biblical parables, are the medium through which faith is restored" (p. 43).

In *Building a Professional Learning Community at Work: A Guide to the First Year*, Parry Graham and William Ferriter set out to restore the faith of educators that their efforts—when coordinated, collective, and collaborative—can have a significant impact on student achievement. In doing so, they weave a story, "the strongest structure for any argument" (Kouzes & Posner, 1999, p. 101) that is both refreshingly candid and powerfully compelling.

In describing the trials and tribulations of Steve and Michael as they attempt to transform a good school into a high-performing professional learning community, Graham and Ferriter write with the honesty and insight that can only be acquired through direct experience. The tale that they tell is clearly not a work of fiction but rather represents the very predictable issues and challenges that any faculty will face when they attempt to engage in the substantive changes necessary to create a professional learning community. It is not easy to move from a focus on teaching to a focus on learning; from working in isolation to working collaboratively; from individual teachers determining what to teach and how to assess their students to collaborative teams establishing a guaranteed curriculum and common formative assessments to inform teacher practice; from isolated teachers determining how to intervene when students struggle and enrich learning when they are proficient to systematic intervention and enrichment that benefit all students—regardless of the teacher to whom they are assigned. Graham and Ferriter do not offer a rosy, optimistic picture of a smooth school transition. Instead, they present, repeatedly, a very powerful message with two unmistakable points—building a professional learning community is really hard work, and it is well worth the effort.

Thankfully, this message goes well beyond the too common but imminently unhelpful lament that "change is hard." The authors present lessons from the front line and specific recommendations to ensure that readers do not miss the moral of each story. The very specific strategies, processes, tools, and templates they offer for overcoming obstacles represent a tremendous resource for educators willing to tackle the challenge of transforming their schools.

There is so much to recommend about this book. The conversational tone makes it extremely easy to read. Although it presents research from both inside and outside of education in each chapter to buttress its arguments, the entire book offers language educators can readily understand because it is the language they use in their day-to-day work.

One of the most common questions we hear from educators who become willing to implement the PLC concept in their own schools is, "But where do we start?" Graham and Ferriter have answered that question, very specifically, in this powerful book. It is a wonderful contribution to the literature on Professional Learning Communities at Work, and we highly recommend it to educators at all levels who recognize that the practices of the past are inadequate to meet the challenges of the present.

—*Richard and Rebecca DuFour*

References

Block, P. (2003). *The answer to how? is yes: Acting on what matters.* San Francisco: Berrett-Koehler.

Kouzes, J., & Posner, B. (1999). *Encouraging the heart: A leader's guide to rewarding and recognizing others.* San Francisco: Jossey-Bass.

Patterson, K., Grenny, J., Maxfield, D., McMillan, R., & Switzler, B. (2008). *Influencer: The power to change anything.* New York: McGraw-Hill.

A NEW BEGINNING

Sitting at his desk, Steve could not believe his luck. Having worked in the Seneca Township School District as a building principal for the past nine years, he knew he was a respected leader with a wide range of experiences, but like most educators, he did not see himself as anything special. That is why his conversation over lunch with district superintendent Patricia Tines had caught him by surprise.

"Steve," said Superintendent Tines, "I've got an important role for you to fill, and I'm hoping that you'll agree to a bit of a change."

Never one to shy away from change, Steve was excited. In fact, an inherent fear of stagnation had always pushed him professionally. He had moved from a successful ten-year career as a high school English teacher into administration, intent on having a greater impact on more students by working beyond the classroom—and once there, he discovered that he loved learning about leadership. Schools were tricky places built on social relationships and influence, but Steve was an old pro at using relationships to drive change. What is more, he spent countless hours reading, determined to understand the inner workings of organizations. He always seemed to get the most out of his teachers, and as a result, his schools always seemed to produce impressive results, regardless of the student population they served. Kids were learning in Steve's buildings, and he was incredibly proud of that.

"Allen Jenkins—the principal at Central Middle School—is retiring next year," continued Superintendent Tines. "I'm sure you know that Central Middle has been one of the flagship schools in Seneca Township since it opened ten years ago. In many ways, it is the heart of our community. . . . I'd like you to be Central's principal, Steve, and I'd like you to begin building a professional learning community from the ground up. What do you think?"

Steve knew immediately that this was an opportunity he would never pass up. He loved his current faculty—they had turned around a struggling building together in the span of four short years—but Central Middle's visibility would make this position one of the most challenging he had ever considered, and Steve loved a good challenge. He accepted without hesitation. "I'm honored that you'd think of me, Pat. Leading Central Middle is the dream of any principal in our district. Count me in!"

Dreaming would not guarantee Central Middle's success, though. Like any high-performing school, Central Middle would need a collection of determined teachers willing to learn from each other, to perfect their craft, and—most importantly—to work tirelessly on behalf of children. Steve understood that in most buildings, untapped power rested in the hearts and minds of teachers working collaboratively. He had seen it happen time after time in small pockets of every school that he had ever led: the elective teachers who found new ways to integrate reading into their classrooms, the math teachers who identified a handful of skills central to student success, the social studies teachers who engaged in research with one another, studying the impact that their practices had on different groups of students.

While Steve had tried to spread the pockets of practice across his entire building in the past, his efforts always felt somewhat scattered. Instead of creating the conditions that would make such collective action a part of the very fabric of his schools, Steve found himself reacting to what he learned: seeing something impressive, introducing it to influential teachers, and then hoping change would stick. "Central Middle School is going to be different," Steve thought to himself. "We're going to get schoolwide collaboration right this time, finding a way for every teacher to be a leader and a learner."

Catching his breath, Steve made his first decision as Central Middle School's new principal: he picked up the phone and called Michael, an old friend and one of Central Middle's most talented, motivated, and influential teachers. "Hey, Michael," said Steve, "What would you think about helping me build a professional learning community?"

Getting Started

What a fantastic opportunity! Superintendent Tines gave Steve the chance to take all of his previous efforts at supporting collaboration and make them the cornerstone of his new building.

But how exactly is that done? How can administrators and motivated teachers take the promise of a professional learning community (PLC) and turn it into reality? Whether starting in a new building or working with the same colleagues from the past fifteen years, how can school leaders transform theories of collaboration into highly effective nuts-and-bolts practices? This book is designed as a guide for accomplishing that difficult task, chronicling the efforts of Steve and his teachers to build a true PLC at Central Middle School and focusing on the successes and challenges inherent in the process.

The lessons in *Building a Professional Learning Community at Work* are drawn from our own experiences working in a variety of roles as practitioners—as teachers, building administrators, consultants, and coaches—at the elementary, middle, and high school levels. From those experiences, we have learned that powerful collaboration can happen anywhere, but it requires hard work, purposeful steps, and a deep understanding of the PLC model. The tools in this book have been tested time and again by our own teachers and our own teams, and our suggestions have helped to improve practices in our own schools. We hope this book serves as an effective introduction to the kinds of steps you can take to polish professional learning in your own buildings.

Each chapter includes these four elements:

1. **An Opening Story**—This book, at its core, is the story of Steve and his teachers, so each chapter starts with a narrative highlighting an important event in their growth together as a learning community. One question you might ask is, "Are the stories true?"

   As an answer, consider the range of movies that attempt to portray true stories. At one end of the spectrum are documentaries, which try to record real events exactly as they happen and real people exactly as they are. At the other end of the spectrum are movies "inspired by real events." (In other words, somebody somewhere did something that is sort of like one of the events in this story, but almost everything that you see here is complete fiction.)

   In between are movies "based on true events"—the stories and people are real, but changes have been made to create a clear narrative. Maybe the traits and actions of several people were combined together into one character, or words that were said at different times are put together into one monologue.

   This is what we have tried to do in *Building a PLC at Work*: create a series of stories that are based on true events from the schools in which we have worked. We have rearranged some characters and added some dialogue, but each of these stories represents the real-life experiences of actual teachers and administrators going through the difficult work of creating PLCs.

2. **Lessons From the Front Line**—This second section of each chapter explores what you can learn from the choices Steve and his teachers made. Like a postgame locker-room conversation between a coach and his athletes, this section spotlights the successful decisions and common mistakes made by the characters in the opening narrative. You get a firsthand look into our minds because we lived each of these experiences. We hope our insights help you when you are faced with similar situations.

   The value in "Lessons From the Front Line" is in the process of learning from any story: you have the opportunity to work through imaginative rehearsals, mentally practicing responses to real events. The chances are good that you will experience many of the same challenges that Steve and his Central Middle School colleagues tackled as you push to become a PLC. Taking the time to think through your own decisions and to see how they compare to the decisions made by our fictional characters will leave you better prepared to lead when the time is right.

3. **Relevant Theory and Research**—Change in schools depends on one of the most challenging tasks faced by leaders in any profession: changing behaviors. It is not enough for school leaders—whether they be principals or teachers working on learning teams—to identify new instructional materials or to find faster ways to get students through lunchroom assembly lines. Instead, school leaders have to actively manage the complexity of human organizations in order to succeed. Questions like, "How can I ensure that all teachers are pulling in the same

direction?" "What kinds of skills and support will teams need to move to new stages of collective action?" and "Which barriers will be the hardest to leap for teachers working together?" are inherently difficult to answer.

Thankfully, researchers have been studying human organizations—including schools—for almost a century. From Russian psychologist Lev Vygotsky (Vygotsky & Cole, 1978), who defined the kinds of tasks that individuals are ready to tackle at different stages of their growth, to American author Clay Shirky (2008), who explains how technology can facilitate transactions between colleagues working in groups, there are countless experts from whom principals and teacher leaders can learn.

In the "Relevant Theory and Research" section of each chapter, we introduce you to some of these experts and connect their findings to the work of professional learning communities. You will hear how Jim Collins' *hedgehog* concept (2001)—widely embraced by companies trying to streamline their products and processes—can help your building to focus on a handful of key ideas and behaviors. Philip Ball's overview of *phase transitions* (2004) shows you the kinds of conditions needed before rapid change can take hold in an organization; and James Surowiecki's explanation of *collective intelligence* (2004) provides insight into the strength found in diverse, independent, and decentralized teams.

Our hope is that this section of each chapter provides you with an approachable framework for understanding—and a language for describing—the complex, yet predictable, changes that are inevitable when schools restructure as professional learning communities.

4. **Recommendations**—In many ways, the "Recommendations" section of each chapter may be the most valuable, offering a collection of suggestions from which to draw while you work through change in your building. In this section you learn how to turn the key principles of your mission statement into stories that faculty members can learn from. We will introduce you to the rationale behind establishing a clear set of nonnegotiables to guide decision making in your building. We stress the importance of striking a balance between supporting and challenging learning teams, share strategies for building relationships through conversations, and emphasize the importance of seeing value in processes instead of products.

As lonely as leading a PLC or working on a struggling learning team can feel when things go wrong, there are always time-tested proactive steps you can use to move your school forward. "Recommendations" introduces you to the best of those steps.

There is no one right way to read this book. If you are motivated by narrative, start with page one and experience how Steve and Michael grow with their colleagues over the course of one full school year together. As the title suggests, *Building a PLC at Work* is organized chronologically. The first chapter shows Steve working to set core principles in place as he interviews a teacher for Central Middle's faculty; chapter 4 takes place in the heart of winter when Central Middle's teachers are exhausted and questioning their decision to collaborate; and chapter 8 is the story of Central Middle's successes—with equal parts looking back and looking forward.

While we have chosen to set *Building a PLC at Work* in the context of one year in the life of a PLC, real-life teams and teachers confront the events our characters experience at different times in the cycle of their work together. The conflict that threatens to tear Michael's team apart in November of their first year working closely together may be the kind of struggle that your team is wrestling with right now. For many readers, selecting individual chapters that offer timely and appropriate advice may be a more productive strategy for tackling the text in its entirety. Either approach will work—each chapter stands alone as a minilesson on PLCs.

To help you decide on the right strategy for reading, here is an overview of each of the eight chapters broken into four broadly themed, chronological sections: summer, fall, winter, and spring.

Summer: Committing to a Common Purpose

Chapter 1—Starting With a Vision

The first chapter begins by describing how Steve—Central Middle School's new principal—uses stories during the interview process to introduce professional learning communities to potential faculty members and to establish several core principles as nonnegotiables. The chapter continues with a description of the PLC model, emphasizing the importance a clear vision plays in creating a true learning community. The chapter concludes with specific recommendations on developing a school vision and how school leaders can use a clear vision to set the foundation for later success.

Chapter 2—Empowering the Core Team

The second chapter explores the important role a core group of respected faculty members can play in building a PLC, beginning with a story about the development of Central Middle School's mission statement. The chapter provides recommendations on the appropriate steps for identifying core team members, with an emphasis on the different kinds of personalities necessary for influencing an entire faculty. After reviewing relevant theory and research, the chapter concludes with a discussion of strategies for ensuring that core teams become catalysts for schoolwide improvement.

Fall: Building a Team

Chapter 3—Creating Trust

The third chapter tackles the challenge of introducing collaborative work in a profession typified by isolation and individual effort, beginning with a story about one team's experiences with members' first opportunities to observe each other in action. This chapter then examines how trust between teachers can influence the work of effective learning teams, focusing on the kinds of actions and behaviors necessary for making collective work safe. By paying attention to the details of team trust, teachers can lay the practical foundations necessary for supporting ongoing conversations focused on teaching and learning.

Chapter 4—Supporting Team Development

Michael and his sixth-grade language arts/social studies colleagues melt down for the first time in chapter 4, after trying to tackle a task for which they were poorly prepared. The lesson Steve and his teachers learn is painfully simple: learning teams, like individuals, are dynamic—not static. They are constantly growing and evolving over time. This chapter describes a continuum of team maturity and provides customized suggestions for supporting teams ready for different developmental challenges. We have included checklists that readers can use to assess the growth of the learning teams in their buildings and offer strategies for dealing with conflict—the most challenging work faced by any group of teachers working collaboratively.

Winter: Weathering the Challenges

Chapter 5—Negotiating Personalities and Conflict

One of the common outcomes of in-depth collaboration is contention. Disagreements will inevitably arise as teachers discuss and debate the teaching and learning process. Chapter 5 begins with a story detailing a conflict among members of a professional learning team over an instructional practice. Readers then explore the root causes of contention within a PLC structure and identify practical ways to deal with disagreements. Special emphasis is given to the elements of team-based conflict Patrick Lencioni (2002) describes in *The Five Dysfunctions of a Team: A Leadership Fable*.

Chapter 6—Experiencing Frustration

An uncomfortable reality for any principal or teacher working in a PLC is that collaboration is not always pretty. In fact, as Steve learns in the story that starts chapter 6, collaboration can be downright frustrating! Frictions naturally develop between colleagues working closely together in any profession, and those frictions can bring collective action to a grinding halt. This chapter introduces readers to the common sources of friction in PLCs, and then explains how you can use twenty-first-century tools to enhance cooperation in your building.

Spring: Looking Forward

Chapter 7—Connecting Data Analysis and Instructional Improvement

Chapter 7 focuses on the most important product of a functioning PLC: improved teaching and learning. The central challenge for any school leader is to keep the work of teacher teams focused on measurable results. Beginning with the story of a group of teachers sharing the results of a common assessment for the first time, this chapter reveals the fears associated with conversations about results. This chapter identifies specific ways the PLC structure can support the use of data to drive decision making and looks at the research concerning the concept of positive deviancy. The chapter also includes data literacy surveys that you can use to assess team readiness for analyzing results, as well as action planning templates for identifying the instructional practices that are best serving students.

Chapter 8—Building a Collective Intelligence

As teachers gradually learn how to work productively in an environment of collaboration and high expectations, teacher teams will become increasingly autonomous and effective. A school marked by high-performing teams requires a different leadership approach. Chapter 8 begins with the story of a high-functioning team reviewing videos of a lesson delivered by one member and focuses on strategies that school leaders can use to deepen and extend conversations about teaching and learning. This chapter also discusses how school leaders can support teams ready to systematically study their practice and implement interventions based on what they learn together.

In *Getting Started: Reculturing Schools to Become Professional Learning Communities*, Robert Eaker, Richard DuFour, and Rebecca DuFour (2002) identify in practitioners working in PLCs a penchant for sitting on the sidelines patiently waiting for others to lead:

> It is important to understand, however, that no school has ever made progress toward becoming a PLC until some of its members took steps to make it happen. There is a natural tendency to wait for someone else to take the initiative to improve our schools. Superintendents wait for more enlightened boards of education or more favorable state legislation, principals look to the central office, department chairpersons look to the principal, teachers look to department chairpersons, and so on. (p. 7)

Our hope is that this book will inspire you to get in the game. If you are a superintendent or an enlightened board of education member, make note of the challenges that Steve and his Central Middle School colleagues face, and identify a handful of strategies to emphasize in your district's leadership-development programs. If you are a building principal, read *Building a PLC at Work* reflectively, considering the current state of your own school. What has your faculty mastered? Where do you need to tighten a few practices or processes? If you are a full-time classroom teacher, use *Building a PLC at Work* to gain a better understanding of the strengths and weaknesses of your own learning team.

Professional learning communities can reinvigorate education in any building serving any grade level with any group of students as long as practitioners—regardless of position—decide to take action. If you are ready to lead, this book will show you where to start.

PART I

SUMMER: COMMITTING TO A COMMON PURPOSE

CHAPTER 1

STARTING WITH A VISION

Sarah thought that the last hour had gone well, but she still had a lot of questions. It was early summer, and she was interviewing for a position teaching sixth grade at Central Middle School, one of Seneca Township's best known schools. The school's new principal, Steve, had spent the last hour asking Sarah about her teaching experience and philosophy, and she was satisfied with the answers she had given.

"Steve, when we spoke last week on the phone you mentioned that you were interested in leading a nontraditional kind of school. I think the term you used was a *professional learning community*. Do you mind if I ask you some questions about what you mean, what you want this school to look like?"

"Please do!" Steve responded excitedly. He had enjoyed getting to know Sarah and was convinced she was the kind of accomplished teacher he wanted as a part of his faculty; however, he also knew it was critical for those he hired to have a clear idea of what he hoped Central Middle School would look like in action so they could decide if it was the right fit for them. Hiring accomplished teachers who could not buy into a school committed to collaboration was a recipe for failure, and Steve was smart enough to know it.

"So what do you mean when you say a 'professional learning community'? How would that be different from a typical school, like the one I'm working at now?"

"That's a good question," said Steve. "Let me start by telling you a story about a woman I used to work with. She was a middle school science teacher, and she was famous for her dinosaur unit. Every year, during the second quarter—and I mean the whole second quarter—this woman would teach her students about dinosaurs. They learned about the different eras in which dinosaurs lived, they learned about how dinosaurs evolved, they made dioramas with different dinosaur habitats. For two months these kids lived and breathed dinosaurs.

"Now, when you went into her classroom, her students were working hard. They were engaged, they had smiles on their faces, and they were learning a ton about dinosaurs. The problem was, dinosaurs weren't part of her curriculum. In fact, not one of the concepts her students learned about was in the state standards for her grade level.

"The more time I spent as an administrator getting into teachers' classrooms," Steve explained, "the more I realized that a lot of teachers had their own 'dinosaur' units: topics that they enjoyed teaching, but that had nothing to do with the curriculum. At first

I wanted to go to these teachers and tell them, 'Hey, teach the curriculum the way it's written!' But the more I thought about it, the more I realized that wouldn't have solved the problem. No one likes a heavy-handed principal, right?"

Besides, Steve knew that the real problem in most buildings was not about individual teachers and their favorite units; rather, it was about the underlying expectations of the environment in which they were working. Teachers who drifted drastically from the curriculum were expected to decide as individuals what they should teach, how they should teach it, and how they should test it—and that is what they were doing. They were making those decisions the best way they knew how.

If he were to change teacher behavior—get them to abandon their dinosaur units—he knew that he would have to change the expectations for how they made their decisions. That was his responsibility, not theirs.

"So how do you solve that problem?" Sarah asked. She understood Steve's frustration with dinosaur units—there was a guy teaching down the hall whose pirate unit was the talk of the town. Sarah just was not sure Steve could really do anything to make people change. Plenty of her colleagues over the past seven years had learned to teach what *the administrators* wanted on the days they were observed and what *they* wanted for the rest of the year without consequence.

"Well, the reality is that it is impossible for me to monitor what's happening in every classroom, every day," Steve continued. "That's why I've decided that, at Central, my primary focus is not going to be to evaluate the individual decisions that people make, but to evaluate the way that people make their decisions.

"You asked me earlier what a professional learning community is. Now, I've been thinking and reading about PLCs for years, and for me it boils down to a couple specific things, starting with the way people make decisions. In traditional schools, teachers make decisions individually—and everyone is going in entirely different directions. In a PLC, people make decisions collaboratively. That means my friend with the dinosaur unit can't decide by herself what she is going to teach. Instead, she's going to have to sit down with all of the other science teachers for her grade level and decide as a team what they are going to teach.

"If she can convince her colleagues that they should be teaching about dinosaurs for two months, then more power to her," said Steve, "but when that team sits down with the state standards and the district pacing guide, I'm guessing that she'll have a pretty tough sell."

Sarah looked a bit puzzled. "So what if that teacher just says, 'Forget it, I want to teach my dinosaur unit anyway'?" she asked.

"Well, that's where it becomes my responsibility," Steve explained. "But I'm no longer asking her to justify her dinosaur unit. Now I'm asking her to justify ignoring the collaborative decision of her peers. That's one thing that I will absolutely not budge on: if you're going to teach at this school, then you have to make the big decisions—especially curriculum and assessment decisions—in collaboration with colleagues."

"What about school leadership? Will you hold yourselves to the same standard of collaboration?"

"Absolutely, the same will hold true for me!" Steve replied. He really did want to be challenged when making decisions that impacted the other adults in Central Middle School. He was convinced that actions decided upon collectively were always better than decisions made in isolation. "If I'm taking steps all by myself, without input from the people who know the details of—and who will be directly affected by—a decision, then chances are the choices I end up making won't be the best."

"Won't this be hard?" pressed Sarah. "I mean, we all have different philosophies about what and how to teach. How can we get everyone to agree?"

"That's another great question, one I don't have the answer to yet," Steve replied honestly. "It's why I want to fill Central Middle School with professionally open and energetic people like you—to help me figure out how to do that. As long as we're all willing to commit to a vision of collaboration—making decisions together to do what is in the best interests of kids—I think we can come up with some pretty good answers."

Lessons From the Front Line

It is no coincidence that this first chapter focuses on Steve's attempts to articulate his vision for Central Middle School. Having an initial vision is critically important in the development of a successful professional learning community. Before joining Central Middle, Steve spent a lot of time creating a picture in his mind of what he wanted the school to look like, and he knew that this picture had to have an underlying vision that was simple, clear, and powerful.

So why is vision so important, and what role does it play in developing a PLC? What difference does it make if the teachers throughout the school have different ideas of what they are working toward and how they should get there?

Say you are a school leader like Steve, with a clear vision of what you want the central purpose of your building to be. How do you communicate those core principles to others? How can you ensure that key stakeholders throughout your school community buy into that vision and turn it into a reality?

For Steve, creating and communicating an initial vision depended on a number of effective practices. First, he made sure he knew what *he* was talking about. He became an expert on the PLC model and the strategies that underlie effective teacher collaboration. Next, Steve was dogged in his early efforts to emphasize his vision. In every conversation, Steve stuck to his message of collaboration as a unifying school theme. Finally, Steve was intent on modeling his vision through action, showing staff members he meant what he said.

This chapter explores the role that a clear vision plays in laying the foundation for an effective PLC. Specifically, it describes some of the central ideas that lie at the heart of a PLC and the importance of building leaders understanding those ideas, from administrators and instructional coaches to motivated classroom teachers. In addition, it discusses ways to communicate the vision to a school community and strategies to model the vision through specific actions. Finally, it looks at how highly successful businesses have used a simple principle known as the hedgehog concept (Collins, 2001) to keep themselves focused on their vision—and what school leaders can learn from these "good to great" companies.

Know Your Subject

In the story that begins this chapter, Steve mentions that he has spent a lot of time reading and thinking about PLCs, and he wasn't kidding. The more the staff got to know Steve, the more they realized just how deep his knowledge of PLC principles went. Steve had been to all of the relevant workshops by leaders of the learning community movement and had read all of the relevant literature. More importantly, Steve had spent time in countless conversations with practitioners about what learning communities actually looked like from a range of different perspectives within the schoolhouse.

At the same time, Steve was always trying to learn more. He continuously engaged others in open-ended conversations about the PLC model, and he brought a high level of humility to the process. Steve recognized that as much as he already knew, there was still so much to learn. In fact, by Steve's own account, he probably learned more in his first year at Central Middle than anyone else.

Steve's depth of knowledge was critically important. While the PLC model may seem simple on the surface, it actually represents a very sophisticated—and in some ways counterintuitive—idea of how an organization works. Because Steve had taken the time to learn about that model, he was well prepared when challenges and opportunities arose.

As Steve emphasizes in the story, the PLC model at its most basic level is about collaboration: people working and learning together. But not everyone believes that collaboration is an effective way to run a school—or any organization, for that matter. Back in the early 1900s, the exact opposite was believed to be true. Early assembly lines were based on the idea that a small group of people at the top of the organization should make decisions, while everyone else should execute those decisions exactly as told. Businesses were supposed to run like machines, with each worker performing a very simple, specific task over and over again without variation. If you wanted to improve the performance of your organization, you just had to improve the efficiency of each isolated task: get workers to do their little jobs even faster, and the business would progress.

That model may not be as outdated as it sounds. In fact, it plays itself out in our schools in the form of "teacher proof" curricula every single day. Teachers are asked to implement scripted lessons exactly as written, with no variation or innovation. Such programs—frequently found in schools serving high percentages of students living in poverty, where testing pressures can be overwhelming—are based on the same scientific management theories that defined American industry for decades: allow senior leaders at the district level to find a successful instructional practice, break down every step of the practice into the smallest possible routines, perform those routines exactly the same way in hundreds of classrooms regardless of student populations, and get the same results every time.

While such programs have, at times, produced measurable results on standardized exams, they often leave teachers discouraged and frustrated (Perlstein, 2007). In addition, they can limit the capacity of an organization to innovate and improve over time. Essentially, they can make teachers and schools static, rather than dynamic.

At the exact opposite end of the organizational spectrum is something called *living systems theory*. Within an organization, according to living systems theory,

> each organism maintains a clear sense of its individual identity within a larger network of relationships that helps shape its identity. Each being is noticeable as a separate entity, yet it is simultaneously part of the whole system. While we humans observe and count separate selves, and pay a great deal of attention to the differences that seem to divide us, in fact we survive only as we learn how to participate in a web of relationships. (Wheatley, 1999, p. 20)

Pretty heady stuff, no? But filled with jargon as that description may be, Steve knew that living systems theory and its focus on networks, systems, and relationships lay at the heart of the PLC model. *Collaboration* meant that he was not going to be the boss, telling everyone how to script their lessons each day. *Collaboration* meant that people throughout the school would be having conversations with each other, learning from each other, and making minute-by-minute, day-by-day instructional decisions based on the collective knowledge of the group. All of those decisions, big or small, would add up to the sum teaching and learning capacity of the school. As Margaret Wheatley (1999) said, "Each being is noticeable as a separate entity, yet it is simultaneously part of the whole system" (p. 20).

While Steve was strong on theory, he knew that theory could only get you so far with busy classroom teachers. So when he talked about PLCs, he did not talk about the differences between scientific management and living systems theory. Instead, Steve borrowed from Richard DuFour (2004a) to boil down his complex vision for collaboration into three concrete and operational expectations. Those expectations, delivered in language approachable to everyone from parents to practitioners, included:

- **A commitment to student learning**—Steve knew the success of the school depended on a deep belief in—and a commitment to ensuring—that all students can learn. He expected that teachers would do whatever it took to make sure that students were successful, and he reiterated that expectation over and over again.

- **No dinosaur units**—While this expectation brought chuckles when introduced to members of Steve's school community, it also resonated because of its painful basis in fact. To combat a sad side effect of the isolation that continues to characterize classrooms in the American schoolhouse, teams of teachers in Steve's building would work on same-subject, grade-level teams—and they would make major curricular decisions *collaboratively*.

- **A focus on results**—Steve planned to empower teachers to make the big decisions, but he wanted those decisions to be based on evidence instead of intuition. Working in teams, teachers would use common assessments to collect data about student progress and adjust curriculum and instruction as needed.

Steve took the time to understand the PLC model, both in theory and in practice. Moreover, he translated that understanding into a clear vision. As the year progressed, the faculty worked with Steve to turn that vision into a reality. But without that first foundation—without Steve's knowledge of PLC principles and his idea of what those principles should look like in practice—none of the later successes would have been possible.

Stay on Message

If you have ever watched successful politicians debate, you have probably noticed that they are really good at staying on message. No matter what questions are posed, no matter what their opponents might say, they always figure out a way to bring their answers back to their central pitch: "I'm going to lower your taxes. I'm going to make America safe. I'll make sure every child in this country has health insurance."

It doesn't matter what their particular point might be. What matters is that they keep making that point, over and over again, until it sticks in people's heads.

In this respect, school leaders have to be good politicians too. In order to drive a vision home—to get it permanently stuck in staff members' heads and to make it part of the collective culture—they have to repeat that message over and over again.

In the conversation between Steve and Sarah, therefore, it is no accident that Steve tells the dinosaur unit story. In fact, he told that same story to every potential teacher he interviewed and to every existing faculty member he met. What made the dinosaur story so effective was that it took complex ideas—curriculum development and alignment, the isolating structure of schools as organizations—and translated them into something that was simple, practical, accessible, and memorable. Almost anyone—including Sarah—could relate to the story. Whether it is the high school U.S. history teacher who spends a month on the Revolutionary War and two days on the twentieth century, or the third-grade teacher who spends a month on poetry and two days on business letters, we all know the teacher Steve is describing.

Steve used storytelling to consistently and continuously reinforce his central vision for the school. Stories were particularly effective because they helped to distill his vision down into simple, specific talking points. Steve knew that implementing a PLC successfully was about much more than just getting people to work together, but he did not want to muddle his message. By telling the same story to every teacher at Central Middle, Steve was able to communicate his vision in a way that everyone could relate to, understand, and remember: at this school, we will all be expected to collaborate.

One of the other strengths of stories is that they are easy to retell, which highlights an additional strategy in vision building: use others to communicate your vision for you. Once Sarah heard the dinosaur story, she turned around and told it to others. Whether speaking with colleagues at her old school or talking to other teachers at Central Middle after she had been hired, Sarah was able to use the dinosaur story as shorthand for Steve's vision of collaboration. The more the dinosaur story was told and retold, the more deeply that vision of collaboration became a part of the initial culture of the school. Because

Steve stayed consistently on message in his conversations, he ensured that the vision of collaboration would be a consistent message in later conversations, even when he was not present.

Steve had learned an important lesson early on: sticking to talking points is essential for creating a vision that others can believe in. As Richard DuFour and Robert Eaker (1998) note in *Professional Learning Communities at Work*: *Best Practices for Enhancing Student Achievement*:

> What separates a learning community from an ordinary school is its collective commitment to guiding principles that articulate what the people in the school believe and what they seek to create. Furthermore, these guiding principles are not just articulated by those in positions of leadership; even more important, they are embedded in the hearts and minds of people throughout the school. (p. 25)

By staying on message no matter the situation, Steve was able to slowly embed his fundamental vision for Central Middle in the hearts and minds of his teachers. If, at the end of Steve's first year at Central Middle, you asked a faculty member to describe what the school was about, the answer—no matter who you spoke to—was always, "Collaboration."

Model the Vision Through Action

It's one thing to consistently talk the talk. But in order to really convince the staff that he was serious about collaboration, Steve also had to walk the walk. In his conversation with Sarah, Steve tells her that he wants to be held to the same standard of collaboration as everyone else. Early in his tenure at Central Middle, Steve made a symbolic move that clearly showed he meant what he said.

Possibly the most important decision that a principal ever makes is who to hire. While other decisions may have a considerable short-term impact, the staff members a principal chooses will have the most substantial long-term impact on student learning. Steve used his vision of collaboration as a central criterion when selecting staff members; he made a point of hiring people, such as Sarah, who were committed to working in a team environment. Steve, however, took the vision one step further by actively involving faculty members in the process of selecting teaching candidates. In other words, Steve took one of his most important decisions—who to hire—and shared that power with his teachers.

Steve scheduled several hiring fairs that summer to fill open positions at Central. At these hiring fairs, he would invite faculty members already on staff to interview faculty candidates. This meant that teachers working in grade levels with openings were active participants in choosing their future teammates. Steve's intention in sharing the hiring decisions was twofold. First, he wanted to send a message that he meant what he said about collaboration. And second, Steve honestly believed that the school would end up with a more effective staff if hiring decisions were made collaboratively. He believed that existing faculty members, working as teams, would end up making better hiring decisions collectively than he would have been able to make individually. In fact, Steve only interviewed Sarah after she had been recommended by a faculty interviewing team.

This is a critical point. Many school leaders emphasize collaboration when talking about the work of others, but tend to deal with important decisions (such as staffing and budgeting) unilaterally. It is easy to understand why: as the person primarily held accountable for school performance, many administrators want to be the ones making big decisions. Their thinking is that if they are penalized for making an error, at least they will be in trouble for their own mistakes, not someone else's.

When a school leader asks others to collaborate on decisions that affect them, while not personally being willing to collaborate on decisions, he or she sends a mixed message: do what I say, not what I do. Steve knew that if he was not willing to model the behaviors he was asking others to adopt, they would be less likely to adopt them.

So Steve took some of his most important decisions and allowed others to participate in making them. He learned quickly that there was a great degree of competence on his staff, as incredibly complex questions were answered by thoughtful teachers exploring issues from a range of perspectives. Sometimes, however, he did end up cleaning up after a mistake that someone else made. By demonstrating to the rest of the staff that he was willing to join in collaborative decision making, Steve increased the odds that others would buy into the vision that he had for Central Middle.

Relevant Theory and Research

Developing and communicating a vision require knowing your subject, staying on message, and modeling the vision through action. But what makes vision so important? Does a school really need to have a clear vision to function effectively as a professional learning community?

Steve's own anecdotal experiences led him to believe that a unifying vision was a critical component to building a successful PLC. Research in the business world supports his belief. In Jim Collins' (2001) influential book *Good to Great: Why Some Companies Make the Leap . . . and Others Don't*, a team of business researchers led by Collins asked the question, what does it take for a good organization to become great? After studying Fortune 500 companies across the country, the team answered their question with a list of common practices implemented by the most successful companies. One of these practices is what the authors call the hedgehog concept.

The name of this concept is based on an ancient Greek parable in which a fox continually tries to outsmart (and to make dinner out of) a hedgehog. The fox is cunning and fast, with sharp teeth and a lightening attack. Day after day the fox implements ever newer, craftier ideas to try to catch the poor hedgehog. In contrast, the hedgehog is slow, with only one trick up his sleeve: rolling up in a ball and playing defense with its sharp quills when the fox attacks. Nevertheless, as basic as it may seem, the hedgehog's single-minded game plan always seems to work.

Extrapolating from this parable to the larger world, Collins (2001) argues that hedgehog-minded individuals and organizations do the following:

> [They] simplify a complex world into a single organizing idea, a basic principle or concept that unifies and guides everything. It doesn't matter how complex the world, a hedgehog reduces all challenges and dilemmas to simple—indeed almost simplistic—hedgehog ideas. (p. 91)

In other words, Collins and his team found that the most successful companies came up with a straightforward, compelling vision that drove everything they did. These companies did not jump on every new bandwagon that came along, flitting from new program to new program. Instead, they focused their efforts on a key strategy and stuck to it, ignoring anything that might distract their focus.

In developing visions, these companies tended to address three important questions. Where the answers to those three questions overlapped, the companies found their hedgehog concept. The three questions are as follows:

1. What can we be the best in the world at?

2. What drives our economic engine?

3. What are we deeply passionate about?

While the first two questions may not sound as if they pertain to the nonprofit education world, they do. Schools may not necessarily compete against each other to be the best, but they certainly strive for excellence (and some would argue that the annual publication of standardized test scores has bred competition to be the best). While schools may not have an economic engine, they do have multiple outcomes that drive their efforts, from test scores to parent participation scores to Friday night football scores. As to the third question, passion is clearly a key ingredient in public education.

Reflecting on these core issues simply must play a key role in the development of a school's vision. While no one has to specifically ask, "Hey, we need to think about those hedgehog questions from *Good to Great*," devoting considerable time, energy, and attention to addressing shared passions, directions, and commitments helps to ensure that a teaching staff remains focused as it works through what can often be ambiguous challenges. As Richard DuFour, Rebecca DuFour, and Robert Eaker note in *Revisiting Professional Learning Communities at Work: New Insights for Improving Schools* (2008), "When educators have a clear sense of the purpose, direction, and the ideal future state of their school or district, they are better able to understand their ongoing roles within the organization" (p. 143).

Answering the three hedgehog questions was critical to Central Middle School's success in developing as a true PLC. Prior to joining Central Middle, Steve visited other schools that had attempted to implement PLCs, some successfully and some not so successfully. In Steve's mind, the successful schools had created a consistent core vision, while the other schools had not. At the successful schools, staff members decided what they cared about, what they could excel at, and how they would gauge their success—they worked to build a "shared knowledge" of commitment and purpose (DuFour, DuFour, & Eaker, 2008). The staff at unsuccessful schools had not taken the time or expended the energy to have the conversations necessary to reach that level of agreement.

So when he moved to his new building, Steve decided to work with his faculty to use DuFour's (2004a) three tenets—a commitment to student learning, a collaborative approach to decision making, and the ongoing use of results—to answer the hedgehog questions:

- **What were they really passionate about?** Making sure that every child would be successful

- **What drove their engine?** The results from common, formative assessments given at all grade levels, which would be used to identify students that needed extra support or who were ready for greater challenge

- **What could they be the best in the world at?** Working collaboratively and learning from each other

Where those three questions overlapped—working collaboratively to ensure that every child was academically successful—became the "Central Vision."

While this might sound easy, it was not. At times, staff members did not want to go through the hassle of making decisions collaboratively—they just wanted to make their own individual decisions and move on. At times, teachers did not want to redouble their efforts to help struggling children—they just wanted to hand the students off to the guidance counselor or the special education teacher and move on. At times, administrators did not want to deal with the headache of empowered teachers—they just wanted to send out a memo and move on.

But if a building faculty truly believes in collaborative decision making, then staff members should be willing to accept some uncomfortable decisions. If they truly believe that every child can be successful, then they must create interventions and support structures that eliminate the opportunity for failure. If administrators truly believe that distributed leadership leads to better results, then it is time to take a deep breath and listen to the requests and opinions of empowered teachers. As we will discuss later, after the staff of Central Middle committed to their Central Vision, that vision became a powerful litmus test for decision making throughout the school.

In *Good to Great*, Jim Collins (2001) notes that the most successful companies continually wrestled with the hedgehog questions and came up with answers that defined who they were as an organization. At Central Middle, everything else followed from a clear and compelling vision. Without such a vision, no organization can become truly great.

Recommendations

If you are interested in creating a professional learning community, developing an initial vision is critical. Without it, a school or team lacks direction and consistency, leading to diffused efforts and miscommunication. With it, an organization is able to move forward on a path toward excellence. The following section outlines our most important recommendations for developing and communicating a vision.

Become an Expert, and Develop Expertise in Others

Before starting down the road to developing a PLC, a leader should understand what the PLC model entails. This means reading about PLCs, speaking to people who have worked in PLCs, listening to experts, and even visiting other schools. Steve put in the necessary time to become an expert and it paid off: he had a clear understanding of the challenges and opportunities that lay ahead, and he was able to speak about PLCs in a way that made the concepts understandable and attractive to others. We strongly recommend that administrators and instructional coaches in schools prepared to go down the PLC path take the time to learn as much as they can about PLC principles.

In addition to developing their own expertise, school leaders must also focus on developing expertise in others. Steve regularly recommended books and articles to his teachers, always happy to engage in a discussion about the details of the PLC model. We recommend that any school leader do the same. By carefully developing expertise in all corners of a building, leaders accomplish two goals. First, they increase the chances that other staff members will be able to successfully put PLC principles into practice; and second, they create fertile ground for professional conversations. As Steve tells Sarah in the story that starts this chapter, he does not have all the answers—he is counting on others to help him find those answers. By distributing expertise throughout the staff, school leaders deepen early conversations and improve the quality of the answers that a staff develops.

The materials at the end of this chapter are designed to provide school leaders—from practitioners to principals—with a basic understanding of the key elements of any PLC. The Capacity of a Professional Learning Community: Four Interconnected Factors (page 17) describes the four parts of a PLC—new structures and procedures, improved communication, enhanced teacher learning, and collective ownership and intelligence—that make the primary goal of improved student learning possible. The checklist that follows the diagram, the Professional Learning Community Capacity Planning Checklist (see pages 18–20), describes each part in greater detail and can be used by leadership teams to identify practical action steps for moving their school forward.

Treat Every Conversation as a Leading and Learning Opportunity

Especially early on, Steve treated every conversation with staff as an opportunity to reinforce the vision of Central Middle School. He stayed on message, and that meant that faculty members were crystal clear on his expectations and vision. Steve also saw early conversations as learning opportunities. Steve knew that he was not the only one with answers, and he was interested in the ideas and perspectives of others. So even though Steve was on message, he was talking with an open mind, ready to hear how his message resonated with others, and interested in what his teachers thought, too.

This two-way conversational style accomplishes many purposes. First, it means that all staff members are constantly in a position to learn from those leading change efforts in buildings and that those leading change efforts are constantly learning from other staff members. At Central Middle, it also meant that faculty members felt respected—validated when Steve listened to their thoughts and empowered when those ideas turned into action. Finally, two-way dialogue from school leaders models a collaborative tone: the *learning* in a professional learning community is largely a result of shared conversations, and leaders should start those conversations—and the learning that accompanies them—from the first day.

Simple tracking sheets like the one included at the end of this chapter (see the Conversation Tracking Sheet on page 21) can be used to systematically reinforce core principles through conversations. By carefully recording the results of individual conversations, school leaders gain a more complete picture of the changing levels of commitment to core principles across an entire grade level, department, or building.

Turn Principles Into Stories

At its heart, a school's vision should be based on a few nonnegotiable principles. Those principles, in turn, become the guide for decision making throughout the school. Explaining those principles to others, however, can be tricky. What does it mean to say that staff members will be expected to "collaborate," or to "work together to ensure the success of every student"?

Stories help in two ways. First, they translate philosophical principles into real-world, day-by-day actions. Second, they create a shorthand way for people to remember complex ideas. In fact, according to cognitive psychologist Daniel Willingham (2009), "The human mind seems exquisitely tuned to understand and remember stories—so much so that psychologists sometimes refer to stories as 'psychologically privileged,' meaning that they are treated differently in memory than other types of material" (p. 51).

Steve's dinosaur unit tale is a good example. After hearing that story, no teacher at Central Middle could turn around, create a "dinosaur" unit, and then plead ignorance. Through an interesting narrative that every teacher could embrace and remember, Steve clearly translated a core element of his vision—making curricular decisions collaboratively—into day-to-day actions.

Try using the Turning Principles Into Stories handout (pages 22–23) to develop your own list of similar stories. Was there a teacher in your building who never let a child fail and always went the extra mile to ensure success? Conversely, was there a teacher who bragged about his high standards while half of the students in his class received failing grades on their report cards? Was there a novice teacher in the school that experienced tremendous success because she was supported by a strong team? Was there a master teacher who learned some new tricks after opening himself up to grade-level collaboration?

The key to articulating complex ideas in ways that resonate does not depend on being an accomplished writer or storyteller. Instead, it depends on nothing more than your ability to choose a few believable stories that faculty members can relate to. Any memorable experience can be turned into a story that contains a clear and memorable message: this is how we will do things at this school, or this is *not* how we will do things at this school.

Recognize Your Responsibility

Building commitment to a common purpose in a PLC depends on the work of another overlooked group of educational stakeholders: teacher leaders. Struggling schools leave vision building in the hands of administrators. In successful schools, accomplished teachers step forward to lead, understanding that the key figures in any successful change effort are influential practitioners who can help colleagues to embrace new patterns of behavior. As DuFour, DuFour, and Eaker (2008) caution:

> When a group has a collective sense of ownership in and commitment to the future they are working together to create, vision can exert a powerful influence on their organization. If the vision represents the proclamation of a single leader or the words on a paper drafted at a Board of Education summer retreat, it will have little impact. (p. 120)

For Sarah, this meant actively working to share Central Middle's common purpose with every member of her growing network of connections in her grade level and department. She, too, became an avid reader and an expert in PLC principles, building a working knowledge of the core concepts of collaboration in tandem with Steve. She was particularly adept at identifying materials that made the learning community process practical for teachers and in helping Steve to translate ideas into actions. She also contributed by constantly starting positive conversations about the exciting opportunities that PLCs would bring to Central Middle. In many ways, her enthusiasm was contagious.

If you are a teacher who is not sure where to begin, consider using the description of professional learning teams included at the end of this chapter (see the Professional Learning Teams handout on page 24) to start conversations with colleagues about your current reality. Like principals, you can also use the Conversation Tracking Sheet (page 21) to make your efforts more thorough and systematic. Building successful PLCs starts with raising awareness, and raising awareness is a task that any teacher can tackle.

Don't Leave Vision Up to a Subcommittee

One final piece of advice is a *don't*: don't farm out the development of a vision to a subcommittee. Unfortunately, this happens too frequently in schools. We all know the drill: a small group of staff members with an intellectual bent sit around and debate where to put the commas and parenthetical clauses in a school's mission and vision statements—and the final product is generic and benign, meaning both anything and nothing at the same time. For example, "We believe that all students should have the twenty-first-century skills to experience true success, develop into productive citizens, and remain lifelong learners" (unless, of course, their math teachers decide that they did a sloppy job on their homework—or their language arts teachers decide that they have atrocious handwriting—in which case they will receive a string of zeros in the grade book).

A school's vision should be influenced by the building principal but decided on by his or her faculty. What is more, conversations around central principles—which can be structured with the Finding Your Hedgehog handout (page 25)—should generate some heat. When an entire staff takes the time to deeply discuss members' core beliefs, sparks are inevitable, as educators debate a shared direction that unites colleagues in a common purpose. Take the time and effort to make that first PLC foundation—the underlying vision—a strong anchor for your building's future growth.

The Capacity of a Professional Learning Community: Four Interconnected Factors

Four interconnected factors determine the capacity of a learning community. While each factor can be addressed individually to benefit student learning, maximum efficiency depends on finding connections between each area.

New Structures and Procedures

Highly functioning learning teams have formalized, collaborative ways of identifying essential learning goals, assessing the extent to which students have mastered those learning goals, and responding to differentiated student needs. Establishing structured procedures for each of these processes is essential for efficient collaboration.

Improved Communication

Teaching has long been defined by isolation. Educators have worked alone to address the needs of their students and rarely looked beyond their own classrooms. Schools functioning as PLCs see teachers engaged in frequent conversations, using communication to build shared understanding about teaching and learning. This collaborative work is built upon established systems for communication within and across learning teams.

Enhanced Teacher Learning

The most effective learning communities are defined by a spirit of reflection, an action orientation, and a focus on "collective inquiry" (DuFour, DuFour, & Eaker, 2008). Teachers are continuously revisiting their instruction together, working to tailor practices to match the individual needs of the student population they serve. Instructional capacity improves as teachers share ideas across classrooms and as they experience systematic training in action research or support for National Board certification.

Collective Ownership and Intelligence

Teachers take ownership of all students and respond as a collective entity to challenges and opportunities. They make efforts to identify and then amplify instructional practices that work—and to eliminate those that are ineffective. Teams create warehouses of best practices that all members of a faculty can draw from to develop an understanding of student needs.

Student Learning

The primary goal of any learning community—improving student learning—is limited only by a school's ability to establish new structures, improve communication, enhance teacher learning, and develop collective intelligence.

Professional Learning Community Capacity Planning Checklist

Building the capacity of a professional learning community requires principals, instructional coaches, and teacher leaders to take practical steps to move their teams and teachers forward. While planning initial efforts to introduce PLC principles in your school, use this checklist to consider the kinds of tasks that your faculty is ready to tackle today, and indicate in the column on the right what investments are necessary to accomplish each task.

Capacity Factor: New Structures and Procedures	
Tasks Our Building/Learning Team Is Uniquely Prepared to Tackle	**Investments Necessary to Accomplish Task (Time, Professional Development, Funding)**
☐ Use curriculum mapping as an opportunity to identify essential elements of the required curriculum. Structured maps can be used as a planning guide for learning teams and eventually become a valuable communication tool for parents.	
☐ Develop tools for standardized lesson planning that highlight key features to be included in shared materials.	
☐ Develop a collection of shared assessments that measure what students know and can do. These common assessments become the foundation for evaluating student performance and for identifying effective instructional practices.	
☐ Develop a collection of rubrics that can be used to evaluate student performance on academic and performance tasks.	
☐ Develop a system for collecting student achievement data from both formative and summative assessment sources.	
☐ Develop formalized processes for identifying students who are struggling academically and then for providing meaningful remediation. These processes often involve school professionals beyond the classroom.	

Capacity Factor: Improved Communication	
Tasks Our Building/Learning Team Is Uniquely Prepared to Tackle	**Investments Necessary to Accomplish Task (Time, Professional Development, Funding)**
☐ Develop a shared mission and vision, a critical first step toward improving communication within any learning community. ☐ Understand the important role that trust plays in team development and incorporate opportunities for shared experiences among members of a team, which helps to make communication safe. ☐ Work through personality profile testing, which identifies the range of communication styles that exists on a learning team and draws attention to the diverse range of personalities that exists within a faculty. ☐ Build time into the school day for both formal and informal conversations among colleagues. This forms the foundation for increased trust and open professional communication. ☐ Use digital forums with discussion board technology or social networking services to open lines of communication by breaking down the physical barriers of time and place that can limit conversations within schools. ☐ Participate in regular meetings focused by predetermined agendas and guided by a collection of norms and team-generated products—a required part of learning teams.	

Capacity Factor: Improved Teacher Learning	
Tasks Our Building/Learning Team Is Uniquely Prepared to Tackle	**Investments Necessary to Accomplish Task (Time, Professional Development, Funding)**
☐ Create time and opportunities for teachers to observe their colleagues so teachers are exposed to new practices and develop a sense of inquiry about instruction. ☐ Work through structured processes for reflecting on instruction. Examples include conducting action research, looking at student work, or Japanese lesson study.	

Building a PLC at Work™ © 2010 Solution Tree Press • solution-tree.com
Visit **go.solution-tree.com/PLCbooks** to download this page.

☐ Rethink instructional practices. Much like the study of medicine, successes and failures in an effective learning team are not attributed to individuals—they are, instead, attributed to the practices of individuals. ☐ Receive training in the analysis of student achievement data. Together, teams learn to look for trends and repeating patterns in results collected from assessments.	

Capacity Factor: Collective Ownership and Intelligence

Tasks Our Building/Learning Team Is Uniquely Prepared to Tackle	Investments Necessary to Accomplish Task (Time, Professional Development, Funding)
☐ Create a structured process for documenting successful and unsuccessful instructional practices that can be reviewed by all members of a faculty. ☐ Drive professional development with in-house presentations, honoring the knowledge that is held within the organization. ☐ Administrators identify the positive deviants within the organization and encourage them to document the impact of their work on students.	

Conversation Tracking Sheet

The most accomplished principals, instructional coaches, and teacher leaders use conversations to systematically reinforce the core principles in their buildings and on their learning teams. Consider using a simple tracking sheet like this one to ensure that conversations become effective tools for spreading core principles in your department, grade level, or building.

Name of Faculty Member: _____

Core Principle Shared: _____

1. Why is this faculty member critical to your change efforts?

2. Who else in your department, grade level, or building has a close working relationship with this faculty member? Are they better prepared to lead this conversation?

3. What was the outcome of your conversation? Was this faculty member receptive to your ideas? What have you learned about this faculty member's level of commitment to, or understanding of, the core principle shared? What will you change about your work because of this new knowledge?

Turning Principles Into Stories

A school's vision should be based on a few nonnegotiable principles that become the guide for decision making throughout the school. Stories help translate philosophical principles into real-world, day-by-day actions. Use the following table to brainstorm a handful of convincing stories from your own experience that you can use to easily communicate complex ideas.

Core Principle: Important decisions in a professional learning community should be made collaboratively.

Potential Story:

☐ Will this story ring true to teachers?

☐ Can this story be retold easily?

☐ Is this story memorable?

Core Principle: Professional learning communities are defined by their commitment to ensuring that every child learns. Failure is not an option.

Potential Story:

☐ Will this story ring true to teachers?

☐ Can this story be retold easily?

☐ Is this story memorable?

Core Principle: Results must be used to drive all decisions in a professional learning community.

Potential Story:

☐ Will this story ring true to teachers?

☐ Can this story be retold easily?

☐ Is this story memorable?

Core Principle: Professional learning teams see themselves as interdependent peers instead of independent operators and accept collective responsibility for the success of all students.

Potential Story:

☐ Will this story ring true to teachers?

☐ Can this story be retold easily?

☐ Is this story memorable?

Core Principle:

Potential Story:

☐ Will this story ring true to teachers?

☐ Can this story be retold easily?

☐ Is this story memorable?

Professional Learning Teams

The following table describes the ways that professional learning teams differ from traditional teacher teams. After reviewing the table with your colleagues, use the questions at the bottom to reflect on your current reality.

Traditional Teacher Teams	Professional Learning Teams
Hold regular meetings that may sometimes be focused on student learning, but are often primarily focused on school routines or procedures.	Hold regular meetings focused specifically on student learning—and only on student learning.
Have inconsistent levels of trust between team members; teachers may engage in collegial conversations, but they tend to avoid conflict with one another. Keeping the peace is a priority.	Have high levels of trust between group members, allowing for productive conflict to occur in a safe environment. This level of trust leads to consensus and commitment on the part of all team members.
Rarely expose teachers to the instructional practices of their peers. Members tend to rely on their own professional experiences when making decisions for their students.	Seek to identify and amplify instructional practices that work. Members are willing to rethink what they do in the classroom based on the collective work of the group.
Members see themselves as loosely connected colleagues. While they may share a common group of students, teachers largely act as individuals when making instructional decisions.	Members see themselves as interdependent, sharing ownership for the success of all students.

1. Which characteristic of professional learning teams do we currently do well? What can we celebrate?

2. Which characteristic of professional learning teams seems the most intimidating? Why?

3. Which characteristic of professional learning teams can we start working on today? What will our first step be? Who can help us in our efforts?

Finding Your Hedgehog

When researching organizations for his book *Good to Great*, Jim Collins (2001) found that the most successful companies came up with a straightforward, compelling vision by looking for overlap in their answers to three simple questions: What can we be the best in the world at? What drives our engine? What are we deeply passionate about? Using the graphic organizer provided here, find your building's hedgehog.

What can we be the best in the world at?	What drives our engine?	What are we deeply passionate about?

Our Compelling Vision (Hedgehog)

CHAPTER 2

EMPOWERING THE CORE TEAM

It was now mid-August, and the faculty of Central Middle was sitting in the media center revisiting the school's mission statement. As Michael listened to the thoughts and opinions of the other teachers in the small group at his table, he recalled his last experience with a school mission statement.

When Michael was a third-year teacher working in a different county, his school went though a reaccreditation process. A subcommittee had drafted a new mission statement and presented it to the faculty for review. Michael could not recall exactly what that mission statement said—something along the lines of, "We will provide a high-quality education to all students"—but he remembered the ensuing discussion in detail. In particular, he remembered the comments made by an English teacher named John.

"I think the statement '*provide a high-quality education to all students*' goes too far," said John. "In reality, the best we can do is provide the opportunity for a high-quality education. It is then the students' responsibility to take advantage of that opportunity. It is not our fault if students don't work hard, if we don't have parental support, or if the town doesn't give us a big enough budget. We can't commit ourselves to something that's out of our hands."

Michael felt this argument sold teachers and students short. Are teachers not professionals capable of more than just *providing the opportunity* for an education? After all, he thought, if you hire an architect and a builder, you expect an actual house at the end of the process—not just the opportunity for a house. Under the same logic, students deserved something more than just the opportunity for an education. It was, in Michael's opinion, the teacher's responsibility as the adult and the professional to see that each child succeeded academically.

But Michael had not said any of these things at the time. Feeling intimidated, he had listened to his more experienced peers and stayed silent. When the final version of the mission statement was approved—reading something along the lines of, "We will provide the *opportunity* for a high-quality education for all students"—Michael was frustrated, knowing that they had missed the boat.

Now Michael had a second chance. A sheet of paper hung at the front of the room at Central Middle, and on it was the following sentence: "We are a collaborative community that _____ high student achievement." The faculty had gotten this far, but now they had to make an important decision: what word should fill in the blank? As Michael listened to the conversation at his table, he heard echoes of the same arguments from his previous school.

"I like the verb *fosters*. It has a nice, active feel, and it lets parents know that student achievement is important to us."

"But isn't that a little soft? I mean, what is really expected of us if all we have to do is foster a good education? Shouldn't we be pushing for more?"

"Then how about something stronger: *prioritizes*? *Emphasizes*?"

Michael raised his hand to speak to the whole faculty. "You know, we're having a really interesting discussion over here at our table. It seems like the main issue is how far we're willing to go to commit ourselves. Basically, what level of accountability are we going to accept? At our table we have the words *fosters*, *prioritizes*, and *emphasizes* so far. But I'd like to propose a stronger word. I'd like to propose the word *ensures*."

From across the room another teacher responded, "But aren't we setting ourselves up for defeat when we say that we *ensure* student learning? How can we ensure learning, especially when we know that some students just aren't going to be successful, and there's nothing we can do about it? Are we willing to tell a parent, 'I'm sorry, I failed in my responsibility to your child because I didn't *ensure* that he was successful'?"

Sarah raised her hand. "You know, before I became a part of this school, I would definitely have agreed that using *ensure* was just going too far. But now, as I think about what it really means to try to be a professional learning community, I think I would be willing to look at parents and admit that I had failed if their children weren't successful in my classroom."

Karen—one of Central Middle School's longest tenured and most respected teachers—agreed with Sarah. "When I look around this room," she said, "I see a group of incredible teachers, and I really believe that we can help any student to be successful.

"Sure, I know that realistically some students aren't going to achieve the way we want them to even though we've tried our best. But shouldn't our goal be to see every child succeed? Shouldn't we commit ourselves to that? Sometimes we will fail, but does that mean we shouldn't expect the best of ourselves? And shouldn't we be willing to admit to—and learn from—our failures?"

The conversation continued, and the faculty came up with a final list of verbs to vote on. Among them were *focuses on*, *prioritizes*, *provides for*, and, finally, *ensures*. Prior to the vote, the principal, Steve, raised his hand.

"This is your school as much as it is my school, and I'm willing to live with whatever mission statement we approve. Before we vote, though, I want to read you a quote from the DuFour article that I gave all of you earlier this month. The article says, 'School mission statements that promise "learning for all" have become a cliché. But when a school staff takes that statement literally—when teachers view it as a pledge to ensure the success of each student rather than as politically correct hyperbole—profound changes begin to take place'" (2004a, p. 8).

The principal sat down, and the faculty prepared for its vote. The choice was unanimous: "We are a collaborative community that *ensures* high student achievement."

Lessons From the Front Line

Michael's experience at his previous school was a common one. Many teachers are uncomfortable with the idea of holding themselves accountable for ensuring student learning—and with good reason. When you tell parents, "I will ensure that your children succeed," and then *any* child struggles, you are admitting to failure. In addition, when you consider that schools and teachers only have limited control over many key factors that can influence the academic success of students, teachers' reluctance to ensure student learning is understandable. What happens when a child comes from a broken family, shows up to school hungry every day because there is no food at home, or cannot see the board because her parents cannot afford to buy her glasses? How can you ensure anything when you cannot control all the variables?

Despite all of these variables and contingencies, the faculty of Central Middle was willing to commit itself to a mission of ensuring student learning—not *providing the opportunity for*, not *emphasizing*, not *fostering*. *Ensuring*.

Why? Why would one faculty make a decision to hold itself truly accountable for a high level of student learning, while another faculty would turn away from that challenge? Both of Michael's schools had talented and capable teachers. Both of the schools had smart and hard-working administrators who believed in the importance of a quality education. Both of the schools served similar student populations. So what made the difference? What tipped the balance at Central Middle?

We have already talked about the importance of establishing an initial vision that paints a picture of what an organization or team should be. The next step is having a core group of people sharing, developing, and promoting that picture of success. This core group becomes the nucleus of the organization, setting the tone and character for what happens over time.

Just as a snowflake starts with a small crystal structure at its center and then repeats that structure over and over again until the flake is formed, the core group plays a significant role in determining the future shape of an organization. At Michael's previous school, that core group of teachers was not there. The right individuals might have been present, but for whatever reasons they were not joined by a fundamental set of principles and values. But at Central Middle, that core group did exist—making all the difference in the world.

In this chapter, we identify the steps that a leader can take to assemble and empower a core team. Specifically, we focus on the importance of balancing personalities and talents; on the need to create opportunities for dialogue within the core group; and on the delicate process of passing ownership of an individual vision to a larger team. Throughout the chapter, we return to the critical question: how can a core group make the difference between a school that *ensures* student learning and a school that simply provides the opportunity for learning?

The Right Personalities

How many times have you sat through training on personality types over the course of your career? How many times have you planned or delivered such a session for your staff? More importantly, how many times have you considered those sessions to be valuable? How many times have they meaningfully changed the way that you—or your school—operates?

Despite the best of intentions, personality-typing activities generally change nothing in most schools. While principals recognize that there are a variety of rich personalities on their faculties, little has been done to make systematic decisions about leadership responsibilities with this information.

Steve, the principal of Central Middle, was different. He recognized early on that establishing a core group of teachers with a variety of personality strengths was necessary for establishing a strong vision in his building. In *Revisiting Professional Learning Communities at Work* (DuFour, DuFour, & Eaker, 2008), Dick Dewey, a former high school principal, makes a similar argument:

> In the early stages of transformation, your quest to build capacity to function as a PLC will likely involve a small coalition of collaborators. Empower these pioneers with the prioritized and embedded time, space, resources, opportunity, support, and training necessary to focus their attention and help them experience success one step at a time. (p. 334)

To be successful, Steve knew that he would need teacher leaders who had different skill sets and put a high value on some very important elements:

- **Other people's feelings**—Moving any vision within an organization requires individuals who can build and sustain supportive relationships with colleagues.

- **Organization, clear rules, and systems**—Significant organizational change would not be possible without detail-oriented individuals who can structure the change process in meaningful ways.

- **Logically thinking problems through to conclusion**—Individuals who can translate concepts into action at the local level are critical for any developing organization.

- **Innovation**—In today's accountability culture, creative thinkers are essential to organizations interested in—and committed to—change.

Steve was a big-picture thinker, an idea guy far more interested in describing the larger vision than in defining the details. To complement his strengths, he knew that he needed a wide range of personalities. As Jim Collins (2001) would say, Steve knew that he needed to have "the right people on the bus" (p. 41). Steve also recognized that no individual would demonstrate strength in each of these four areas. Instead, he began looking for several teachers who would together form a cohesive, well-rounded core team that he could count on as allies.

When hiring new staff members and meeting with Central Middle's existing faculty, Steve actively sought people who could see the big picture and carry that vision to other members of the faculty. He identified people who could translate ideas into details at the curricular and instructional levels. He identified people who could serve as diplomats by managing team relationships within the faculty, and he identified people who could collect and analyze data to see if his school was moving in the right direction.

Despite the different personalities, however, there were two things that *all* of the members of Steve's core team had in common: a strong belief in the same central principles and the ability to influence others. In the story that begins this chapter, Michael, Sarah, and Karen, all allies that Steve had identified as potential leaders early on, were very different people. Michael was an innovator and maverick, constantly pushing and challenging himself and his colleagues to think about teaching and learning in new and interesting ways. Sarah was a diplomat, quietly working to create consensus and maintaining strong interpersonal relationships. Karen understood the culture of Central Middle better than anyone and had great credibility with peers and parents alike. But each firmly believed in Steve's vision and remained steadfastly committed to ensuring student learning, pursuing strong and purposeful collaboration, and embracing ongoing reflection. For Michael, Steve, Karen, and Sarah, these ideas were nonnegotiables, and their different personalities and styles became indispensable assets in pursuit of common principles.

These teacher leaders whom Steve had identified also shared an ability to influence others. Michael's influence was driven largely by his deep knowledge of K–12 education and his reputation within the district and the state as a master teacher. Sarah was also an excellent teacher, but her growing influence came from her ability to build strong relationships and to use those relationships to gently nudge the thinking of others. Karen's influence was built on the years of successful practice and positive interactions with her peers at Central Middle. Because of their complementary personalities and powers of influence, Michael, Sarah, and Karen came to play prominent roles as core members both in the revision of the school's mission statement and later in the development of the character of their own professional learning team.

Early Dialogue

The lifeblood of any successful professional learning community is conversation. Sometimes this conversation is structured, taking place in planning meetings designed to develop a shared sense of purpose between key staff members. Other times this conversation is unstructured: stopping by another teacher's classroom after hours or maintaining a discussion thread on the faculty website.

Either way, the *learning* aspect of a professional learning community is no accident—it is a direct result of the sharing of ideas, the collaborative exploration of new approaches, and the sometimes-contentious process of making communal decisions (DuFour, DuFour, & Eaker, 2008; Hord, 1997). Each of these activities relies on regular, open, and meaningful conversations. To lay the proper groundwork, this dialogue should begin with the core members of a school's faculty.

Central Middle School used a variety of means of communication early in the process. Like the other buildings in the Seneca Township School District, Central Middle's staff members had access to Blackboard™, a web-based application that supports threaded discussions. With the support of Michael—a tech savvy teacher who had extensive experience with digital communities—Steve used Blackboard as a forum for ongoing conversations between faculty members. These online conversations allowed every teacher to participate actively by starting and contributing to various discussions and to participate passively by reading what their colleagues had to say in a nonthreatening electronic environment.

Central Middle's digital conversations covered a wide range of school topics. Teachers discussed the benefits of block scheduling, developed a clear definition of a PLC, and decided on the essential components of working teams. The asynchronous nature of the conversations eliminated the traditional barriers to open communication in schools: time and place. Teachers were able to join in the conversation at times that fit with their own personal schedules by logging on from any computer with an Internet connection.

Steve also scheduled several early strategy meetings during the summer with his core group, giving them opportunities to talk through the ideas and principles that define a PLC. These meetings were essential, helping members to form strong working relationships based on an awareness of each other's personal and professional skills. Central Middle's core team quickly recognized individual strengths and weaknesses and began to accept leadership roles and responsibilities appropriate for their abilities. These strategy meetings led to a deep sense of mutual trust and shared purpose among the colleagues that Steve knew would lead in the development of a PLC.

While some of this early dialogue focused on decision making (for example, agreeing on a revision to the schoolwide schedule that would be appropriate for both core and elective classrooms), the majority was built around a natural and ongoing process that created connections and strengthened core principles. Schools are incredibly dynamic and complex organizations, and making decisions that are ultimately in the best interests of students is never a linear or simple process. Opportunities for organic dialogue create threads connecting individuals to each other in ways that support the spread of innovations—and ensure that decisions are based on good information and input from a variety of people.

Therefore, as Central Middle School wrestled with accountability, it is no accident that Karen and Sarah bought into a commitment to ensure student learning; both had already been talking and thinking about that commitment for months. Through dozens of conversations, Karen, Sarah, and other core group members had worked their way to a point at which they believed in and understood what ensuring student learning entailed. So when the faculty needed to decide on a verb to use in the mission statement, Karen and Sarah were able to lead.

Trusting Good People to Do Good Things

Trust is a common theme throughout this book. At this early stage in Central Middle School's development as a professional learning community, it was absolutely critical. From the teachers' perspectives, they were always waiting to see if Steve was for real. He said he wanted to promote collaboration and distribute decision-making responsibility, but what would happen when the teachers wanted to do something that he did not agree with? At every point in the process, teachers were watching him—and the rest of the administrative team—to see if they would really walk the walk. And this meant that, especially with core team members, Steve had to earn trust.

Trust is not built overnight, however. As the old adage says, when building trust, actions speak louder than words. In *Getting Started: Reculturing Schools to Become Professional Learning Communities* (Eaker, DuFour, & DuFour, 2002), Rebecca DuFour describes the trust-building process:

> Trust is built over time. It goes back to the idea of leaders modeling their priorities through their behaviors. Teachers learn to trust their leaders when leaders do the things they are asking others to do. . . . People, over time, will see that the norms leaders set and the commitments they make really do drive the work. They must recognize that leaders are going to do what they say they'll do, rather than just talk about it. (p. 89)

Open conversations went a long way toward earning Steve's trust, but Central Middle's principal also made several early decisions that signaled his intentions. One of those decisions (detailed in chapter 1) was to let core team members control much of the interview process for new hires. Michael and Karen led teams that met with Central Middle's teacher candidates, and existing teachers had a big hand in making the final decisions about who should be hired. The core group was also given real responsibility at the organizational level. Working together, they planned the bell schedule for the new year, worked on schoolwide discipline and academic intervention plans, and created professional development activities for in-service training.

Implicit in Steve's attempt to earn the teachers' trust, however, was another level of trust: he had to believe that his core group of teachers would make good decisions. As the building principal, he started with a picture in his head of a vision and a set of central principles. As he identified a group of people to work with him in instituting those principles, he had to be willing to let go—believing that key people could push the process more powerfully than he could have done alone. In the story that started this chapter, Steve participated in the discussion about the mission statement, but he did not control it. Instead, he had faith that people like Michael, Sarah, and Karen would lead the rest of the faculty in a positive direction.

The decision to trust teacher leaders to make good decisions requires a spirit of risk taking on the part of principals, but distributing leadership is always a risk well rewarded. As Gayle Moller and Anita Pankake (2006) explain:

> The distribution of formal power and authority demands courage from the principal, who must trust that others will fulfill their responsibilities. This combined leadership of the principal and the teachers can result in changes that one person could never initiate and sustain, or even envison. . . . Working to build relationships and then creating structures to distribute power and authority are essential for professional learning to thrive. (p. 11)

The final—and most important—level of trust essential for the development of a strong core team in a PLC is the trust that teachers have to have in each other. When Sarah argued that "ensuring student success" is a worthwhile target, she expressed a single-minded confidence in the expertise and abilities of her colleagues that Karen reinforced when she said, "When I look around this room, I see a group of incredible teachers, and I really believe that we can help any student be successful."

Karen and Sarah's confidence began in the formal and informal conversations they had been a part of for the past several months, and it was strengthened by the knowledge that all of the core team members believed in the same central principles. Trust among teachers became the foundation of the collaboration that occurred over the rest of the year. Its genesis within the core team was critical—especially as challenges and disagreements inevitably arose.

Relevant Theory and Research

At some deep level, there is a fundamental difference between a professional learning community and a "business as usual" school—a difference that is difficult to explain. The two types of schools simply *feel* different. This difference goes beyond a superficial comparison of school practices and procedures, and enters the realm of school character and culture. In a successful PLC, the whole really is greater than the sum of its parts.

Insight into the unique character of PLCs—and the role of core individuals in their formation—can be found in Philip Ball's (2004) book *Critical Mass: How One Thing Leads to Another* and in Malcolm Gladwell's (2002) book *The Tipping Point: How Little Things Can Make a Big Difference*. Ball is a scientist and writer interested in the ways in which the laws of physics can help explain interactions among people. Gladwell is a journalist who has studied the epidemic nature of ideas and social practices. Two lessons from their books are particularly important for understanding how influential individuals can shape the development of PLCs. The first relates to phase transitions—such as the point at which water boils from a liquid into a gas—and the second relates to the roles that different personality types play in spreading ideas.

Phase Transitions

In *Critical Mass*, Ball (2004) explains that a *phase transition* is a physical switch from one state to another. One of the interesting things about phase transitions, Ball notes, is that the individual particles don't change during the switch. Molecules of H_2O look the same whether they are in liquid or gas form, but the collective state of the particles changes dramatically. Another interesting characteristic of phase transitions is that, rather than happening gradually, they happen all at once, spreading quickly throughout a system. At 210 degrees, water is a liquid; but heat it just two degrees more, and water suddenly makes a dramatic transition into a gas. The collective nature goes through a substantial shift!

In order for a phase transition to occur, something called *nucleation* has to happen. When water freezes, the molecules do not all crystallize at once; instead, a few *seed* crystals appear, and the crystallization process then spreads throughout the liquid. These seed crystals are formed by irregularities in the water, which could be a piece of dust or a scratch on the inside surface of the water's container. These irregularities are called *nucleators*. If no nucleators are present, it is actually possible for water to stay in liquid form below 32 degrees, or above 212 degrees.

Ball (2004) argues that phase transitions are also evident in social interactions. One example might be the spread of "the wave" at a sporting event. The spectators are already in a heightened state because of the excitement of the event. Different groups of people throughout the stands might, then, try to get the wave started, serving as nucleators. Many attempts fail, but one finally catches on—and suddenly the whole crowd is participating in a collective behavior.

Another example, which Ball (2004) explores in depth, is traffic congestion. Have you ever been driving on a busy highway where cars and trucks were moving quickly even though there was a considerable amount of traffic, when seemingly out of nowhere, you see red brake lights in front of you and the quick-moving traffic slows to a frustrating crawl? What caused the traffic to change? One minute you were zipping along without a problem, and then all of the sudden the traffic switched to slow motion.

Ball would suggest that the traffic went through a phase transition. Even though there were lots of cars on the road, the traffic was moving quickly—just like water at 34 degrees still flows smoothly. But the whole system was in a near-critical state. All it took in this situation was for one car to change lanes too quickly, causing someone to hit his brakes, and suddenly the whole system went through a transition. After that first person hit his brakes, the one behind him followed, and so on. Just like that initial water crystal, the single braking driver worked as a nucleator, starting a chain reaction and pushing the whole system into a new collective state.

When the faculty of Central Middle wrote their mission statement, they too went through a phase transition. They changed from a group of teachers excited and nervous about working with a new principal to a cohesive faculty committed to a specific vision. Without question, Steve had already laid much of the groundwork for that transition. He had recruited new teachers interested in working in a collaborative school, sought out existing faculty members that he knew would be influential change agents, and talked about his vision of a PLC at every opportunity. In fact, if the temperature of the faculty could have been taken on the day they discussed their mission statement, it was probably a healthy 210 degrees!

During that meeting, something happened to the nature of the entire organization. In order for that phase transition to occur—changing Central Middle from a traditionally structured school to a PLC—the faculty needed something, or someone, to start the chain reaction. In physics terms, the faculty needed a nucleator. At Central Middle, members of the core group served as the nucleators, catalysts for the phase transition. Specifically, Michael, Sarah, and Karen made comments that helped push the faculty past their metaphorical boiling point.

While the model of a phase transition sheds light on how an organization can shift from one form to another, it does not do much to explain why those core team members—those nucleators—were able to start the chain reaction. What made Michael, Sarah, and Karen so influential? To answer that question, we turn to Gladwell's (2002) *The Tipping Point* and consider three different personality types: Connectors, Mavens, and Salesmen.

Connectors, Mavens, and Salesmen

Gladwell (2002) explores the phenomenon of changes in society, and how an idea or practice can tip from obscurity into popularity. He focuses on a number of social phenomena, such as the dramatic drop in crime in New York City in the mid-1990s and the spread of popularity of Airwalk sneakers in 1995 and 1996. In his analysis of various social trends, Gladwell identifies three different types of people who help to make trends happen: Connectors, Mavens, and Salesmen. Gladwell goes on to argue that Connectors, Mavens, and Salesmen all play different roles in the spread of ideas.

Connectors are people with oversized Rolodexes; the kind of people who seem to find friends easily and make a point of staying in contact with both friends and acquaintances. Connectors have a special gift for creating and maintaining relationships, becoming ideal conduits for the spread of ideas. If a Connector is excited about something, she will tell her friends—and she has *lots* of friends.

Mavens are information hounds. In the education world, Mavens take the time to research ideas and become experts on new innovations and trends. When you have a question about guided reading strategies or the latest pay-for-performance plan being debated by the state legislature, Mavens are the people you turn to. Mavens are not just interested in knowledge for its own sake; they like to share their ideas to help others. This makes Mavens indispensable in the spread of any innovation or trend because people respect the opinions of Mavens and listen to their recommendations.

Salesmen are convincers with an intuitive understanding of the art of persuasion. They are able to use charisma and an amiable disposition to convince naysayers of the benefits of any idea. Rather than the used-car salesmen stereotype, howeer, Salesmen project a sense of honest commitment to an innovation, and their influence is a combination of both their charisma and their sincere desire to help others.

At Central Middle, Steve looked for a variety of personalities for his core team that included a combination of Connectors, Mavens, and Salesmen. By the time the faculty sat down to create its mission statement, those core team members had already been using their various personality strengths to spread and support PLC principles so that the idea of ensuring student learning was at a metaphorical tipping point.

At the faculty meeting, the collective efforts of these different personalities finally came together. Connectors used their network of relationships to bring various constituencies into the conversation, Mavens used their knowledge and respected expertise to convince others of the importance of PLC principles, and Salesmen used their charisma to sell the faculty on a schoolwide commitment to ensuring student learning. The principal had laid the groundwork by identifying and bringing together a core group of people who were committed to a common vision, and that core group had the right combination of personalities to serve as nucleators to start a chain reaction that quickly spread throughout the school.

Now, did Steve plan it this way, constructing an elaborate plot that finally came to fruition? Hardly. Instead, he had identified and assembled a collection of teachers with complementary personalities; he allowed that core group to work together, get to know each other, and amplify their understanding of PLC principles through dialogue. Then he trusted those teachers to champion their shared beliefs when the right moment came.

In Michael's previous school, for whatever reason, those nucleators did not act. Maybe their colleagues were not close enough to the boiling point, or maybe the nucleators thought that they were alone in their convictions. But at Central Middle, that core group tipped the faculty balance toward an initial commitment to becoming a true PLC.

Recommendations

If you are interested in creating a learning community in your school, the formation of a core group committed to the central vision of your work is critical. Here are the most important recommendations for anyone at this stage in the process to consider.

Decide on Your Nonnegotiables

School leaders must figure out early on exactly what their central principles are. For a true professional learning community, these are likely to include a commitment to ensuring student learning, a belief in the power of true collaboration and in a model of distributed leadership and decision making, and in an ongoing process of reflection and inquiry. It is essential that school leaders are able to define the principles they consider to be nonnegotiables before moving forward. A clear focus will help principals identify and select teacher leaders who share their initial vision. A wavering commitment to—or understanding of—a set of central principles only leads to confusion and inefficiency within core team members.

Establish the Core Team, and Spend Time Discussing Your Central Principles

In *Leading Change*, John Kotter (1996) emphasizes the importance of developing a strong core team or, as he calls it, a "guiding coalition." He argues that "a strong, guiding coalition is always needed—one with a high level of trust and shared objectives that appeal to both head and heart. Building such a team is always an essential part of the early stages of any effort to restructure a set of strategies" (p. 52).

The most important prerequisite for core team members is a belief in a school's central principles. After that, effective leaders work to find individuals with different personality strengths who share a high level of connectivity and influence, both inside and outside the organization. Once the core team is established, it is important that administrators spend time with the core team, encouraging conversations throughout the group and creating opportunities for participants to discuss and debate the building's central principles, translating them into practical ideas and statements. At this point in the process, school leaders must be open to additions or revisions to their original principles. It is particularly important for doubting members of a building's core team to have opportunities to share their reservations. A leader's willingness to respect the voice of supporters and skeptics alike will build trust and commitment between administration and influential teachers. Core team members are experts with a deep understanding of the dynamics of human relationships within a building; effective leaders allow this knowledge to shape the central principles of a learning community without compromising their nonnegotiables.

The materials at the end of this chapter can help school leaders to carefully plan their core teams. Included are a brainstorming tool, Who Are the Personalities in Your Organization? (page 40), that can be used to identify potential core team members and a tracking tool, Balancing the Core Team (pages 41–42), that can help to ensure that the teachers you are identifying as leaders have influence across your entire building.

Ensure a Collective Process

For the leader pushing a new vision, there is an important fact that has to be accepted: at a certain point, it's no longer the leader's vision, but rather a collective vision.

As long as everyone on the team commits to a central set of principles, the details will work themselves out—even when the details feel like the most important thing in the world and heated disagreements result over simple challenges. When the principles underlying the decision-making process are pervasive throughout a school—if the best interests of students are the goal *despite* the conflict over details—then the organization can be successful and move forward in the face of any challenge.

For leaders, this means being willing to let go of details while reinforcing principles. For participants in the process, this means being willing to compromise, recognizing that mistakes and frustrations are a natural part of the organizational learning process. As DuFour, DuFour, and Eaker (2008) argue, "Educators can clarify a general sense of direction at the outset of an improvement initiative, but a shared vision emerges over time as a result of action, reflection, and collective meaning based on collective experiences" (p. 145).

Both of these behaviors—letting go of details and being willing to compromise—are facilitated by opportunities for ongoing conversations focused on a building's core principles. The handout Creating Opportunities for Dialogue (page 43) can help you to systematically create these opportunities for your faculty.

Value Relationships

When establishing a core team, it is important to develop professional and intellectual connections, but it is equally important to establish congenial relationships. Once friendships have been formed, it is significantly easier to negotiate controversial topics or decisions. People need time to get to know each other, feel comfortable working together, and develop trust.

For teacher leaders, developing trust is essential for becoming an influential member of a school faculty. Lacking any kind of organizational decision-making power, teacher leaders can only change the behavior and commitments of colleagues when they are committed to actively building positive relationships with peers. The checklist Building Relationships With Teachers (page 44) can help teacher leaders to think through simple actions for extending their influence across grade levels or departments.

Regardless of their role, accomplished leaders of learning communities always find time for feeding relationships.

Who Are the Personalities in Your Organization?

Establishing a core team is an essential task for principals interested in creating a learning community. Members of a core team will greatly influence the direction and success of your efforts. Use this handout to brainstorm the strengths and weaknesses of existing faculty members or new candidates. Remember, the best core teams contain teacher leaders who put a high value on the following:

- Relationships and other people's feelings
- Organization and clear rules and systems
- Logically thinking problems through to conclusion
- Thinking outside the box

Relationship Builders Within Our Organization	System Thinkers Within Our Organization
Problem Solvers Within Our Organization	**Innovators Within Our Organization**

Balancing the Core Team

To guarantee that ideas spread across an entire building, it is also essential that core teams include members who are influential in every grade level and department in a school. Use the following tracking table to ensure that your core team has the kind of broad representation to ensure success.

Department Name	Potential Core Team Member	Personality Type	Is Person Considered Influential by His or Her Peers?	
		☐ Relationship Builder ☐ System Thinker ☐ Problem Solver ☐ Innovator	Yes	No
		☐ Relationship Builder ☐ System Thinker ☐ Problem Solver ☐ Innovator	Yes	No
		☐ Relationship Builder ☐ System Thinker ☐ Problem Solver ☐ Innovator	Yes	No
		☐ Relationship Builder ☐ System Thinker ☐ Problem Solver ☐ Innovator	Yes	No
		☐ Relationship Builder ☐ System Thinker ☐ Problem Solver ☐ Innovator	Yes	No
		☐ Relationship Builder ☐ System Thinker ☐ Problem Solver ☐ Innovator	Yes	No

Finally, it is also important that your core team have a nice balance between relationship builders, system thinkers, problem solvers, and innovators. Before making any final decisions about who to reach out to as an ally, use the following tally sheet to monitor the composition of your developing core team.

Relationship Builders	System Thinkers	Problem Solvers	Innovators

Building a PLC at Work™ © 2010 Solution Tree Press • solution-tree.com
Visit **go.solution-tree.com/PLCbooks** to download this page.

Creating Opportunities for Dialogue

In order to share a collective vision, members of your core team must have opportunities to engage in meaningful dialogue with one another. Efforts to structure core team social outings, core team goal-setting meetings, and the creation of electronic discussion forums for ongoing conversations allow influential faculty members to identify their own strengths and begin to recognize their individual roles in the development of the organization. They also allow core team members to develop a measure of trust in one another and a synergy as a group that is essential to continued success. Use this handout to consider different kinds of opportunities that you can provide for your core team to interact.

Opportunity	Ease of Implementation (Easy, Possible With Effort, Challenging but Possible, or Impossible)	Ideas for or Barriers to Implementation	People to Contact to Assist With Implementation

Building Relationships With Teachers

For teacher leaders, the only guaranteed way to become influential is to systematically build trusting relationships with colleagues. Use the following checklist of simple strategies to track your efforts to improve the interpersonal connections with teachers on your team, in your department, or at your grade level.

Teacher With Whom You Are Trying to Build a Relationship	Trust-Building Strategy to Try	Outcome of Effort
	☐ Stop by for an informal conversation before or after school with colleague. ☐ Freely share resources related to current unit of study with colleague. ☐ Celebrate the work of colleague publicly beyond team. ☐ Share the workload for an upcoming activity with colleague. ☐ Own up to a mistake that caused conflict with colleague. ☐ Assume positive intentions when involved in a disagreement with colleague. ☐ Coplan and teach an upcoming lesson with colleague. ☐ Write a handwritten note of thanks or praise to colleague. ☐ Ask for guidance from colleague. ☐ Find a way to laugh with colleague. ☐ Other:	

PART II

FALL: BUILDING A TEAM

CHAPTER 3

CREATING TRUST

Karen had just had two firsts in the same day. Earlier, for the first time since her student teaching days, she had observed one of her grade-level colleagues in action. Immediately afterward, she had observed the school principal teaching a lesson in her classroom, *and* she had given him constructive criticism!

The ball had started rolling back in early October. Steve, Central Middle's principal, mentioned in a casual conversation that he was interested in providing teachers throughout the building with opportunities to observe their teammates teaching. Karen, a member of the sixth-grade language arts/social studies professional learning team, took him at his word and asked when her team could start. A week later, Steve sent out an email asking the team to let him know when they wanted coverage, indicating that he would be happy to guest teach a lesson in each person's classroom.

Just like that, Steve was teaching Karen's students while she went and observed one of her teammates.

Karen had enjoyed the visit. She chose to observe Jennifer, a second-year teacher, for about twenty minutes. Several weeks earlier, the team had collaboratively planned a unit on poetry that included three full days worth of station work, and Jennifer's class was a bit ahead of Karen's. Karen was interested in seeing how Jennifer ran stations, hoping to pick up a trick or two before her class started them. Jennifer was far more comfortable with small-group work than Karen had ever been.

Karen had returned to her own room a little earlier than expected, sitting down quietly in the back while Steve completed his lesson. In social studies, Karen's sixth graders were currently studying the Middle Ages. Steve prepared a lesson comparing medicinal practices in the Middle Ages to those of today. As she watched and listened, Karen smiled to herself. Steve had been a high school teacher, and it showed. The lesson he prepared was way over the heads of Karen's dumbfounded tweens.

Towards the end of the lesson, Steve was failing badly, and he knew it. You could see the flicker of fear in his eyes, worried that he would lose some measure of credibility with Karen because of one poorly delivered lesson. Thankfully, Karen's kids were well behaved, and she was a trusted member of Steve's core team. Otherwise, Steve's reputation as an instructional leader might have taken a hit at the hands of a group of disinterested twelve-year-olds.

Later in the day, Steve stopped by Karen's classroom. He asked, "So, did you enjoy the opportunity to get into Jennifer's classroom?"

"I really did. You would never know she's a second-year teacher," said Karen. "She has excellent classroom-management skills. Her students are completing the same poetry stations that I'll be starting in a couple of days, and I picked up two or three great ideas about how to run them. She was doing some neat things that I never would have thought of."

"That's great!" said Steve. "I'm glad it was worth the time. So, I noticed that you caught the tail end of my lesson. It didn't go very well, did it? I'm a bit embarrassed, I guess, but I'm supposed to teach that lesson in Jennifer's class tomorrow so that she can observe Sarah. Can you help me improve it? It seemed like the kids were sort of zoning out at times."

Karen was momentarily speechless. When Steve had struggled in her classroom, she was certain that there would be a few awkward moments in their work together at some point in the near future—but she did not think it would be because Steve would come to *her* looking for teaching advice! Impressed by his actions, though, Karen explained that her students had struggled with some of the concepts that Steve was trying to introduce. "This is the first time that many of them have ever heard of 'humors' in the medical sense," she said. "I'm not sure that everyone understood what they were."

"Any recommendations on how I could make things more clear?" asked Steve. "I'm actually determined to get this right, no matter how many trials it takes!"

Together, Steve and Karen spent a few minutes improving his lesson. The original worksheet that Steve was using was full of pretty complicated questions, and the readings on medieval medicine were not easy to get through either. Karen suggested that Steve hand out some type of graphic organizer to help students visually organize information as they were working. "A simple Venn diagram and a reading partner," she said, "would go a long way towards making the lesson more approachable, don't you think?"

"That's a great idea, Karen. When you haven't been in the classroom in a while, it's easy to forget how hard teaching really is. My high schoolers were pretty self-reliant. They didn't need very much support from me for anything. Because I'm an engaging speaker, I could pretty much stand and deliver for an hour—which didn't require thoughtful lesson planning at all. If nothing else, I think this process of covering classes will do me some good by teaching me a little humility."

"Well, it's nice of you to say that, but I can promise you I wouldn't want to trade my job for yours any day!"

Karen caught up with Jennifer later that day to tell her how much she enjoyed the visit. She had picked up lots of great ideas and was looking forward to her own poetry stations more than ever. "I especially liked the roles you assigned to students to keep everyone on task," she said. "I think I'm going to do the same thing when we start our stations on Monday."

"Thanks! The students ended up doing a really good job with the stations, better than I expected. So how were your students with Steve?" Jennifer asked. "He's supposed to be covering my class tomorrow."

Karen answered, "They were good, but not because of Steve's lesson! It's funny—you can tell that he was probably a great teacher when he was in the classroom, but he's definitely rusty. You don't need to worry about your students misbehaving—he is the principal, after all—but you may have some blank looks when you get back. He has this activity on medicine in the Middle Ages, and at least half of what he's talking about is over the kids' heads. He stopped by just now for a few suggestions on how to improve things, so hopefully he'll be better tomorrow than he was today.

"I have to say, I'm really impressed he was willing to teach. That was pretty brave—in twenty-five years, I've never actually 'observed' a principal, let alone given one advice about teaching. And it sure was great to get out of the room for a bit to come see you with your students. Your lesson was terrific."

"Thanks again!" beamed Jennifer. "I'll try to warn the kids to be good for their guest teacher!"

Lessons From the Front Line

Karen was rightfully shocked when Steve came to her room looking for instructional advice. After all, in an age where administrators are expected to be all things to all people, showing weakness to a faculty member was a move that many principals would think twice before considering. Steve intuitively understood, though, that building positive relationships with all of the adults in his building was absolutely critical—and he knew that the best relationships are built on trust. His goal was to extend the lessons about trust that he had learned when building his core team to his entire faculty (a strategy explored in chapter 2).

The central power of a professional learning community is the collective decision making and adult learning that take place on a daily basis as a result of powerful conversations— such as the conversation between Jennifer and Karen about Jennifer's station activities. Powerful conversations between colleagues do not just happen. Powerful conversations occur only when participants believe their voices will be heard and valued. In other words, powerful conversations occur only when participants trust each other.

So how do school leaders create a trusting environment? What did Steve do to create a school community in which his sixth-grade language arts/social studies teachers were actually excited about inviting one another into their classrooms? Conversely, how do administrators convince teachers to trust them, and how do administrators deal with their own insecurities about placing too much power in the hands of teachers?

In a profession driven by personal interactions, shared experiences form the foundation of every successful relationship. When teachers work together, get to know each other, and create a bank of common experiences, they build strong interpersonal bonds that allow for meaningful change. Principals who share decision making with teacher teams create additional opportunities for collaborative conversations about critical issues and demonstrate confidence in what teachers know and can do—laying the cornerstones of positive long-term relationships.

Most importantly, school leaders must model and reward the types of behaviors that they hope to see. At Central Middle School, Steve felt strongly that observations between peers would improve teaching and learning, so he made time in his own schedule to ensure that Karen and Jennifer could watch one another teach. He also sought out feedback from a colleague, trusting her to provide guidance in a productive and professional manner—and sending a powerful message about what reflective practitioners look like in action.

This chapter discusses various approaches school leaders can take to create an atmosphere of trust in their buildings. Specifically, we explore effective strategies for developing shared experiences among staff members and empowering learning teams, as well as providing examples of ways in which administrators can model and reward the types of behaviors they hope to see demonstrated in their schools. Finally, we look at Roland Barth's work (2006) on the power of positive relationships and the role they play in a school's health and success.

Creating Shared Experiences

Building a successful professional learning community is difficult work, both at the school and individual team level. After all, PLCs really are not about structures and processes. Those things are important in a PLC and easier to address because they are transparent and concrete. At their core, however, PLCs are about conversations and relationships. And conversations and relationships are tricky.

In a traditional school, conversations and relationships usually stop at amiable. The least effective teacher in the school can be the most popular person on staff, so long as he is the best storyteller in the teachers' lounge. The truth is, most teachers just don't talk about practice with one another. We talk about our families, our weekend camping trips, or the new hit TV show—we talk about the struggles and successes in our personal lives, but we keep our professional lives behind closed doors. In a traditional school, Karen would have never sought to learn from Jennifer, the newest teacher on her hallway. It would have been an admission of weakness at best—and of complete incompetence at worst!

This hesitance to expose our practices and to talk about the teaching and learning that is (or isn't) happening in our rooms represents a significant barrier to individual and school improvement. To move beyond the barrier of congeniality—to deepen professional relationships and conversations—a faculty needs to build on a collection of shared professional experiences that bind them together. As learning community expert and one-time director of school improvement initiatives for the state of Missouri Terri Martin (2008) writes:

> Collaborative relationships are about teachers supporting teachers in order to promote success for students. Unlike collegial relationships, in which the emphasis is on supporting teachers on a more personal and social level, collaboration is all about the professional side of teaching. (p. 150)

Strangely enough, some of the most powerful shared experiences are completely unplanned. They just happen. But shared experiences can also be manufactured by school leaders who plan meetings effectively or schedule substitute teachers so that grade levels have release time to meet with one another. The following strategies can help building principals manufacture successful shared experiences for the teachers in their schools.

Reframe Informal Interactions Between Colleagues

We started this section by downplaying congenial relationships, but congeniality *is* important. People who like each other work more effectively together. School leaders should never overlook regular opportunities for staff members to get together and socialize. Such activities span from holiday parties to team-building workshops designed to generate camaraderie and a sense of school spirit. As Daniel Kain (2003) notes in *Camel-Makers: Building Effective Teacher Teams Together*:

> Teams ought to be fun . . . and teams should not wait for someone else to make them have fun—having fun ought to be a priority for teams from the start. This can be in the context of work, but it can be especially effective as it extends beyond the work situation. . . . Making connections outside of work can help teamed teachers become more cohesive and effective. (p. 101)

Moving beyond congeniality, teachers and principals alike must also seek out informal, professional opportunities to interact by spending regular time away from their primary workspaces visiting classrooms and starting up conversations with colleagues. At Central Middle, a formal visit between Karen and Jennifer served as a catalyst for multiple informal conversations about teaching and learning that successfully changed the focus of collegial interactions from personal to professional. Karen and Jennifer now see their time together as an opportunity to reflect, rather than simply as a chance to exchange pleasantries.

Provide Structure and Expectations for Formal Interactions

A common belief in schools attempting to build PLCs is that any type of collaboration is good collaboration. Just throw the teachers together, lock the doors, and something positive is sure to happen! In reality, not all shared experiences are positive, and not all types of collaboration lead to the outcomes that PLCs strive to generate. As Richard DuFour, Rebecca DuFour, Robert Eaker, and Thomas Many (2006) argue in *Learning by Doing: A Handbook for Professional Learning Communities at Work*, "The fact that teachers collaborate will do nothing to improve a school. The pertinent question is not, 'Are they collaborating?' but rather, 'What are they collaborating about?'" (p. 91). It is important that formal, shared experiences (faculty meetings, professional learning team meetings, peer observations) have structure and that school leaders are clear about their expectations for those experiences.

Prior to the events described in this chapter's story, Steve and the entire sixth-grade team met to lay some specific groundwork for peer observations. Together, they developed a set of shared expectations for the process, emphasizing that peer observations represented opportunities to learn, not to judge. The observer's role was that of student, not critic. Teams were to identify specific teaching and learning behaviors on which they would focus. The sixth-grade teachers, for example, were interested in studying different approaches to student grouping. Finally, Steve suggested a set of simple ground rules for peer observations; teachers were asked to focus on student interactions with instructional materials, keeping the focus of the observations on outcomes rather than evaluations.

By carefully crafting clear structures and expectations, professional learning teams create a sense of comfort and safety for shared experiences. Peer observations and interactions become far less intimidating when they are based on preset parameters. Jennifer was not nervous about Karen's visit because she knew Karen was entering her classroom as an ally looking for evidence of accomplishment rather than an enemy looking to criticize her practice. While it is impossible to script the development of positive relationships, school leaders can help by structuring safe environments for common shared experiences.

Create Multiple Communication Forums

Dialogue is the foundation of shared professional experiences: teachers having conversations, asking questions, throwing out ideas, and sharing perspectives. Because schools are such busy places—and educators such busy people—it can be difficult to make these conversations happen. School leaders can address this challenge by creating multiple forums for dialogue.

The most obvious forums involve face-to-face interactions, whether in whole-faculty meetings, professional learning team meetings, department meetings, or some other configuration. When faculty members get together in these settings, it is important to engage teachers in collaborative conversations about teaching and learning. For example, rather than holding monthly faculty meetings focused on "administrivia," make faculty meetings time for cross-grade dialogue, professional learning team presentations, or whole-staff conversations that are led by practicing classroom teachers. By focusing common time on opportunities for constructive dialogue—and by creating frequent opportunities for teachers to be seen as building leaders—principals and instructional coaches create professional shared experiences and actively define the kinds of interactions that are expected among peers.

Moving beyond face-to-face conversation, school leaders can use electronic communication to connect teachers in creative ways. Professional learning teams, and even whole schools, are beginning to use asynchronous tools such as discussion boards and synchronous tools such as chat rooms to host online discussions and post grade-level resources.

Interestingly enough, electronic conversations offer a measure of safety that face-to-face interactions can lack. Participants have time to consider their words before "speaking," and often spend time carefully revising and editing their thoughts before contributing to digital forums. Asynchronous discussions run smoothly, without risk of one or two participants dominating the conversation. There is a sense of equitable participation in electronic conversations that is often missing in faculty meetings, empowering new teachers—or teachers with contrary viewpoints.

While electronic conversations will not appeal to every member of a school faculty, they are an avenue for creating additional shared experiences—and as such, they should play a role in the communication plan of every building.

For Steve, a building principal who embraced digital dialogue early in the development of his school's vision, electronic conversations had proven to be invaluable. In the discussion forums he was using to engage his faculty members, several points of contention and core misunderstandings about PLCs became clear. Because his faculty was relatively new to the concepts related to collaborative teams, learning about misconceptions was incredibly valuable, giving Steve insights that would help him polish the foundational beliefs of his building.

Steve was also excited when faculty members communicated concerns in the electronic forums he had created. While he had hoped for a culture in which everyone was comfortable expressing doubts in whole-faculty meetings, he had been a building principal long enough to recognize that face-to-face meetings can be intimidating places. Voicing uncertainties in front of seventy colleagues late on a Monday afternoon is a sure ticket to *outsider* status; but raising concerns online is a different story. Steve had structured his digital conversations to allow for anonymous posts and regularly referred to strands of conversation in his work. His faculty members knew that Steve was listening, and as a result, they were willing to bring challenging perspectives to the group that may once have been overlooked in Steve's buildings.

Make It Matter

Time is one of the most precious—and most limited—resources in a school. But time is necessary to create a bank of shared experiences that form the foundation of trusting relationships. That means two things. First, school leaders—whether they work at the building or learning team level—need to find time to make shared experiences happen, and second, shared time must be time well spent.

In the story that introduced this chapter, Steve accomplished both of these goals. First, he created time for peer observations by agreeing to guest teach in each classroom. Like Steve, the most innovative school leaders go to great lengths to create common time for teachers (DuFour, DuFour, Eaker, & Many, 2006), using building administrators and guidance counselors to monitor a whole grade level as they watch *Flowers for Algernon* in the auditorium, giving grade-level teachers ninety minutes of common meeting time, or pulling teacher assistants to monitor students during arrival and homeroom, squeezing an extra half-hour to forty-five minutes for professional learning team meetings. When school leaders give of their own time—and find creative ways to repurpose the time of non-classroom-based educators (such as guidance counselors, teacher assistants, front office staff, and administrators)—they can create ongoing opportunities for teachers to have critical shared experiences during the school day.

After finding/creating the time, school leaders must then make the time matter. Steve did not cover Karen's class so that she could get her photocopying done. He covered it so she could engage in a powerful professional activity: observing a peer. The types of shared experiences that matter are those in which teachers are engaged in substantive conversation or reflection on core teaching and learning issues. Observing peers, analyzing student learning data, developing common assessments, reflecting on instructional strategies, celebrating successes—when school leaders carve out time for teachers to engage in these practices, they create opportunities for the types of shared experiences critical for building trusting relationships and actively redefining what professional interactions look like within their buildings.

"Push Out" Decision Making

One of the most important ways for school leaders to create shared experiences and develop an environment of trust is by "pushing out" decision making—empowering professional learning teams to make key decisions. When school leaders give teacher teams real decision-making authority, they accomplish multiple goals. They give teams a task to accomplish that requires substantive dialogue which creates a shared experience. They also send a message to teachers that they are trusted, modeling the type of behavior they wish teachers to exhibit. What is more, they increase the quality of decisions. As we discuss in more detail in chapter 8, "Building a Collective Intelligence," decisions made by teams, especially when members are familiar with the context and responsible for implementing the decision, are usually more effective than decisions made by individuals removed from the situation.

When it comes to distributed decision making, an administrator often wrestles with two difficult questions. First, how do I ensure that teacher teams are making good decisions? And second, how do I ensure that all of the different teams in my building are not making decisions that go in a hundred different directions? The answer is that a school leader must remain apprised of teams' decision-making processes, use the school's vision as an explicit litmus test for decision making, and be willing to push back on team decisions by asking for justification when necessary.

Teacher leaders encourage distributed decision making by successfully guiding team conversations and ensuring that the school's vision—a vision that team members have helped to collectively craft—remains at the center of grade-level or department decisions. As teams successfully make decisions that reflect the core principles of their building, distributed decision making becomes less risky and more rewarding for principals. Anthony Byrk and Barbara Schneider (2002) call this the building of relational trust and note that "relational trust . . . grows over time through exchanges where the expectations held for others are validated in action" (pp. 136–137).

At Central Middle, Steve pushed out as many decisions as possible because he had confidence in his colleagues. Schoolwide leadership teams made decisions about the master schedule and the instructional budget, while grade-level teams made decisions about anything from grading practices to homework policies. In the words of DuFour, DuFour, and Eaker (2008), "The best way principals can help others learn to lead is to put them in a position where they are called upon to lead, and then provide them with feedback and support as they move forward" (p. 312).

Pushing out decision making, however, did not mean writing figurative (or even literal) blank checks to his faculty. Steve engaged in ongoing conversations with members of every team in his building and was open about his own reservations around controversial—or particularly consequential—decisions. *Empowering principals*, like Steve, are those who actively participate in conversations. They build time into their schedules for team meetings, recognizing that the best strategy to avoid being surprised by a decision is to know about the decision—or the sentiments leading up to the decision—well in advance.

Empowering principals also use the clear vision described in chapter 1, "Starting With a Vision," as a litmus test for schoolwide decision making. When teacher teams are engaged in making important decisions with potentially far-reaching consequences, the question that school leaders should ask is this: how does this decision align with our school vision? When teams throughout a school explicitly tie decisions to a set of commonly agreed-upon core principles and values, those decisions are going to be naturally aligned.

Along these same lines, empowering principals push teams to achieve defensible consensus. *Defensible consensus* means that a team has reached a level of agreement around a decision and can clearly articulate how that decision supports the school's goals. For example, early in the year at Central Middle, the sixth-grade language arts/social studies teachers made a controversial decision. The team decided that they would not count homework as part of a student's grade, and they would never put zeros in their grade books for missing assignments. No matter when a student turned in an assignment, he or she would receive credit for it based on its quality, not its timeliness.

When the team presented their decision to Steve, he pushed back. How would teachers explain this grading policy to parents? How could they expect students to take due dates seriously when assignments were accepted late for full credit? How would the team hold students accountable for developing responsible work behaviors given that assignments could be turned in anytime? And how did the team's decision explicitly align with the school's mission? All of these were reasonable questions that forced the sixth-grade team to defend the consensus they had achieved with thoughtful answers connected to the core values that defined Central Middle School.

What was perhaps most important about the conversation between the sixth-grade team and Steve in this example was that it happened within an environment of collaborative dialogue. The team presented its decision, looking for feedback and approval, rather than simply implementing the decision without any warning. Steve was honest in his push back. As we said earlier, distributed decision making does not mean a blank check, and it does not mean school leaders have to agree with every decision teams make. One piece of a trusting environment is being willing to openly communicate reservations or differing opinions.

Of course, the flip side of defensible consensus is that, when teams achieve it—that is, when they have good answers to all of administration's questions—principals need to be willing to let the decisions stand. In the case of the sixth-grade homework and grading policy, the team developed a strong rationale before approaching Steve. They planned to send home a detailed letter to parents explaining the policy; they developed a rubric that would give students and parents specific feedback about work behaviors; they even developed a *working lunch program*, where students with missing assignments would complete required tasks during their lunch period in classrooms.

Perhaps most importantly, the sixth-grade team explicitly tied their practice to the school's core values—an action that teacher leaders in a professional learning community must always take. As they argued, if Central Middle's mission was to ensure student learning, then should teachers not do everything in their power to keep students from receiving zeros in the gradebook and require that work be completed regardless of the time line?

While Steve was not completely comfortable with the team's homework policy, he trusted the professional opinion of his teachers, and he was proud of the work they had done together to craft an approach aligned with Central Middle's mission and based on a nuanced understanding of the nature of sixth-grade students. By being open about his reservations but supporting a team-generated decision that was clearly connected to Central Middle's core business, Steve earned the trust of the sixth-grade team. He knew that if he was going to push out decision making, he also needed to be willing to accept and support decisions that he did not entirely agree with—otherwise his teachers would be unwilling to invest mental energy in any decision pushed out in the future.

Our point is not that school leaders must support every decision made by teacher teams or that school leaders should never make decisions unilaterally. Clearly, there are situations that require administrators to make decisions without faculty input—and there are times when administrators believe it is in the best interests of a school to overrule decisions made by teacher teams. After all, there are a range of factors far beyond the classroom influencing decisions of which the typical teacher may have no awareness. If, however, school leaders want to create an environment of trust within their schools, they must model that trait in their own actions and relationships whenever possible.

In fact, one of the benefits of distributed decision making is that each decision pushed out to teacher teams is like a small deposit in the schoolwide trust account. Then, when leaders are faced with the need (or the perceived need) to make unpopular decisions, they have built up enough credit from colleagues to ensure that unilateral actions do not undermine the school's culture of trust.

Model and Reward the Behaviors You Want to See

While pushing out decision making is one powerful way in which school leaders can demonstrate that they trust the judgment and professionalism of the school staff, there are a variety of ways to model and reward the types of trusting behaviors necessary for a successful PLC to develop.

In the story that started this chapter, Steve takes several steps to reward and model specific behaviors. Perhaps most importantly, Steve allows Karen, a classroom teacher, to observe him teaching. After all, he expects his teachers to embrace peer observations. Following the observation, Steve engages Karen in dialogue about his teaching, just as he hopes the members of the sixth-grade team will engage in a dialogue with one another around their own teaching practices. By doing so, Steve sets a powerful example for the teachers in his building. His actions make it clear that collaborative conversations around practices are to be valued.

There are multiple opportunities for school leaders to model the reflection and professional dialogue so important to learning communities. Many principals begin by working together with teachers to generate a shared list of expectations for administration. Then, they gather feedback measuring the extent to which administrators are meeting these expectations every semester via surveys. They make the results transparent to the entire school community as principals engage their faculties in ongoing discussions about ways in which building leadership can improve.

For teacher leaders working on professional learning teams, modeling reflection and professional dialogue happens in both formal and informal interactions with colleagues. Demonstrating a willingness to become students engaged in collective inquiry of the current reality, teacher leaders encourage their peers to rethink and improve their practices. As teachers skeptical of change begin to see frequent examples of responsible professional behavior in action, those behaviors become the norm across entire schools.

The point is, if you want the teachers on your learning team or in your building to engage in honest, open dialogue about their professional practice, start by modeling. If you are unwilling to embrace collaborative reflection about the work you do each day, it is unrealistic to expect those behaviors to become a part of the fabric of your learning community.

Once trust and reflection take hold in a building, they must be regularly rewarded. As Anthony Muhammad (2009) notes, rewarding teachers for collaboration aligned with your school's mission should happen early and often:

> The positive school cultures I observed consistently celebrated the things the school valued. These celebrations were both planned and impromptu, and all were authentic. Recognition was genuine and not manufactured for the sake of giving the appearance of false appreciation in the midst of low productivity. These schools set clear expectations for all stakeholders—students, teachers, administrators, support staff, and parents. When these expectations were met, the achievements were celebrated proudly and publicly. (p. 106)

At Central Middle, rewards and celebration stretched far beyond simple incentives or prizes. In Steve's school, rewards included extra time and access to additional resources. He extended an offer to teachers throughout the school to create opportunities for peers to observe each other, knowing that observation is the type of activity that can spark dialogue and deepen professional relationships. Now, not every teacher was comfortable with the idea of colleagues taking notes from the back of class. However, when the sixth-grade language arts/social studies staff took Steve up on his offer, he gave of his own time to make sure that the peer observations became a reality.

Other accomplished administrators actively work to support teams with professional development dollars or informal recognition at the school level. They often send teams beginning their first efforts at developing common assessments to off-site workshops to refine their skills on the clock. Faculty meetings become impromptu forums for recognizing teams that have mastered particularly effective practices (Moller & Pankake, 2006).

For Steve, the most valuable rewards he could offer were genuine words of praise, appreciation, and congratulation—and he offered them on an almost constant basis. Understanding that a positive relationship with the principal is often the single most important factor in a teacher's willingness to put in extra effort, Steve was always looking for ways to informally thank his teachers.

Every conversation that he shared was an opportunity to encourage—and the encouragement paid off. Steve's teachers felt appreciated and were willing to do anything for him. More importantly, Steve's model spread through all levels of the organization, as teachers and support staff members found regular opportunities to offer informal commendations to one another. A culture of celebration was spreading, and the result was a sense of trust and togetherness that was undeniable.

School leaders may not have a pot of gold, but they do have a variety of tools and resources they can use to reward effective behavior. When leaders take the time to recognize and incent the types of professional activities that lead to collegial relationships and productive dialogue, they reinforce a developing culture of trust and professional improvement.

Relevant Theory and Research

In an article in *Educational Leadership*, Roland Barth (2006) makes a bold pronouncement: "The nature of relationships among the adults within a school has a greater influence on the character and quality of that school and on student accomplishment than anything else" (p. 8). Anyone who has spent time developing a professional learning community understands that relationships form the cornerstone of every transaction within a building. Without positive relationships, schools fail.

So what do effective relationships look like? Barth (2006) describes four stages of relationships that he has observed in schools:

1. **Parallel play**—If you have ever been on a play date with two-year-olds, you know what parallel play looks like: happy toddlers, each busily engaged in coloring or rolling a toy truck, and completely unaware of the fact that another toddler is sitting two feet away, absorbed in his or her own independent activity. The two children are playing at the same time, but their play is in parallel with each other, never intersecting. In a school, this describes the two teachers who work across the hall but have no idea what happens in each other's classrooms. They spend eight to ten hours a day no more than one hundred feet apart, but they might as well be living on separate continents.

2. **Adversarial relationships**—While open adversarial relationships sometimes exist in schools (such as the feuding history teachers who have been making snide comments about one another to generations of students) these types of relationships are usually more subtle. Maybe it is the veteran fifth-grade teacher who refuses to share her lesson plans with the struggling first-year rookie next door. Or the art teacher who hoards construction paper like a miser, deaf to the complaints of classroom teachers who have run out of supplies by midyear.

3. **Congenial relationships**—These are the relationships that stay in the personal realm. Congenial friendships exist between the English teachers who meet every Thursday after school for a cup of coffee, but never discuss the critical elements of an effective essay. Congenial relationships help us enjoy and look forward to our work day, but they rarely help us improve as professionals.

4. **Collegial relationships**—These are the relationships that have an impact on performance, for example teachers talking about practice, planning together, developing common assessments, and analyzing student data. When teachers are able to establish positive professional relationships, they improve their individual and collective capacities to improve teaching and learning.

According to Barth (2006), effective schools minimize parallel play and adversarial relationships while emphasizing congeniality and collegiality. Barth makes a number of recommendations to create what he calls a *culture of collegiality* that emphasizes positive professional relationships.

First, educators must regularly talk about professional practice and share craft knowledge. In a school attempting to become a PLC, this happens primarily in professional learning team meetings in which teachers talk about curriculum, assessment, and instruction and reflect on best practices. The next chapter specifically explores strategies for helping teacher teams to focus on curriculum and instruction.

Barth (2006) also recommends that school leaders create opportunities for teachers to observe each other, much as Steve did in the story at the beginning of this chapter. In describing his own experiences as an administrator trying to start peer observations among teachers, Barth makes an interesting point. The teachers at his school initially resisted the peer observation process, largely because they did not see Barth embracing collaborative reflection himself. This became readily apparent when a teacher finally asked him, "Why is it that we're supposed to observe each other, but you never have other administrators observing you?"

So, at the next faculty meeting, Barth introduced an invited guest: a principal from a nearby school. That visiting principal observed Barth facilitating the faculty meeting and provided feedback at the end of it. From that point forward, teachers in the building were much more willing to invite peers into their classrooms because they had seen their principal model the behavior for them.

While many education leaders might see the development of a PLC as a simple matter of Xs and Os—craft your mission statement, place teachers into teams, develop common assessments, and then introduce intervention and enrichment opportunities—Barth reminds us that none of this is possible without solid collegial relationships. In sports, the team with the most talented players often loses to the team that knows how to play well together. The same is true in schools: when educators work together as a unified team, they are able to transcend their individual talents and accomplish something truly extraordinary with their students.

Recommendations

Earlier in this book, we emphasize the importance of developing a common vision and assembling a core group of professional learning community champions. At this point, however, the focus of school leaders must turn to engendering a deep sense of trust throughout a building and strengthening the collegial relationships within professional learning teams. Here are our top recommendations for making this happen.

Recognize the Importance of Trust

Trust may be the most important ingredient in the development of highly functioning PLCs. In *Trust Matters: Leadership for Successful Schools*, Megan Tschannen-Moran (2004) argues that "professional learning communities share three important features: the adults in them act and are treated as professionals, there is a focus on learning, and there is a strong sense of community. For these three features to characterize a school's culture, trust is required" (p. 107).

When team members are not sure whether or not they can trust each other—when they are not willing to let down their guard and have open, honest conversations—not much happens. For teacher leaders working on learning teams, this means making a point of monitoring the sense of trust within grade levels or departments and constantly seeking out information about the quality of the relationships developing between teammates. Informally, teacher leaders use one-on-one situations to ask peers about the support that they need to work through their initial efforts at collaboration. Trust monitoring, however, should also be accomplished formally. Consider giving teachers quarterly or midyear surveys that explicitly ask about the relationships on their learning teams. A sample survey, The Trust on Our Team Survey (page 63), is included at the end of this chapter.

The responsibility for monitoring the levels of trust on professional learning teams also extends to administrators and instructional coaches. If you are a building principal or instructional support teacher, consider using the Record of School Relationships handout (page 64) to keep track of the different levels of trust in your building. Gather information for ratings from formal observations and informal conversations with classroom teachers and team leaders. Also, remember to update your records on an ongoing basis. Human relationships rarely remain stagnant.

One caution, however. When administrators ask about relationships, they will some-times get earfuls about the negative actions or attitudes of specific staff members. Resist the impulse to wade into team dynamics and fix problems. One of the best ways to earn staff members' trust is to demonstrate impartiality and discretion. One of the quickest ways to kill that trust is to take sides in personal spats.

Build Relationships One Conversation at a Time

We cannot overemphasize the importance of informal conversations when school leaders are out and about in the building. Administrators and classroom teachers are incredibly busy, and so many of the conversations that occur between them are formalized: staff meetings, observation conferences, IEP meetings, and so on. But those brief, informal opportunities—catching a colleague in the hall between periods, stopping by a classroom during planning, or even walking out to the parking lot together at the end of the day—can serve as the building blocks of professional relationships.

Sometimes administrators, instructional coaches, and highly motivated teacher leaders are tempted to use these encounters to push their own ideas or agendas. While this may be appropriate from time to time, effective leaders use these quick conversations primarily as opportunities to ask questions and recognize positive behavior. Ask about trends in student performance on the latest common assessment or the strengths and challenges of the new writing program. Comment on the quality of the conversations at the last professional learning team meeting or the high level of engagement during the most recent informal walkthrough. This approach builds rapport and sends the personal message that building leaders—whether principals or classroom teachers—are actively interested in and focused on the teaching and learning happening in the building.

Model, Model, Model

The real success of a PLC is its reliance on bottom-up interactions, driven by the day-to-day efforts of teachers and teacher teams throughout the building. But trust in a PLC comes from the top down. When teachers are concerned that they cannot trust building leaders—worried that a critical comment at the staff meeting could earn a reprimand or that a team decision could be arbitrarily overturned—they carry around a defensive wall that is tough to break through. Those defensive walls are what keep learning teams from being truly successful. As we discuss in more detail in the next chapter, "Supporting Team Development," teacher teams can only become high-performance units when individual members feel comfortable having open—and sometimes frank—discussions with one another.

For this reason, it is critically important that school leaders model positive, trusting relationships. When building leaders expose themselves to (or even actively invite) critical feedback, they make it safe for teachers to do the same. When building leaders push out decision making and then support the decisions that are made, they create the confidence and safety that are necessary for innovative thinking. In every conversation and decision, accomplished school leaders ask themselves the question, How do my actions model the types of behaviors that I, in turn, want teachers to exhibit?

If you are looking for an easy way to begin this modeling, consider giving the Professional Learning Community Administration Survey (pages 65–66) to your faculty and publicizing the results. Most administrators are not used to being evaluated by teachers, so this might be an uncomfortable experience for you; however, by allowing yourself to be evaluated, you will send a strong message about the kinds of reflective behaviors you value and that you hope to see spread across your building.

The Trust on Our Team Survey

This survey is designed to collect information about the levels of trust on our learning team. For each of the descriptors below, please indicate (1) the extent to which you agree or disagree with each statement by circling one of the three letters on the left-hand side, and (2) the level of importance that you place on each indicator by circling one of the three numbers on the right-hand side.

D = Disagree, N = Neutral, A = Agree   1 = Very important, 2 = Somewhat important, 3 = Not important

My colleagues willingly share their materials, resources, and ideas with me.	D	N	A	1	2	3
I feel welcome in my colleagues' classrooms before and after school.	D	N	A	1	2	3
I feel welcome in my colleagues' classrooms during their instructional periods.	D	N	A	1	2	3
I feel comfortable with my colleagues in my room during my instructional periods.	D	N	A	1	2	3
I believe that my colleagues have good intentions in their interactions with me.	D	N	A	1	2	3
I believe that my colleagues have good intentions in their interactions with students.	D	N	A	1	2	3
I know that I can count on my colleagues.	D	N	A	1	2	3
I believe that my colleagues are honest.	D	N	A	1	2	3
I am not afraid to share student learning results with my colleagues.	D	N	A	1	2	3
I believe that my colleagues are competent and capable teachers.	D	N	A	1	2	3
I believe that I can learn from my colleagues.	D	N	A	1	2	3
I believe that everyone on my team makes meaningful contributions to our work.	D	N	A	1	2	3
I believe that everyone on my team is pulling in the same direction.	D	N	A	1	2	3
Our team celebrates the personal and professional successes of individual members.	D	N	A	1	2	3
Our team celebrates our collective accomplishments.	D	N	A	1	2	3
I look forward to the time that I spend with my colleagues.	D	N	A	1	2	3

Final Thoughts: On the back of this page, please describe the kind of support you think your team would need in order to improve the overall levels of trust between teachers.

Record of School Relationships

Providing effective support to a diverse collection of learning teams depends on an accurate assessment of the current state of relationships between colleagues on each team. School leaders interested in tracking the nature of the relationships across their entire organization can use the following record, which is based on the four basic types of relationships defined by Roland Barth (2006):

1. **Parallel play**—Relationships where teachers and teams who work across the hall from one another have no idea what happens in each other's classrooms. They spend eight to ten hours a day no more than one hundred feet apart, but they might as well be living on separate continents.

2. **Adversarial relationships**—Relationships based in subtle competition. Maybe it is the veteran fifth-grade teacher who refuses to share her lesson plans with the struggling first-year rookie next door, or the art teacher who hoards construction paper, deaf to the complaints of classroom teachers who have run out of supplies by midyear.

3. **Congenial relationships**—Relationships that stay in the personal realm. Congenial friendships exist between the English teachers who meet every Thursday after school for a cup of coffee, but never discuss the critical elements of an effective essay. Congenial relationships help us enjoy and look forward to our work day, but they rarely help us improve as professionals.

4. **Collegial relationships**—Relationships that have an impact on performance, for example teachers talking about practice, planning together, developing common assessments, and analyzing student data. When teachers are able to establish positive professional relationships, they improve their individual and collective capacities to improve teaching and learning.

Learning Team	Date of Rating	Type of Relationship Noted				Evidence for Rating
		Parallel	Adversarial	Congenial	Collegial	
		Parallel	Adversarial	Congenial	Collegial	
		Parallel	Adversarial	Congenial	Collegial	
		Parallel	Adversarial	Congenial	Collegial	
		Parallel	Adversarial	Congenial	Collegial	
		Parallel	Adversarial	Congenial	Collegial	
		Parallel	Adversarial	Congenial	Collegial	

Professional Learning Community Administration Survey

This survey is designed to collect information about how effective administration has been at supporting learning community development in this building. For each of the statements below, please indicate (1) the extent to which you agree or disagree with each statement by circling one of the three letters on the left-hand side, and (2) the level of importance of each expectation by circling one of the three numbers on the right-hand side.

D = Disagree, N = Neutral, A = Agree   1 = Very important, 2 = Somewhat important, 3 = Not important

Mission and Vision Setting One responsibility of administrators in a learning community is to focus efforts on a clear mission/vision.						
Our school has a clear mission statement.	D	N	A	1	2	3
Our mission statement was developed collectively.	D	N	A	1	2	3
Our mission statement is frequently referenced by all faculty members in formal and informal meetings.	D	N	A	1	2	3
We have defined vision statements or guiding principles that describe what our mission should look like in action.	D	N	A	1	2	3
Resources—both financial and human—are allocated toward efforts that support our mission.	D	N	A	1	2	3
Hiring decisions are made with our mission in mind.	D	N	A	1	2	3
Scheduling decisions support our mission.	D	N	A	1	2	3
Community partnerships support our mission.	D	N	A	1	2	3
Learning teams have the flexibility/freedom to make decisions when they are aligned with our mission.	D	N	A	1	2	3
Decisions that are not aligned with our mission are questioned by our administration.	D	N	A	1	2	3
We review our mission and vision regularly and revise it when appropriate.	D	N	A	1	2	3

D = Disagree, N = Neutral, A = Agree   1 = Very important, 2 = Somewhat important, 3 = Not important

Atmosphere of Trust

Learning communities also depend on an atmosphere of trust and mutual respect that administrators encourage and promote.

Administrators are honest.	D	N	A	1	2	3
Administrators have a sense of humor.	D	N	A	1	2	3
Administrators systematically engage teachers from all grade levels and departments in key decisions.	D	N	A	1	2	3
Administrators celebrate all school accomplishments—athletic events, art achievements, and so on—equitably.	D	N	A	1	2	3
Administrators are visible throughout the school day.	D	N	A	1	2	3
Administrators recognize the personal and professional accomplishments of all faculty members.	D	N	A	1	2	3
Administrators hold all faculty members to clear and appropriate standards of performance.	D	N	A	1	2	3
Administrators respect and value dissenting opinions.	D	N	A	1	2	3

Action Orientation

Administrators in highly functioning learning communities promote an action orientation.

Administrators actively engage teachers in conversations about new instructional strategies.	D	N	A	1	2	3
Administrators promote and praise creative efforts—even when they are not successful.	D	N	A	1	2	3
Administrators model openness toward data.	D	N	A	1	2	3
Administrators help teams to use data to drive decisions.	D	N	A	1	2	3
Administrators realign resources and repurpose positions to meet identified student needs in our building.	D	N	A	1	2	3
Administrators find time and resources for teams to pursue continuous learning.	D	N	A	1	2	3
Administrators promote a collective responsibility for results.	D	N	A	1	2	3
Administrators hold all members of our school's faculty—from support staff to classroom teachers—accountable for student achievement.	D	N	A	1	2	3

2 of 2

CHAPTER 4

SUPPORTING TEAM DEVELOPMENT

Tom was not quite sure what had gone wrong, but his good intentions had clearly resulted in disaster.

Back at the beginning of November, Tom, Central Middle School's assistant principal, had conducted a formal observation of a seventh-grade language arts class. He was blown away by what he saw. The class was reading the novel *The Outsiders* by S. E. Hinton and learning about character development. Throughout the observation, students worked in teams on differentiated tasks as the teacher worked with small groups of students every five to ten minutes, providing feedback on progress and targeted instruction on various topics. From what Tom could tell, every student was engaged and motivated for the entire class period. He heard students having incredibly meaningful conversations with each other and saw students capturing their thoughts with sophisticated writing.

After the observation, Tom learned that the entire activity had been created by the seventh-grade language arts professional learning team. The team had developed a pretest that was administered to all students. Then the team created differentiated tasks based on the pretest. In addition, the teachers had analyzed results from the pretest as a team, to identify students who might struggle with particular concepts, and were planning to deliver a common posttest to measure the effectiveness of their teaching.

"At last," Tom thought, "a concrete example of the power of professional learning teams!" At the beginning of the year, the principal had asked Tom to work with the sixth-grade language arts/social studies teachers directly to help them improve their work as a team. Now he could show them exactly what the outcomes of collaboration could look like.

Tom had immediately approached Michael and Karen, two of the sixth-grade language arts/social studies team members, telling them that he would cover each of their classes for thirty minutes one day so they could observe what the seventh-grade language arts teachers were doing. Both Michael and Karen responded with an enthusiasm that did not seem completely genuine, but they agreed nonetheless.

Now, two weeks later, Tom was seeing the disappointing results of his good intentions. He had wandered into Sarah's sixth-grade social studies class for an informal walkthrough and observed a disorganized mess. Students appeared to be working at different stations throughout the room—the word *working* being a generous characterization. In reality,

Tom overhead conversations about weekend plans, a debate over who had the meanest dog, and tips on how to master the newest PlayStation® game.

Sarah was seated at a table with a small group of students, keenly aware of the unproductive chaos around her, explaining in a frustrated tone what the key differences had been between the Spartans and ancient Greeks. As Sarah became aware of Tom's presence, she shot him a look that communicated multiple messages—"Help!"; "Please don't fire me!"; and "How could you do this to me?"—all at the same time.

Later, during Sarah's planning period, Tom stopped by her room.

"Hey, Sarah . . . so what exactly happened in class today?"

"Disaster! That's what happened. Michael and Karen came to our professional learning team meeting earlier this week talking about what the seventh-grade teachers were doing and told us that you wanted us to try to be more like them. So I was here until 9:00 last night trying to create a bunch of differentiated learning stations—and then I came in at 6:00 this morning to copy them for everybody. You saw how it turned out: a disaster."

Tom was a little confused. After all, he had never told Michael or Karen that he wanted them to be more like the seventh-grade learning team. He had just mentioned how impressed he had been by the unit on *The Outsiders* that they had developed and thought the sixth-grade teachers might like the chance to see what they were doing in action. He explained all of this to Sarah.

"Well, that's not how it was communicated to us," snapped Sarah.

"So the team agreed in one meeting to just scrap all your lesson plans and create entirely new ones?" Tom asked.

"Um, I wouldn't say that the 'team agreed.' Michael and Karen just sort of told us that this is what we should do because that's how professional learning teams are supposed to look. No one wanted to argue with them—especially because they said that you made it clear that you wanted us to do this—so we just kind of followed their lead."

"And how did it fall to you to make all the lesson plans?"

"I don't know. Karen pointed out that I'm the resident expert on ancient Greece, which we're currently studying in social studies, so it just seemed to make sense for me to do the work. To be honest, I wasn't really sure what the seventh-grade lessons looked like, so I did my best to try to copy what Michael and Karen told us that they had seen."

Tom immediately apologized. He could tell how frustrated and exhausted Sarah was and knew how badly she probably felt about the poor lessons she had developed. Sarah was an accomplished teacher—and a bit of a perfectionist—who took great pride in her instruction. Failure was not an option for her. To make matters worse, he knew that Sarah's struggles started when Michael and Karen misunderstood his intentions in having them observe the seventh-grade language arts teachers. "I'm really sorry that this all fell on you," he said.

"That's okay, I'll survive. I guess this PLC thing is a little more complicated than we thought it would be."

Lessons From the Front Line

Sometimes, the best of intentions can go astray. After all, Tom's actions were well meant and in the spirit of professional learning community principles: he was encouraging collaboration, he wanted teachers to be able to learn from each other, and he was attempting to provide concrete examples of what success could look like. By working to focus the sixth-grade teachers on specific behaviors rather than beliefs, he was following the advice of Richard DuFour and Robert Eaker (1998):

> It is much more difficult to monitor the presence of beliefs than it is to monitor the presence of behaviors. While asking the question, "What do you believe?" could provide interesting answers that are worthy of consideration, finding shared answers to the question, "What are you prepared to do in support of those beliefs?" will be much more effective in advancing school improvement. (p. 96)

Despite his positive intentions, however, Tom ended up making a bit of a mess of things in the sixth-grade hallway. Why was that? Why did the opportunity to observe teachers who had successfully translated Central Middle's vision into action fail to drive positive innovation for the sixth-grade learning team?

The answer is *team development*. Tom failed to recognize that different teams develop at different rates, passing through stages that have a profound influence on the type of work they are capable—or not capable—of tackling. What is more, his own responsibilities had prevented him from finding the time to truly understand the team he was trying to support.

In this particular instance, Tom had little firsthand experience with the sixth-grade team's work. He had been to one or two of their meetings since the year began, but had been called away from both. Informal conversations with the teachers and a superficial review of meeting notes formed the foundation of his beliefs and opinions about the team's strengths and weaknesses. Tom simply did not know that the sixth-grade team had yet to develop the skills and dispositions necessary to wrestle with challenging new instructional practices together.

They had not yet developed formalized meeting structures—team norms, roles, expectations, and discussion protocols—to help them talk through Tom's suggestion. In addition, the team was not yet accustomed to taking on more complex teaching and learning tasks, such as developing gradewide differentiated lessons. Essentially, Tom was asking the sixth-grade team to run before they had learned to walk.

Complicating matters was the fact that Tom had never personally worked as a member of a collaborative learning team during the course of his career. While he had been an accomplished teacher for nearly ten years, his work was done in isolation. Instructional decisions were easy because they did not require consensus. These traditional experiences served as a barrier for Tom, preventing him from truly understanding the challenges that teachers faced in their efforts to collaborate.

Chapter 3, "Creating Trust," explored the concept of trust and the importance of building positive relationships within a team. Trust and relationships, however, are not enough to get teams through difficult conversations and decisions. Teams also need clear guidelines and a solid structure to help them in their work. Furthermore, both school leaders and teachers need an understanding of the developmental continuum that teams go through—and a common language to discuss that development.

This chapter explores the types of practices and strategies that can support positive team development. Specifically, we look at the four developmental stages and the progression of focus that professional learning teams typically work through. Additionally, we discuss strategies that school leaders can take to support positive development and challenge teams to constantly improve. Finally, we look at how research in child development might inform the work of professional learning teams.

The Stages of Team Development

Learning how to work well with others in a group setting is not easy. Managing personalities, creating consensus, and developing a team identity are all challenging, emotionally loaded activities that require time and skill to accomplish.

In schools, that difficulty is compounded by the fact that few teachers have direct experience with collaboration. As DuFour, DuFour, and Eaker (2008) note, "For more than 30 years, any serious study of the culture of teaching has reached the same conclusion: Teachers work in isolation" (p. 170). While teachers work right next door to each other, often developing strong congenial relationships, they rarely have the opportunity (or obligation, as the case may be) to work with each other in close, collegial relationships. Teachers are accustomed to working independently, making individual decisions about their classrooms—and many like it that way.

Because of the inherent difficulty of working with others, and because most teachers are used to working independently, when professional learning teams are put together and members suddenly asked to work in cooperation—to make collaborative decisions about what will happen in their classrooms—many teachers experience considerable frustration.

Back in the 1960s, Bruce Tuckman (1965) explored the ways in which teams develop over time and created a theory to describe that development. He found that teams tend to go through four common stages marked by specific issues, challenges, and behaviors. He labeled these stages *forming*, *storming*, *norming*, and *performing*. The following summaries of those four stages are adapted from a presentation by Glen Alleman (2004) and identify the typical characteristics and behaviors associated with each stage.

Forming

This initial stage in which a group comes together typically lasts only for the first several meetings. While forming, team members exhibit polite behaviors, feeling out their roles in the team and testing their relationships with each other. Members often sense excitement, anticipation, and anxiety about becoming members of a team and doing collaborative work. It is common for a few individuals to dominate discussions or deliberations as the group begins to define its tasks and acceptable group behavior.

Storming

During this stage, conflicts emerge within the team, especially around interpersonal issues. Individuals clash over control of the group and its work—and as team members disagree, they may blame the resulting conflict on teamwork. As teams storm, it is not unusual for passive aggressive behaviors to emerge and for some members to attempt to sabotage the group's work. As this stage continues, group members may become defensive or competitive, and may choose sides within the team. Additionally, team members may establish unrealistic goals or workloads and end up frustrated as goals are not met.

Norming

In the norming stage, teams begin to work together more productively and a positive team identity emerges. Members begin to take pride in—and see the value of—collaboration, sharing conversations that are generally positive. As interpersonal relationships improve, it is common for teams to actively attempt to avoid conflict and keep the sense of smooth sailing. At this point, new leaders may emerge, and meetings are likely to focus on achieving consensus, with the team making effective use of formal roles and rules to maintain harmony.

Performing

At this point, a team reaches a high level of functioning. Strong interpersonal relationships lead to members feeling a real sense of attachment to the team. These relationships (and the trust that underlies them) allow team members to disagree in constructive ways. Formal team roles and rules become less important as the team is able to work in a more organic fashion. Finally, the team internalizes reflective processes, identifying and executing self-chosen tasks that focus on continuous improvement.

What makes group development so difficult for school leaders is that even though every learning team will move through Tuckman's stages in the same order, different teams move ahead at different rates. In addition, most teams cycle back and forth between stages, for example, progressing from storming to norming, but then returning to storming when confronted with a new challenge or disagreement.

To put it simply, progress for learning teams is not continually forward and not always linear and smooth. As Robert Eaker and Richard and Rebecca DuFour (2002) write:

> The structural and cultural changes required to advance a traditional school on the continuum of becoming a PLC are inherently non-linear and complex. Progress is typically incremental, characterized more by starts and stops, messiness, and redundancy than sequential efficiency. (p. 2)

Progress is, however, identifiable in every case.

In the story at the beginning of this chapter, it is clear that the seventh-grade language arts teachers had reached a more advanced stage than their sixth-grade language arts/social studies peers in both team development and work focus. The seventh-grade teachers were working well together as a team, reflecting on instruction and identifying practices that would impact student learning in a meaningful way. Conversely, the sixth-grade team struggled to communicate with one another and to use student learning as the focal point for collective efforts. The central mistake made by Tom, the assistant principal, was in not realizing that the two teams were at different stages—and in expecting the sixth-grade team to take on a task for which it was not yet ready.

Two important steps would have made Tom's approach more productive. First, he could have taken the time to better understand the sixth-grade team by regularly attending team meetings, holding informal conversations with team members, and actively reflecting on team progress. Second, Tom could have worked to identify the sixth-grade team's current stage of development (most likely the storming stage) and provide members with the type of support necessary to move their group forward.

While both of these tasks would likely have been a challenge given the range of other tasks that Tom was responsible for as the assistant principal of a large middle school, it is arguably the determining factor in his ability to effectively support the development of his learning team. Without shared experiences and a sophisticated understanding of the strengths and weaknesses of his colleagues, it was just not possible for Tom to effectively design a course of action for the sixth-grade teachers he was responsible for supporting.

Taking Action to Drive Positive Change*

Another challenge for educators working to create a professional learning community is that learning teams tend to pass through similar stages in terms of the nature of their work. In general, professional learning team efforts progress from a focus on teaching (for example, what students should be learning and what assessments should look like) to a focus on learning (for example, monitoring whether or not students are mastering required content, supporting students who are not successful, and challenging those who are).

The good news for school leaders—whether serving in formal leadership roles like Tom or as teacher leaders embedded in learning teams—is that they can take specific actions to support teams that are developing at different rates. To understand these actions, it is essential to recognize the kinds of work that learning teams engage in as they grow together.

Filling the Time

The first question that novice teams typically ask is: "Okay, so what is it we're supposed to do, exactly?" Initial meetings can be rambling affairs, especially for teams that lack clear work guidelines. As teachers try to become comfortable with a collaborative way

---

* This section was previously published as "One Step at a Time" by Parry Graham and William Ferriter, *Summer JSD*, July 2008. Reprinted with permission of the National Staff Development Council, www.nsdc.org. All rights reserved.

of doing business, meetings can swing from one extreme to the other. New challenges emerge, such as struggling to find enough topics to fill collaborative time or trying to tackle too many topics and tasks in hour-long meetings. Frustration is inevitable for groups grappling with new responsibilities.

The best way for school leaders to help teams move out of this stage quickly is to set clear work expectations. According to DuFour, DuFour, Eaker, and Many (2006), "Principals must do more than assign teachers into teams and hope for the best: They must establish clear parameters and priorities that guide the work of the teams toward the goals of improved student learning" (p. 99). Providing teams with specific tasks to complete, such as identifying essential curriculum objectives for the next quarter or creating common assessments, lends direction to what can be an ambiguous and overwhelming process. Sample agendas, suggested team roles, and sets of norms that can be adapted are helpful tools for developing teams and serve to focus attention on behaviors rather than beliefs. When school leaders fail to give teams suggested tasks and basic structures for meetings, collaboration can quickly become confusing, or worse yet, be seen as a waste of time by teachers comfortable with isolation.

Specific expectations keep a group focused, providing tangible proof of progress to administrators, but more importantly, to collaborating teachers as well. As teams complete individual tasks successfully, confidence in collective action grows, and there is cause for real celebration.

Sharing Personal Practices

A common next question asked by professional learning teams is, "What is everyone doing in their classrooms?" Teachers ask this question for a variety of reasons. They may be genuinely interested in what other teachers are doing and hope to pick up new ideas. Or, it may be that talking about what others are doing feels like collaboration. Initially, there is great value in these conversations. Sharing practices can serve as a first step toward making instruction transparent. More importantly, conversations about instructional practices can be comfortable, helping to establish positive patterns of interpersonal dialogue between members of a learning team.

Unfortunately, many teams get complacent and fail to move beyond the simple sharing of instructional practices. While such conversations are a good beginning, the real work of PLCs is reflective and inquiry oriented, resulting in teacher learning and improved instruction.

School leaders can help teams move toward more meaningful work by requiring team members to arrive at collaborative decisions around curriculum, assessment, or instruction. For example, teams could be required to create a series of shared minilessons that all teachers will implement in their classrooms, shifting the focus from individual efforts to collective exploration of effective instruction.

Planning, Planning, Planning

As teachers become more comfortable with each other, teams will begin to ponder, "What should we be teaching and how can we lighten the load?" Planning—a task that all teachers are responsible for and consumed by—is, hence, seen as a logical place to begin collective efforts.

At this stage, school leaders may begin to see a self-imposed standardization of the curriculum emerge within teams. In other words, collaborating teachers begin teaching roughly the same thing at roughly the same time in roughly the same way. One of the advantages of this stage is that both less experienced and less effective teachers benefit from the planning acumen of more experienced and more effective colleagues. Another advantage is that the team is able to delegate responsibilities and workload. Rather than each teacher individually planning every lesson, different team members can take responsibility for different lessons and share their work.

The primary disadvantage of this stage is that teams often fail to focus on the results of their instruction. Unless challenged, planning often remains centered on *inputs*—what the teacher is doing—but student learning is about *outputs*. The most effective way for school leaders to move teams forward is to structure and support efforts to utilize student achievement data in the planning process. School leaders must ask teacher teams to answer basic questions about results: Are your students learning what you want them to learn? How do you know?

Developing Common Assessments

New thinking related to student outputs will force teams to ask, "What does student mastery look like?" This question can cause controversy primarily because it taps into teachers' deepest philosophies about education. Should the focus of a classroom be on basic skills, or should it be on applying knowledge in real-world situations? Which is more important, being able to get the right answer or being able to explain your work?

In the PLC process, learning teams first struggle with these questions while developing common assessments. Shared assessments force teachers to define exactly what it is that students should learn—and what kind of evidence is necessary for documenting success. Novice teams may work to avoid common assessments, steering clear of the discomfort of difficult conversations—but common assessments are essential if teams are to shift from a focus on teaching to a focus on learning. According to DuFour, DuFour, Eaker, and Many (2006), "Common assessments represent the most effective strategy for determining whether the guaranteed curriculum is being taught and, more importantly, learned" (p. 56).

Wrestling with fundamental beliefs requires teachers to develop the interpersonal skills necessary for working through contention. Having had the opportunity to set individual direction with little intervention, many experienced teachers lack the skills necessary for finding common ground. While teams with positive interpersonal relationships thrive on the mental synergy generated by complex conversations about teaching and learning, teams struggling with personalities (and still in the storming stage) need real support. School leaders should consider moderating difficult conversations and modeling strategies for building consensus and making joint decisions. Rather than focusing efforts on solving problems, school leaders must build teaming capacity and conflict-resolution skills within members of their faculty.

At this point in their development, it is also essential to provide teams with a common language about development. At Central Middle, the sixth-grade language arts/social studies team members felt like failures, frequently asking themselves, "What are we doing wrong? Why is this so hard?" Had team members known ahead of time that their struggles were an inevitable part of the team-building process, they would have been less likely to see themselves as unsuccessful. Tom eventually began explaining the phases of team development to all of his teachers, highlighting storming around common assessments as something to be embraced, rather than feared. By doing so, he gave team members a language and framework with which to work through disagreements and the ability to see conflict as a natural by-product of working well together.

It is also important to note that teams may need additional training in assessment during this stage of development. While teachers often possess an intuitive understanding of student strengths and weaknesses, common assessments require a measure of standardization—both of task and of judgment—to provide reliable comparisons and stimulate productive conversations among peers. Investing energies into measures of performance that are simplistic or unreliable only serves to frustrate teams and stall future work. Spending time on a study of the core differences between assessments *of* learning and *for* learning—as well as reviewing strategies for selecting or developing appropriate assessments for a wide range of different outcomes—guarantee that joint evaluation of student learning will be effective and embraced by developing teams.

Analyzing Student Learning

After creating and administering common assessments, the next question is perhaps the most challenging: "Are students learning what we think they are supposed to be learning?" By this point, teams have become more productive, disagreements are less frequent, and group members feel positive about their collaborative work. A developing sense of collective identity allows professional learning teams to begin to shift their focus from teaching to learning, actively exploring the relationship between instructional practices and outcomes. This shift, however, requires extensive technical and emotional support.

Technically, teachers will need frequent and easy access to user-friendly results that will both inform and improve their practice. In some schools and districts, these data are collected and organized by professionals working beyond the classroom—principals, data coaches, central office specialists. Other schools and districts embrace digital solutions to this challenge, providing teachers with districtwide formative assessment systems, handheld student responders, or netbook computers that make easy data collection and manipulation possible (Ferriter, 2009).

As teams begin to embrace a focus on results, teachers are likely to want significant training on data analysis and interpretation. Using data effectively is a complex and nuanced process—and it remains an area in which most teachers lack experience and expertise. School leaders who provide structures, tools, and suggestions for effective data analysis are rewarded with highly motivated teams driven by results. Many successful learning communities repurpose positions, hiring teachers trained in data analysis to assist teams in identifying and interpreting trends in student learning. We discuss specific recommendations for dealing with the technical aspects of common assessment data in chapter 7, "Connecting Data Analysis and Instructional Improvement."

Emotionally, common assessment data reveal varying levels of student success across classrooms, leading to initial feelings of guilt, inadequacy, and even defensiveness. Teachers are put in the delicate and controversial position of publicly facing what they inevitably—yet inaccurately—view as their individual successes and failures. This intensely personal reaction is understandable from professionals invested in meaningful work yet confronted with unyielding outside evidence.

When handled properly, however, analysis of student learning can lead to rich conversations about effective instruction. According to DuFour, DuFour, and Eaker (2008):

> Without relevant information on their respective strengths and weaknesses, teacher conversations regarding the most effective ways to help students learn a concept will deteriorate into sharing of uninformed opinions—"This is how I like to teach it." Improving teacher practice requires informed and precise conversation about effective techniques, and the best way to provide teachers with the tools for that conversation is to ensure each receives frequent and timely information regarding the achievement of his or her students in reaching an agreed-upon standard on a valid assessment in comparison to other similar students attempting to achieve the same standard. (p. 27)

When teachers have these types of conversations, and as they spot patterns in student data, they can work as a unit to respond in productive ways. On highly functioning teams, the collective intelligence of the group provides a never-ending source of strategies and solutions for addressing shared challenges. However, getting teams to this point requires emotional support and patience.

In helping teacher teams to move forward, we encourage school leaders to create safe environments in which teachers can discuss common assessments and model nonjudgmental approaches to data. Separating the person from the practice is an essential first step for teams examining results. Possible starting points for safe conversations about outcomes include leading teacher teams in discussions of videotaped lessons, providing teachers with comparative student data for a study of achievement levels, or structuring grade-level book studies focused on the characteristics of quality instruction.

School leaders should also walk the walk, sharing school data reflecting their own work, such as faculty or parent surveys, in public forums. By modeling a data-oriented approach, school leaders send the message that data analysis is about improving practices, not judging personalities.

Differentiating Follow-Up

While teacher teams will almost naturally move to the next stage of team development, focusing on how to respond instructionally to student data, school leaders can help facilitate this transition in two important ways: by asking teams to reflect on the right questions and by giving teams the resources they need to craft appropriate responses.

As teams become more adept at analyzing student data, school leaders should no longer be in the role of directing team development. Instead, they should serve as collaborative partners in ongoing conversations focused on teaching and learning. At Central Middle, the seventh-grade language arts team appeared to be able to analyze data and act upon it. The team began by developing a preassessment to identify student proficiency prior to instruction. Next, they created differentiated activities that attempted to meet students where they were and help them progress forward. Finally, they administered a posttest to collect information on student learning. Teams at this point in the process are typically performing at a high level, taking collective responsibility for the performance of their students rather than responding as individuals.

The most effective way to further develop a team at this level of functioning is to pose a variety of questions, both to the team, collectively, and to its individual members: "Which instructional practices are you finding to be most effective across your team? How do you know they are the most effective? What concepts do your students struggle with the most? Why do they struggle with them? Are your students able to apply knowledge to novel problems? How do you know?" By posing such provocative questions and demonstrating flexibility as teams pursue various approaches for student intervention and enrichment, school leaders encourage the professional ownership that defines our most accomplished educators.

More importantly, however, school leaders must begin to identify concrete ways in which they can directly support differentiation efforts. Traditionally, this has meant identifying appropriate professional development opportunities or providing substitute teachers so that teachers can plan responses as a group. Interested teams are often sent to training sessions or engaged in partnerships with sister schools sharing similar student populations. Leaders can also find funding for after-school tutoring sessions, honoring the time and talents of teachers filling what were once voluntary roles.

Supporting differentiation also means making a commitment to nontraditional thinking about school structures and processes beyond the classroom. The most effective administrators are willing to reallocate positions within the school, focusing resources on serving struggling students. Rethinking the role of nonclassroom educators like guidance counselors, secretaries, teacher assistants, media specialists, assistant principals, and literacy coaches creates a pool of human capital that can be tapped to address the knotty challenges involved in differentiating learning opportunities for all students.

Learning community expert Austin Buffum (2008) sees these kinds of efforts as something more than simply marshalling resources. They are, instead, opportunities to bolster the confidence of teachers working in new ways:

> Teachers are . . . more willing to try new things when the administration is effective at finding the necessary resources to turn a new idea for teaching into reality. When teachers engage in collective inquiry and begin to ask for

new resources based upon their research, administrators must build trust by writing grants, providing teachers the opportunity to observe other classrooms or schools, asking the PTA to help purchase manipulatives, and so on. (p. 64)

To put it simply, action on the part of those working beyond the classroom is essential to maintaining the momentum of a learning community. While school leaders can begin to move out of a directive role with individual teachers and teams, their efforts to coordinate available resources, support innovative approaches to differentiation, and engage faculty members in new work determine how successful a faculty will be at meeting the needs of every learner.

Reflecting on Instruction

Teams that are performing at a high level eventually ask themselves one final question: "What instructional practices are the most effective with our students?" This final question brings the process of learning team development full circle, connecting learning back to teaching. Teams at this point are engaged in deep reflection and inquiry, tending to tackle innovative projects such as action research or lesson studies.

At this point, school leaders should actively facilitate a team's ability to take on its own projects and explore the teaching–learning connection. Efforts might include giving teachers the opportunity to conduct in-depth lesson studies or providing release time to complete action-research projects. When multiple teams in a school are at this level, leaders might want to consider ways to facilitate cross-team conversations, which create opportunities for practices and perspectives to migrate across grade levels and subject areas, thus spreading innovations schoolwide.

Regardless of where your school is in the professional learning community process, rest assured that your teams are living, breathing social organisms that are constantly changing. As a school leader, it is essential to respect and support each team as they work to grow.

Relevant Theory and Research

Team development can be boiled down to three maxims. First, every team is different, but all teams walk a similar path. Second, teams need new challenges to move forward, but too great a challenge can push them backward. And third, just as teachers must differentiate their practices for students, school leaders must differentiate their practices for teams.

Research in child development, interestingly enough, lends credence to these maxims. The theory of zones of proximal development (Vygotsky & Cole, 1978) suggests that individuals can master progressively more complex skills with support and guidance. Correlations can be made between this theory and the growth of learning teams. By thinking of teams as coherent entities with their own personalities and growth paths, school leaders can craft effective strategies to support and challenge team development.

Lev Vygotsky was a Russian psychologist born around the turn of the century and, although he died at a relatively young age, he introduced a number of important child-development theories that are still considered relevant today. One of those theories concerned what he called the *zone of proximal development*, or ZPD (Vygotsky & Cole, 1978).

The ZPD represents the difference between what a child is currently able to do independently and what she can potentially do with support. For example, imagine a child who is able to independently add two-digit numbers together, but struggles with two-digit subtraction. If this child were able to successfully subtract two-digit numbers with some adult help, then we could say that two-digit subtraction is within her ZPD—she cannot do it by herself, but she is in a cognitive developmental stage that is close (proximal) to mastery of the skill. With some support and practice, she could gradually come to master two-digit subtraction independently.

In addition, while some skills are within a child's ZPD, some skills are simply too complex and cannot yet be mastered. In the previous example, two-digit multiplication would likely lie outside the child's ZPD; she would need to master several intermediate concepts and skills before being able to multiply two-digit numbers.

If this sounds like common sense to you, we agree. People master skills and concepts in successive stages. With support and guidance, people can gradually come to master skills and concepts of increasing complexity or difficulty; however, some skills and concepts are simply too difficult for a person to immediately acquire, necessitating the mastery of intermediate skills or concepts.

This common-sense theory also applies to professional learning teams. Just as certain skills and concepts lie within an individual's ZPD, certain tasks and processes lie within a team's ZPD. Thinking in terms of team ZPD means that teachers and school leaders should be engaged in continual reflection on a number of related questions:

- Where is a team currently in terms of its development?
- What new tasks and processes lie within the team's ZPD?
- What types of support or guidance will help the team master these new tasks and processes independently?
- What new tasks and processes lie outside the team's ZPD and should be avoided for the time being?

In the story that started this chapter, Tom, the assistant principal, introduced new tasks and processes that were outside the sixth-grade team's ZPD, setting the team up for failure. What Tom might have tried, instead, was to take one specific task—say developing a common assessment on ancient Greece that all sixth-grade language arts/social studies teachers could have given to their students—and work with the team to provide guidance and support in accomplishing this task. After creating one common assessment with Tom's support, the team might then have been able to go on to create another common assessment independently. In this way, Tom could have helped the team gradually move toward the more complex tasks accomplished by the seventh-grade team, but at a rate that recognized the sixth-grade team's ZPD.

The idea of team ZPD provides an effective mental model for considering team evolution. In addition, the stages of team development (forming, storming, norming, and performing) and the progression of focus described earlier in this chapter provide a specific framework for tracking and supporting team growth over time. By combining the ZPD model with the team development strategies outlined in this chapter, principals, instructional coaches, and teacher leaders working to drive change from the classroom can avoid the type of mistake that Tom made at Central Middle and support and challenge team growth effectively.

Recommendations

It is apparent to us that there are recognizable patterns to the development of professional learning teams and that school leaders should both recognize and respond to these patterns appropriately to support growth. Following are our most important recommendations for challenging and supporting professional learning teams as they develop.

Lay the Proper Groundwork

There are three types of groundwork that school leaders must ensure are in place to support team development. The first is structural. Teachers must be organized into explicit teams and must have time during the school day to meet. Second, teachers need specific procedural expectations. Some procedural expectations should be left up to teams to decide. For example, teams should create their own sets of meeting norms, choose the roles that they would like to use during team meetings (such as timekeeper, recorder, and facilitator), and decide how they will come to team consensus. Other procedural expectations should be decided upon by school leadership. Consider requiring all teams to create meeting agendas, keep copies of meeting minutes, and distribute meeting minutes to administrators.

The third type of groundwork involves undertaking team tasks. Learning teams that are just beginning their work together need specific jobs to perform. Logical starting points might include identifying essential curriculum, developing a common assessment, or creating a team action plan. Explicitly focusing learning teams on the types of tasks that are appropriate within a PLC organizes their work, encourages the productive use of time, and minimizes frustration.

School leaders should set an early meeting specifically focused on procedural expectations with any faculty new to the work of learning communities. This type of meeting could begin with an overview of the PLC structure, move to an explanation of the tasks that will be expected of teams for the first two months, and conclude with time for teams to create their own sets of norms and expectations. Addressing this groundwork in a formal way at the beginning of the year gets everyone off on the same foot and increases the chances that teams will settle into comfortable meeting routines.

Teacher leaders are often critical for ensuring that teams identify and undertake appropriate tasks because they possess firsthand knowledge of the strengths and weaknesses of their learning teams. In the most successful schools, principals and instructional coaches work closely with teacher leaders to identify the kinds of professional development needed for moving each unique learning team forward. To better organize professional development efforts in your building, consider asking teachers to fill out the Professional Development for Learning Teams checklist (page 84) included at the end of this chapter.

Educate Participants About the Process

There are a lot of things that can go wrong when trying to develop a PLC. As demonstrated in the story that started this chapter, miscommunication and misunderstanding happen more frequently than participants would like or expect. When this occurs, it can be extremely frustrating because missteps can feel like failures.

What feels like failure, however, is usually just a natural result of trying to improve a school's traditional way of doing business. We strongly recommend taking every opportunity to educate faculty members about the potential frustrations associated with the PLC process. By explicitly talking about the difficulties of implementing a PLC, you give teachers a framework and language to understand and discuss their own frustrations. As Peter Noonan, assistant superintendent for curriculum and instruction in Fairfax County, Virginia, found:

> Making fundamental changes in schools is historically one of the most difficult tasks for any administrator. As educators, we are afraid of making mistakes that will negatively impact the next generation of kids. This is certainly a noble reason to slow down the process of change, but often results in the status quo and no movement forward. Consequently, we fall back to what we have always done. To break down the walls of fear and paralysis, we must create a new vocabulary laden with research, philosophy for the 21st century, and instructional best practice. (2008, pp. 48–49)

The need for a new vocabulary is especially true of teams in the storming stage of professional learning team development. When participants know in advance what storming looks like—and understand that it is a natural part of growing together—they feel empowered to work through the frustration.

If you are a teacher leader working on a learning team, regularly engage your colleagues in conversations about your collective development. Have collaborative peers brainstorm topics about which they think they may end up storming (for example, participants not staying on task during meetings), record those topics on index cards, and then write a possible strategy to address the storming on the reverse side of the card. By collecting and organizing team-generated solutions for common collaborative conflicts, your learning team will have a customized list of ideas to help them get through the storming stage. Also, consider reviewing the handout Weathering the Storm: Storming Strategies and Suggestions for Learning Teams available for free download at **go.solution-tree.com/ PLCbooks** in one of your next team meetings. By doing so, you will build the weathering capacity of your colleagues.

Continuously Reflect on and Adjust Leadership Practices

In order to avoid mistakes similar to the one made by Tom in the story at the beginning of this chapter, leaders—whether they are principals, instructional coaches, or motivated teacher leaders—need to continuously reflect on the growth of the learning teams in their buildings. At what stage of development is a particular team? Is it focusing on teaching tasks or learning tasks? What processes are within the group's ZPD, and what leadership strategies are most appropriate to help the team move on to more advanced collective actions?

In order to seriously consider and answer these questions, school leaders must be "tapped in" to the work of learning teams. If you are a building principal or an instructional coach working beyond the classroom, being tapped in means reading and rereading meeting notes, sitting in on planning sessions, and having formal and informal conversations with team members. Gayle Moller and Anita Pankake (2006) encourage school leaders to make time for "stop-bys":

> Principals are unable to attend every scheduled meeting. However, they can, with a little planning, "stop by" to check in on how things are going with most meetings. Finding time to stop by . . . allows principals to be in tune with what's going on and who is involved with what's going on. As brief as stop-bys might be, they still provide an opportunity to gather information about the focus of the meeting and the participants. (p. 80)

Being tapped in also means convening regularly as a leadership team. When administrators take the time to meet and share with each other their impressions, thoughts, and questions about the professional learning teams they are charged with supporting, they are engaged in creating their own high-functioning team. Consider reviewing the Professional Development for Learning Teams documents (see pages 84–90) together, looking for patterns in the type of support that your learning teams need in order to succeed.

For teachers on learning teams, being tapped in means systematically collecting perception data from time to time to use as a form of self-reflection. Administering the Learning Team Collaboration Survey (pages 85–88) may provide you with a more complete picture of the strengths, weaknesses, and general PLC understandings of each of the teachers on your team.

Strike a Balance Between Supporting and Challenging

One of the common snares for administrators and highly motivated teacher leaders in a PLC is impatience—wanting to see positive results right away and pushing teams too hard when their work does not initially meet lofty expectations. Another common snare is inattention—putting time and energy into the early stages of PLC development and then failing to stay engaged in the process as other day-to-day priorities emerge.

The trick, of course, is to find the sweet spot between these two extremes. One of the best ways we can recommend to remain focused is to continually refer to the Stages of

Team Development reference guide (pages 89–90) included at the end of this chapter. By doing so, you will have a regular reminder that teams are ready for different tasks at different times as well as a list of appropriate tasks that you may want to encourage teams to consider.

Administrators and other school leaders will also want to maintain ongoing conversations with core members of the faculty. Back in chapter 2, "Empowering the Core Team," we talked about the important role core faculty members play in the early development of a PLC. By maintaining open, regular, and informal lines of conversation with those key players, school leaders can keep up to date on the status of team development and have a strong sense of where the team still needs to make progress.

When a core member indicates frustration that a team is not moving along quickly enough, this could mean it is time for a little extra challenge. Conversely, when a core member shows clear signs of fatigue or sounds overwhelmed, it could mean that it is time to slow things down and provide a little extra support. And, when core members start asking administrators, "So when are you going to be stopping by one of our meetings?" it probably means it is time to leave the paperwork behind for the morning and catch up on where learning teams are in their development!

Professional Development for Learning Teams

The work of learning teams presents new challenges that must be addressed with systematic professional development. Team members must acquire two broad categories of skills: team-based collaboration skills and skills for instructional reflection. Using the following checklist, indicate the kinds of professional development that you believe would best move your team forward.

Team Name: _____   Teacher Name (optional): _____

My team needs immediate support in (select 1–3 items) . . .

Team-Based Collaboration Skills

- ☐ Developing team norms and protocols
- ☐ Determining how group conversations and meetings will be structured
- ☐ Determining how consensus will be reached
- ☐ Determining how violations of team norms will be addressed
- ☐ Determining how the results of team work will be recorded
- ☐ Conducting effective conversations
- ☐ Finding common ground and working towards consensus
- ☐ De-personalizing discussions of curricular, assessment, and instructional practices
- ☐ Building trust between colleagues
- ☐ Setting goals and reflecting on results
- ☐ Uncovering hidden disagreements
- ☐ Embracing conflict as a positive tool for continued growth
- ☐ Using protocols for priority setting
- ☐ Conducting team-based, self-directed action research and/or lesson study
- ☐ Amplifying "lessons learned" across our entire grade level and/or department
- ☐ Understanding the characteristics of adult learners and continuing education
- ☐ Other: _____

Instructional Reflection Skills

- ☐ Identifying required state and district curricular expectations
- ☐ Prioritizing learning objectives based on an understanding of our students
- ☐ Designing a logical sequence for addressing required elements of the curriculum
- ☐ Understanding the difference between formative and summative assessment
- ☐ Connecting assessments to specific learning goals
- ☐ Measuring higher-order thinking skills
- ☐ Developing performance-based assessments
- ☐ Creating reliable assessment instruments such as rubrics
- ☐ Using data collection and analysis tools such as student responders, netbooks, and Microsoft Excel™
- ☐ Understanding the differences between data analysis and data interpretation
- ☐ Developing discussion protocols for conversations related to data
- ☐ Identifying common areas of student mastery and misunderstanding
- ☐ Understanding the unique characteristics of both low and high achievers
- ☐ Defining strategies and identifying tools for differentiating lesson plans
- ☐ Investigating the relationships between instructional practices and student learning outcomes
- ☐ Developing protocols for lesson study and action research
- ☐ Developing protocols and practices for peer observation
- ☐ Other: _____

Learning Team Collaboration Survey

This survey is intended to help us learn about our current collaborative practices and our goals for collaboration. Please complete this survey with the members of your learning team as honestly and thoughtfully as possible. By gathering reliable information about our current practices, current areas of concern, and future goals, we can constantly work to improve the quality of education we provide our students.

Please return this survey to _____ **by** _____.

Your learning team: _____

Your Definitions

As a learning team, please discuss your ideas of the following concepts and how they relate to the work that you do together:

Collaboration:

Content:

Assessment:

Instructional strategies:

Student achievement data:

The Current Situation

As a learning team, please indicate the extent to which each of the statements below is true by circling one of the four numbers using the following scale:

1 = Very true   2 = True   3 = Somewhat true   4 = Not true

1. As a learning team, we collaborate regularly to decide what content we will teach in each of our classrooms.	1	2	3	4
2. As a learning team, we collaborate regularly to decide what assessments we will use in each of our classrooms.	1	2	3	4
3. As a learning team, we collaborate regularly to decide what instructional strategies we will use in each of our classrooms.	1	2	3	4
4. As a learning team, we collaborate regularly to analyze student achievement data.	1	2	3	4
5. As a learning team, we make decisions to adjust instructional practices based on analysis of student achievement data.	1	2	3	4
6. As a learning team, we have the necessary skills to analyze student achievement data in order to make instructional decisions.	1	2	3	4
7. As a learning team, we have the skills to address controversial topics, such as differences in student learning across classrooms.	1	2	3	4

As a learning team, please answer the following questions, providing as much detail as possible.

1. Our learning team identifies students who are struggling academically through the following practices or assessments:

2. When our learning team identifies students who are struggling academically, we respond by:

Future Goals

As a learning team, please answer the following questions, providing as much detail as possible.

1. Eventually, we would like to see our learning team collaborating in the following ways to do the following things:

2. Eventually, as a result of team collaboration, we would like to see our students achieve the following things:

3. In order to reach our goals as a learning team, we need to address the following barriers and challenges:

4. In order to reach our goals as a learning team, we need to develop the following skills:

5. In order to reach our goals as a learning team, we need the administration to support us in the following ways:

6. Our greatest success as a learning team is the following:

Stages of Team Development

While the process of developing a professional learning team may feel uniquely personal, there are certain stages of development common across teams. By understanding that these stages exist—and by describing both the challenges and opportunities inherent in each stage—school leaders can improve the chances of success for every learning team. Use the following quick reference guide to evaluate the stages of team development in your building and to identify practical strategies for offering support.

Characteristics of Stage	Strategies for Offering Support
Stage: Filling the Time	
• Teams ask, "What is it exactly that we're supposed to do together?" • Meetings can ramble. • Frustration levels can be high. • Activities are simple and scattered rather than a part of a coherent plan for improvement.	☐ Set clear work expectations. ☐ Define specific tasks for teams to complete (for example, identifying essential objectives or developing common assessments). ☐ Provide sample agendas and sets of norms to help define work.
Stage: Sharing Personal Practices	
• Teamwork focuses on sharing instructional practices or resources. • A self-imposed standardization of instruction appears. • Less-experienced colleagues benefit from the planning acumen of colleagues. • Teams delegate planning responsibilities.	☐ Require teams to come to consensus around issues related to curriculum, assessment, or instruction. ☐ Require teams to develop shared minilessons delivered by all teachers. ☐ Structure efforts to use student learning data in the planning process. ☐ Ask questions that require data analysis to answer.
Stage: Developing Common Assessments	
• Teachers begin to wrestle with the question, "What does mastery look like?" • Emotional conversations around the characteristics of quality instruction and the importance of individual objectives emerge. • Pedagogical controversy is common.	☐ Provide teams with additional training in interpersonal skills and conflict management. ☐ Moderate or mediate initial conversations around common assessments to model strategies for joint decision making. ☐ Ensure that teams have had training in how to best develop effective common assessments. ☐ Create a library of sample assessments from which teams can draw.

1 of 2

Stage: Analyzing Student Learning	
• Teams begin to ask, "Are students learning what they are supposed to be learning?" • Teams shift attention from a focus on teaching to a focus on learning. • Teams need technical and emotional support. • Teachers publically face student learning results. • Teachers can be defensive in the face of unyielding evidence. • Teachers can grow competitive.	☐ Provide tools and structures for effective data analysis. ☐ Repurpose positions to hire teachers trained in data analysis to support teams new to working with assessment results. ☐ Emphasize a separation of "person" from "practice." ☐ Model a data-oriented approach by sharing results that reflect on the work of practitioners beyond the classroom (for example, by principals, counselors, and instructional resource teachers).

Stage: Differentiating Follow-Up	
• Teachers begin responding instructionally to student data. • Teams take collective action, rather than responding to results as individuals. • Principals no longer direct team development. Instead, they serve as collaborative partners in conversations about learning.	☐ Ask provocative questions about instructional practices and levels of student mastery. ☐ Demonstrate flexibility as teams pursue novel approaches to enrichment and remediation. ☐ Provide concrete ways to support differentiation. ☐ Identify relevant professional development opportunities; allocate funds to after-school tutoring programs. ☐ Redesign positions to focus additional human resources on struggling students.

Stage: Reflecting on Instruction	
• Teams begin to ask, "What instructional practices are most effective with our students?" • Learning is connected back to teaching. • Practitioners engage in deep reflection about instruction. • Action research and lesson study are used to document the most effective instructional strategies for a school's student population.	☐ Facilitate a team's efforts to study the teaching-learning connection. ☐ Create opportunities for teachers to observe one another teaching. ☐ Provide release time for teams to complete independent projects. ☐ Facilitate opportunities for cross-team conversations to spread practices and perspectives across an entire school. ☐ Celebrate and publicize the findings of team studies.

PART III

WINTER: WEATHERING THE CHALLENGES

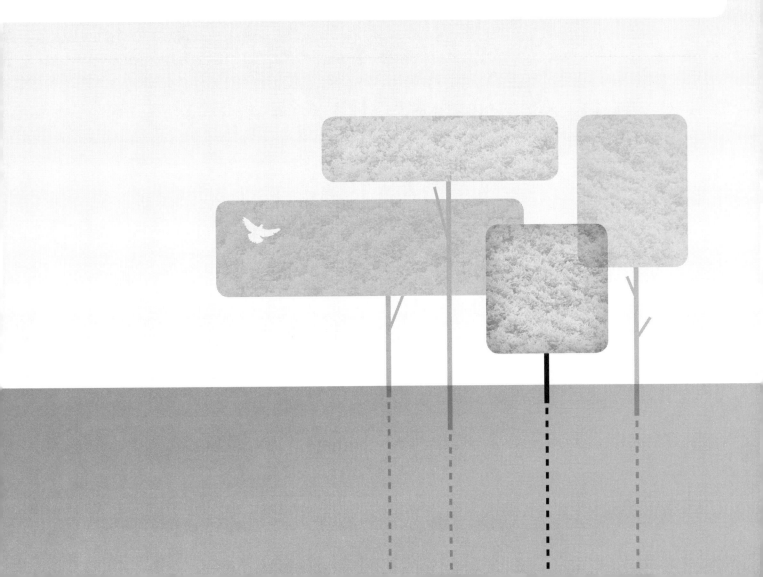

CHAPTER 5

NEGOTIATING PERSONALITIES AND CONFLICT

Unless Karen was completely misreading her, Jennifer was expressing some serious nonverbal cues of frustration. The team was talking about a literature unit they would begin teaching in January, after the winter break, and divvying up responsibility for planning it. Throughout the conversation, Jennifer's body language had been closed and negative: arms crossed, sour look, chair backed away from the rest of the circle.

Hoping to draw her into the conversation, Karen reached out. "So, Jennifer, do you agree with the decision that we should start with a series of activities focusing on problematic vocabulary from the book?"

"Actually, no."

Everyone at the table looked up. Jennifer's tone suggested strong emotions, and no one could remember the last time she had disagreed with a group decision.

"Okay, Jennifer, what is it, exactly, about the decision that you don't agree with?" Michael asked.

Jennifer turned to him. "Well, Michael, there are a number of things about the decision that I don't agree with." The sarcasm in Jennifer's voice was shocking, and everyone in the room felt the temperature drop about ten degrees. Michael shifted in his chair in a way that Karen didn't like. "This does not look good," she thought to herself.

Jennifer continued. "When we did the short story unit, I developed a bunch of activities on vocabulary, but then it turned out no one used them. I don't see any reason to spend all of the time and effort to create materials if we're just going to end up doing our own thing anyway."

Michael fired back. "Well, the reason I didn't use your vocabulary activities was because you got them to us about a week later than you said you would. Because it didn't seem like you were going to finish them, I went ahead and created my own stuff. So actually, I ended up doing double the work. I created all of the daily reading comprehension guides for the team—which I sent to you well before the unit began—and then I had to go back and create vocabulary activities because yours were so late. If you had gotten them to us on time, I would have been happy to use them."

Jennifer's eyes narrowed, and the floodgates of months of pent-up frustration opened. "Are you kidding me? I didn't even *want* to do those activities in the first place! I spent last summer developing a whole series of comprehension handouts for the short story unit, but you *assigned* me the vocabulary activities instead, so that work was wasted. If you had taken the time to ask me about what I wanted to plan, you would have known that I had zero interest in developing the vocabulary activities!"

"*Asked* you?" Michael responded. "Look, one of our norms is 'silence is consent.' We don't hand out any engraved invitations to participate on this team—it's up to you to speak up."

Sensing that the situation was getting completely out of hand, Karen jumped in. "This isn't getting us anywhere. It's a stressful time of year, we're all working hard. Let's just cancel today's meeting. We can come back to this after everyone's had a chance to calm down."

Jennifer stood up and walked quickly from the room, being certain not to make eye contact with Michael, who waited until she was gone.

"Is she serious? Does she realize how hard I've been busting my butt to get stuff done on time so that she can use it in her class? And now she's complaining that we haven't spent enough time listening to her? This is ridiculous. She's bringing the team down, and she knows it—that's the issue."

Karen got up and left, heading to Jennifer's classroom. She knew that both Jennifer and Michael had valid points. As the most accomplished teacher on the team, Michael was contributing the lion's share of the materials for collaboratively planned units, and everyone was grateful for his hard work. At the same time, Michael did tend to dominate team conversations, and Jennifer rarely got a word in edgewise. She had been late on several team-based responsibilities, but she was only a second-year teacher. Couldn't Michael cut her some slack?

"Hey Jennifer, you okay?"

Jennifer was seated at her desk with her head in her hands. As she looked up, Karen could see the defeat in her eyes.

"Look, I'm sorry. I know I'm letting everyone down and not getting stuff out on time. I just feel so overwhelmed. I'm sorry that I'm the dead weight on the team."

Karen was surprised. She thought of Jennifer as light years ahead of the typical second-year teacher, and she had no idea that Jennifer was feeling this swamped.

"Jennifer, I know you're a good teacher—I've been in your classroom, remember? If you were feeling this way, why didn't you tell us? If we're giving you too much work to do, just let us know."

"And let the team down? Plus, how can I say anything in those meetings? If Michael's not talking, Sarah is—and every time I do offer something it gets shot down. It's like, if you can't quote the research chapter and verse, Michael won't even listen to you."

Karen paused and reflected. There had been a few times when Jennifer offered ideas in meetings, and she was right that the team never acted on them. The team's meetings tended to be freewheeling affairs, and the strongest personalities—Michael and Sarah—did tend to dominate. Jennifer was not alone in her frustration: Karen sometimes felt left out of the conversations, as if it were really a two-person team and Karen and Jennifer were just along for the ride.

"Look," Karen said, "I'll make you a deal. I'll talk to Michael and try to smooth things over. But you need to try being more assertive in meetings. Don't let us push you around. If you don't agree with something, or if you feel strongly about an idea, speak up! Maybe we can figure out some ways to make the meetings more democratic. I agree with you that it seems like some people talk way more than others."

Jennifer nodded. "Well, at least we have break coming up soon. A little time to cool off is probably a good idea. I just wish I didn't feel like our team is failing and that it was entirely my fault."

Lessons From the Front Line

What a mess! All of the goodwill and progress that the sixth-grade language arts/social studies team had made in the past few months seemed to have been thrown out the window. Teammates were clearly frustrated with their meetings, angry about domineering colleagues, seething about missed work deadlines—and they had been hiding their true feelings from each other for months.

The unfortunate truth is that nothing about the sixth-grade team's blowup is really *that* atypical. As professional learning teams work toward deeper levels of collaboration and interdependence, conflict is inevitable. In fact, conflict can eventually become a positive tool that teams can use to continuously improve. In the story, though, conflict seems to be nothing but negative.

If disagreement and confrontations are inevitable for professional learning teams, what can they do about it? Luckily, there are a number of different steps teams can take to move beyond conflict. Specific conversational techniques such as creating mutual respect, separating facts from stories, and practicing active listening can minimize the emotional damage—and maximize the productive outcomes—of professional disagreements. In addition, teams can take specific steps in the way they structure their meetings to draw out potential conflicts and frustrations before they escalate.

For the administrators supporting struggling learning teams, team-based conflict can feel like quicksand: once you step in, there's almost no way out. Administrators should tread cautiously when it comes to interpersonal team dynamics, but there are strategies they can employ to help solve problems. Most often that support should come from the sidelines, but there are situations in which school leaders need to roll up their sleeves and take an active part in managing team disagreements.

This chapter focuses on the disagreements that arise in collaborative work and how to deal with them. We begin by reviewing specific conversational strategies outlined in the book *Crucial Conversations: Tools for Talking When Stakes Are High* (Patterson, Grenny, McMillan, & Switzler, 2002). We then identify ways in which professional learning team members can structure team meetings to mitigate the damage in disagreements. After considering the role that school administrators should (or should not) play in team conflict, we conclude the chapter by exploring the typical interpersonal challenges that teams face, as described by Patrick Lencioni (2002) in his book *The Five Dysfunctions of a Team: A Leadership Fable.*

Holding Crucial Conversations

Confrontation—most of us will do just about anything to avoid it. When confrontation does rear its ugly head, we often react with strong emotions, doing and saying things that we later regret.

In the story that begins this chapter, Jennifer has been frustrated for months, feeling as though her colleagues wouldn't listen to her. She was also struggling to keep up with the increased collegial expectations of working on a learning team, worried that her teammates would think less of her if she did not pull her own weight. While she didn't know it, Jennifer was not alone. Anthony Muhammad (2009) argues that teachers "new to a particular culture," who he calls Tweeners, often try to hide their struggles from colleagues and administrators (p. 43). He writes:

> Administrators often assume everything is running smoothly because of the Tweeners' high level of compliance and sunny disposition, but the teacher may be experiencing significant difficulty and trials. This causes some Tweeners . . . to live in two worlds: a private world of struggle and doubt, and a public world of false enthusiasm and positivity. These two worlds are on a collision course to what I call the *moment of truth.* (p. 48, italics in the original)

Jennifer has reached her moment of truth, hasn't she? Rather than voicing her frustrations, Jennifer has remained silent, choosing quiet seething over open confrontation. But when that confrontation did finally happen, all of her pent-up anger came spilling out in a way that increased the emotional ante for everyone on her team.

The real challenge for those interested in restructuring schools as learning communities is that many teachers are Tweeners, new to the culture of collaboration. Dealing with confrontation is just not something that most teachers are comfortable with. As a result, many teachers on professional learning teams live in Muhammad's two worlds, displaying confidence yet avoiding conflict at all costs.

The danger in this decision is that while most of us may be inclined to avoid conflict, especially with teammates and friends, the fact is that we're not always going to agree with our colleagues. In response, many professional learning teams do what the sixth-grade language arts/social studies team did: avoid disagreements to maintain a shallow layer of harmony, while frustration and anger boil beneath the surface. According to Betty Achinstein (2002), this practice can be detrimental to systemic change efforts:

> The kinds of organizational learning purported to result from building community among teachers are deeply linked to how they manage the difference amid their collaboration. The processes of conflict are critical to understanding

what distinguishes a professional community that maintains stability and the status quo from a community engaged in ongoing inquiry and change. (p. 446)

The key to avoiding making the same mistake is to turn hostile confrontations into productive conversations. In their book *Crucial Conversations*, Kerry Patterson and his coauthors (Patterson, Grenny, McMillan, & Switzler, 2002) discuss strategies for holding effective conversations when the stakes are high. Professional learning team participants would be well served to follow their advice. Their strategies included four important recommendations: identify your motive, make it safe, master your own emotions, and work to understand others' perspectives.

Identify Your Motive

During a crucial conversation, the first step is to figure out what you want to get out of the conversation. In other words, what is the real issue? For Central Middle's sixth-grade language arts/social studies teachers, the real conflict was not about developing vocabulary activities—even though that was what triggered the blowup. The real issue for Jennifer was feeling as though her colleagues did not value her ideas. For Michael, the issue was respect: he was doing the bulk of the work on the team, and he saw Jennifer's complaints as taking him and his hard work for granted. He wanted his contributions to be recognized and appreciated.

In order for Jennifer to start a positive conversation that allows her to discuss and move beyond her frustrations, she has to begin by being honest with herself and her teammates about the real issues. Once she does, the next step is to ensure that the resulting conversation is a safe one.

Make It Safe

Safety is the key element in any crucial conversation and a theme that repeats time and again in the literature about PLCs. As soon as we perceive ourselves as under verbal attack, the defensive walls go up, turning a collaborative conversation into a competitive confrontation.

The first step in making any conversation safe is to communicate that you care about your colleague. Had Jennifer begun her confrontation with Michael in a safe manner, Michael's response probably would have been very different. Consider this approach: "Michael, I would like to share some frustrations that I have about our team meetings, but I first want to say how much I appreciate and respect all the hard work you've been doing for our team." In that type of scenario, Michael, like the rest of us, would be much more likely to believe the speaker cared about him and his interests and thus listen to constructive feedback.

The next step in making conversations safe is to create a sense of mutual purpose. Even though two professionals may have a difference of opinion, it helps matters tremendously when both feel that they are playing on the same team and running toward the same goal. Had Michael emphasized this shared commitment when speaking to Jennifer, it could have changed the course of their disagreement: "Jennifer, I hear what you're saying. You put a lot of time and energy into those vocabulary units, and I understand your frustration that they weren't used. I also know that even as a second-year teacher, you've made great contributions to our common units. I respect your hard work, and I know we both want our students to do well and our team to be successful."

The final step for making conversations safe is to speak honestly about concerns using structured responses such as *Don't/Do statements*. For example, Jennifer could have used a Don't/Do statement to express her difficulty keeping up with the professional learning team workload: "Michael, I *don't* want you to think that I take you or your hard work for granted. I really appreciate all of the activities and units that you've created for our team. At the same time, I *do* want you to understand that I am feeling overwhelmed. There have been times when I have had to prioritize grading papers and planning for my own class over planning for the team, because I just haven't had enough time to do both."

Master Your Own Emotions

In the opening story, both Jennifer and Michael got carried away by their emotions. In order to keep a conversation productive, it is important to master your emotions and keep them from pushing dialogue into dangerous waters.

One strategy to accomplish this is to separate facts from stories. Jennifer had crafted a story in her mind about Michael from bits of evidence in their interactions—the failure of her team to use the lessons she developed, Michael's success at nearly everything he tackles, and the fact that she cannot get a word in edgewise during team meetings—that suggested he did not value her contributions to the group. This apparent lack of respect left Jennifer frustrated. Similarly, Michael had a story in his head that Jennifer slacked off and held the team back.

To keep their conversation professional and productive, both Jennifer and Michael need to stick to the facts when speaking to one another. For Jennifer, it might sound something like this: "The last time I created a vocabulary unit, you didn't use it in your classroom. I'm sure you had a good reason for not using it—maybe it didn't fit your students' needs—but that left me feeling as though my time and effort were wasted. In addition, at the last team meeting I suggested we allow people to volunteer for creating lessons rather than assigning them on a rotating basis, and you never responded to my suggestion. That left me feeling as though you didn't respect my opinion."

By focusing on the facts that led to her emotional response, Jennifer allows Michael the opportunity to respond rationally instead of emotionally. Sticking to facts also makes it easier to listen to another person's point of view, which leads to the final strategy.

Work to Understand Others' Perspectives

A crucial conversation cannot be about convincing another person of your opinion or perspective. It has to be about coming to a shared understanding. For this to happen in our example, both Jennifer and Michael have to try to see the situation through each others' eyes. This requires a focus on listening and an assumption of rationality and good faith.

In the conversation at the beginning of the chapter, both Jennifer and Michael expressed important sentiments, but neither person listened to the other. Michael did not pay attention to Jennifer's disappointment about being ignored, and Jennifer did not listen to Michael's dissatisfaction about his disproportionate workload. In order to move beyond their emotional roadblock, each of them needs to work to understand the other person's frustration, as difficult as that may be.

In addition to focusing on listening, Jennifer and Michael would be well served to assume that the other person is acting rationally and in good faith. For Jennifer, this means accepting that Michael is not out to get her or to hurt her feelings. Instead, he is doing what he believes is best for the team. Sure, Michael might dominate conversations. But from his perspective, he is trying to pass along best practices that he has acquired over the course of his accomplished career. And Jennifer does not mean to slow down or handicap the team—she genuinely feels overwhelmed and a bit intimidated by working with her more experienced colleagues. When the stakes are high, begin by trusting that your colleagues have good intentions.

Productive conversations over controversial issues in professional learning teams are equal parts art and science. On the one hand, members of learning teams have to be able to express their honest opinions and concerns. On the other hand, confrontations such as the one that happened between Jennifer and Michael can set a group back several steps in terms of its development. By using the strategies that Patterson and his colleagues (2002) recommend in *Crucial Conversations*, educators can work through difficult issues in ways that maintain emotional safety and lead to productive gains.

Structuring Team Meetings

In chapter 4, "Supporting Team Development," we discussed the stages that professional learning teams tend to go through, and we pointed out a number of strategies to support their collective efforts. One of the primary strategies, especially for teams in the earlier stages of development, is to follow clearly defined structures. In the story that began this chapter, Michael told Jennifer that it was up to her to speak up during team meetings; in practice, however, some team participants feel intimidated in unstructured situations and may avoid speaking up as a result. Well-structured meetings and conversations help to address this challenge.

Structure can come in a variety of forms. Specifically, teams in the earlier stages of development should carefully create explicit structure around meeting formats and decision-making protocols in order to facilitate productive conversations (DuFour, DuFour, Eaker, & Many, 2006).

Agendas, Minutes, and Roles

As cliché as it may sound, time still remains the most valuable resource in any school—particularly in PLCs in which teachers are being asked to collaborate and take collective action. Accordingly, one of the chief frustrations of any teacher working in a PLC is seeing valuable time wasted. When team meetings are unstructured and disorganized, a dangerous tension builds: while teachers feel compelled to show up at the appointed time and place because of administrator expectations, they resent the unproductive use of their time. This resentment can spill over into uncomfortable gripe sessions and toxic atmospheres.

By creating agendas prior to meetings, keeping accurate sets of minutes, and assigning clear roles, a learning team can avoid the disorganized environment that is fertile ground for arguments and confrontations. The first step is to have an agenda. Many teams create an agenda for the next meeting in the last five minutes of their current meeting or assign a meeting facilitator to put together an agenda in between meetings. By specifying beforehand what will be discussed, teams can limit disorganization and random conversations.

Team minutes are helpful because they document discussions and decisions. Too often participants leave a meeting thinking one decision was agreed upon, only to find out later that something entirely different was implemented. By creating documentation, minutes allow teams to function without confusion or misunderstandings. Meeting minutes can also become an important forum for celebration. Encourage your teachers to track progress towards shared goals in their minutes and to refer back to archived records whenever they're questioning the value of their time together. While there is no "right way" to structure PLC agendas and meeting notes, the Team Agenda Template (pages 111–113) included at the end of this chapter can serve as a starting point for teachers trying to organize the time that they spend together.

Finally, team roles can provide a healthy structure for conversations and decision making. Common roles include discussion facilitator, timekeeper, and recorder. Explicit roles help to keep meeting participants focused and on track, reduce the odds of one or two individuals regularly dominating conversations, and help to draw in less vocal team members. The handout Team Roles to Consider (pages 114–115) describes a set of possible team roles to use when organizing the work of your learning team. Teams can add more roles—such as the "Devil's Advocate" introduced in chapter 7, "Connecting Data Analysis and Instructional Improvement"—to try to tackle specialized tasks together.

Decision-Making Protocols

One of the key factors contributing to the conflict between Jennifer and Michael is ambiguity around decision making. Over the course of several meetings, Jennifer had been assigned work responsibilities that she did not want, and the team made several decisions with which she did not agree. In each case, this resulted from unproductive (but common) approaches to decision making: the loudest voices dominate and majority rules.

In a collaborative setting without explicit team-created rules for making decisions, the loudest voices tend to be listened to. This is a dangerous approach to decision making for two reasons. First, it leaves other participants feeling frustrated, believing that their opinions and voices do not count. Second, it results in less-effective decisions. When the ideas of a few dominate, it limits the creative input and potentially effective ideas of less dominant members.

When teams do explicitly agree to a decision-making protocol, it is often a *majority rules* approach. For a decision to be implemented, it simply needs the support of a majority of team members. This can have negative ramifications, both in terms of team dynamics and effectiveness. A majority rules approach can create divisions within a team, leading to an unhealthy concentration of decision-making power. The real power of a professional learning team should derive from the *united* commitment of its members, not from a 60 percent voting block.

Teams that rely on majority rules also tend to be less effective because they ignore critical feedback and handicap implementation. A team that simply votes 3–2 and moves on never takes the time to understand the reasons for dissent, and those reasons may have real merit. In addition, the participants on the losing side may decide to simply ignore decisions with which they disagree, undermining the collective effectiveness of the team.

We recommend decision-making protocols that encourage critical discussion and seek input from every team member. Two simple methods for gaining input are fist-to-five and thumbs up/thumbs down. With *fist-to-five*, each team member is asked to put up his or her hand when it is time to make a decision, displaying individual levels of agreement with any given decision. If the participant completely agrees with the decision, he holds up five fingers. If the participant is completely opposed to the decision, she holds up a closed fist. The numbers in between represent varying levels of agreement (for example, a three indicates lukewarm approval, but with no desire to hold up the decision if others agree). Highly effective teams generally agree that if any team member holds up a two or lower, the decision should be postponed until all reservations have been discussed. The Fist-to-Five Ratings guide (page 116) included at the end of this chapter can serve as a starting point for professional learning teams interested in building consensus before making key decisions.

A similar protocol is *thumbs up/thumbs down*. With this approach, team members indicate their agreement to a decision by holding their thumbs up or their disagreement by holding their thumbs down. A sideways thumb indicates some reservations, but not serious enough to warrant further discussion. Again, many teams decide that any thumbs down results in a postponed decision until dissenting teammates have had the opportunity to have their concerns addressed.

Nevertheless, there may be times when not all members of a team can agree with a decision, even after considerable discussion. In these cases, DuFour, DuFour, Eaker, and Many (2006) propose a somewhat controversial approach:

> The definition of consensus we prefer establishes two simple standards that must be met in order to move forward when a decision is made by consensus. A group has arrived at consensus when:
>
> 1. All points of view have been heard.
>
> 2. The will of the group is evident even to those who most oppose it.
>
> This definition can, and typically does, result in moving forward with a proposal despite the fact that some members of the organization are against it (p. 165–166).

The important point to remember is that team decision making should be an inclusive rather than an exclusive process that involves real discussion and debate and that leads to shared understanding. In chapters 7 and 8, "Connecting Data Analysis and Instructional Improvement" and "Building a Collective Intelligence," respectively, we talk in more detail about the importance of shared understanding and team dialogue and how teams can leverage these concepts to become truly high performing.

The Administrator's Role in Team Conflict

One thing missing from the story at the start of this chapter is an administrator. This is not uncommon in most schools—administrators are not privy to or involved in many of the disagreements that happen within teams, and that is usually a good thing.

But there are times when administrators feel compelled to step—or are unwittingly pulled—into team conflicts. The danger here is that when administrators do step into the pool of team confrontation, they can create dangerous ripple effects for two primary reasons. First, administrators often have an incomplete understanding of the relationships within a team, failing to clearly see the potential ramifications of their actions. What may initially appear to be a simple misunderstanding might actually have years of history and complexity behind it. An administrator's decision to resolve the conflict, no matter how straightforward and sensible the solution may seem, might actually exacerbate the situation.

For example, if Steve (Central Middle's principal) had heard second hand about the incident between Jennifer and Michael, he might have decided to tell the sixth-grade language arts/social studies professional learning team that Jennifer should not be responsible for planning any more common lessons. From Steve's perspective, this would solve the problem: Jennifer would not feel as overwhelmed and Michael would not have anything to complain about. But this decision would probably make things worse. Michael's sense that Jennifer was pulling down the team would be validated, likely leading him to ignore her input even more. And Jennifer's concern that her colleagues did not respect her would also be validated: the principal of the school would be telling her whole team that she cannot keep up.

The second reason behind administrator ripple effects is that administrators represent power. In dysfunctional situations, teams may make controversial decisions and try to compel members into following those decisions, but it is administrators who have the true power of coercion. Teachers know this, and some try to manipulate that power to get their way. For example, in the unfortunate (but not uncommon) situation when teammates "tell" on each other to an administrator—for example, Mrs. Jones always shows up late to team meetings, Mr. Smith gives his kids the answers for the common assessment beforehand to make his scores look better, and so on—the teammate's intent is to compel a change in someone else's behavior: get Mrs. Jones to show up on time for meetings, and get Mr. Smith to stop handing out the answers beforehand.

When administrative power is wielded, it may have the immediate effect of changing behavior—Mrs. Jones becomes punctual, and Mr. Smith never hands out the answers again—but it can worsen the situation. Mrs. Jones may show up on time for meetings, but she no longer contributes in a productive way. Mr. Smith may never hand out the answer key, but he also stops caring about how his students do on common assessments.

The bottom line is that team conflict represents a thorny patch for administrators, but there are times when administrative intervention is warranted. Organizational behavior experts call this the "contingency model" of leadership, or "situational leadership" (Owens & Valesky, 2007). The idea is that leaders have to be flexible depending on the situation, and that leadership style is contingent upon individual teams' needs. Professional learning teams that are still struggling with basic issues of trust and decision making may benefit from directive leadership from an administrator, whereas teams at a more advanced stage of development may be better served by solving problems themselves.

When it comes to administrator involvement in team conflict, we recommend five core behaviors that school leaders should employ. While simple and based in common sense, these behaviors will help to ensure that principals don't make a difficult situation even worse.

1. **Listening without commitment**—When teachers have concerns, administrators should be willing to listen. But listening does not necessarily require action. Especially when it comes to team dynamics, administrators would be well advised to listen carefully without conveying any clear sense of commitment. Use careful and cautious language during these conversations, remembering that an innocent comment ("Sure, that makes sense to me") can turn into something entirely different ("The principal said that he agrees with me") by the end of the day.

2. **Basing crucial conversations on facts that *you* have witnessed**—It may be that Mrs. Jones is continually late to meetings, and that she needs to know that this is unacceptable behavior. But do not base a conversation with her on hearsay. Show up to a couple of meetings unannounced, observe the behavior firsthand, and then address it. This ensures that her crucial conversation is based on facts and not supposition, and it minimizes the chances that Mrs. Jones will blame her teammates for any slap on the wrist.

3. **Trying to coach before commanding**—Many teachers struggle with the challenges of collaboration and team dynamics. Before telling Michael that he needs to ease up, or Jennifer that she needs to buckle down, take the time to understand the support they may need to be successful. Let Michael borrow a copy of *Crucial Conversations* and offer to pay to let him take a two-day workshop on effective team facilitation. Set Jennifer up with a mentor who can support her as she struggles with the challenges of being a second-year teacher. Assume that people can do better with the right coaching—and then find a way to provide that coaching.

4. **Collecting feedback to improve systems**—Often, the unproductive behavior of professional learning team members is a response to ineffective systems, not a

manifestation of intractable character flaws. Michael is not a mean person, and Jennifer is not a slacker; rather, they are both working within a system that does not yet have the right structures in place. If administrators are out collecting feedback on the successes and challenges of collaborative work—both formal feedback through surveys and informal feedback through regular conversations with colleagues—they can work to improve systems proactively.

5. **When all else fails, being flexible (to a point)**—Let's face it, there are some people who just should not work together. Every now and then, individual teams will get to a point of such interpersonal dysfunction that there is no way of fixing things. At this point, administrators have to be flexible. This might mean allowing a six-person team to split up into two three-person teams. In extreme situations, it might also mean moving individual teachers to different teams or grade levels over the summer. While we caution against too much fiddling with teams (the fallout can sometimes be more destructive than the original situation), there are times when flexibility with team composition is warranted.

Relevant Theory and Research

As we have said throughout this book, we believe that stories have the power to engage and to explain. A good story takes complex ideas and makes them approachable and relevant, turning the theoretical into the practical.

In *The Five Dysfunctions of a Team*, Patrick Lencioni (2002) uses a modern-day fable to demonstrate the problems teams face. His book tells the fictional story of DecisionTech, a Silicon Valley start-up that has fallen on rough times. The company's executive team has become a dysfunctional collection of strong-willed egos, a group that is a "team" in name only. As the book begins, the company's board of directors has hired a new CEO, Kathryn, whose job it is to turn the company around.

The book then chronicles Kathryn's work as she slowly transforms the company's top executives into a high-performing team. Kathryn does so by working through the five dysfunctions that Lencioni believes all teams experience. Based on his research and consulting work in the American business sector, Lencioni's hierarchy of team dysfunctions serves as a particularly useful model for professional learning teams attempting to improve their own work practices.

Throughout the book, Lencioni uses stories to demonstrate each of the five dysfunctions and provides tips and strategies on how teams can successfully navigate each challenge. According to Lencioni (2002, p. 188), the five dysfunctions are as follows:

1. An absence of trust

2. A fear of conflict

3. A lack of commitment

4. An avoidance of accountability

5. An inattention to results

Absence of Trust

Lencioni (2002) believes that the first dysfunction teams typically experience is an absence of trust. To Lencioni, *trust* means that teammates accept that their colleagues' intentions are good and allow themselves to be vulnerable in front of one another, recognizing and acknowledging their own weaknesses and shortcomings.

There is certainly an absence of trust between Jennifer and Michael in this chapter's story. Neither takes the other person's comments in good faith, and neither appears willing to acknowledge any shortcomings. Jennifer has been hiding the fact that she is feeling frustrated and overwhelmed, and Michael has been seething about Jennifer's late work without being willing to speak with her about it in a safe and open way.

According to Lencioni, teams have to work to establish trust. They need to create shared experiences over time, while at the same time taking steps to develop credibility within the team. In addition, teams need to take the time to identify and recognize the unique attributes of their members. One of the reasons Jennifer does not trust Michael is that she does not see him as having compassion for her situation as a second-year teacher. In Jennifer's eyes, Michael is not credible as someone who cares about her. In turn, Michael does not trust Jennifer because she has failed to meet work deadlines established by the team. For him, she has no credibility as a hard-working and dependable colleague.

Lencioni suggests that teams take the time to regularly engage in group reflection on team and individual strengths and areas for improvement. In addition, professional learning teams should focus explicitly on building shared instructional experiences. This is one of the reasons that Karen feels comfortable approaching Jennifer in the story. Back in chapter 3, "Creating Trust," Karen had the opportunity to observe Jennifer teaching, creating a sense of reciprocal credibility and professional respect between the two colleagues. Peer observations, sharing students across teams, coteaching lessons—each of these strategies represents an opportunity to develop trust on a learning team.

Fear of Conflict

The next dysfunction that Lencioni identifies is a fear of conflict. He argues that conflict—instead of personality attacks—can be a positive thing. In the early stages of development, however, many teams find it difficult to distinguish between productive conflict and hostile disagreement, so they steer clear of just about anything that sounds contentious—until, of course, the big blowups occur.

In the story that begins this chapter, Jennifer avoided bringing up her frustrations and disagreements because she wanted to avoid a confrontation. Similarly, Michael avoided calling Jennifer on the fact that her work was late because he did not want to risk the uncomfortable conflict that would likely ensue. Instead, each one bottled up his or her emotions, waiting for the confrontation that eventually occurred.

Lencioni makes a number of recommendations for addressing a team's fear of conflict. First, begin by collectively acknowledging that conflict can be productive. If a disagreement appears to surface, a facilitator (if the team has appointed one) can encourage an extended discussion of the disagreement, using positive language to describe the point of contention: "This is great, let's dig a little deeper on our opinions around this issue."

Another step is separating personality from practice, which we explore in greater detail in chapter 7, "Connecting Data Analysis and Instructional Improvement." Conflict should focus on practices or ideas, not individual people. One way to approach this is for teams to appoint an official Devil's Advocate whose role it is to challenge ideas. This helps to depersonalize disagreements: the Devil's Advocate is not trying to be difficult or hold a grudge, it is his or her role to challenge ideas and practices.

Lack of Commitment

The next dysfunction of a team is a lack of commitment. In our story, Jennifer was never invested in the team's short story unit because she had been assigned work she did not want to complete. As a result, she ended up prioritizing her own work—lesson planning and grading papers—over the work of the team, justifying this decision by her lack of commitment.

This is a particularly difficult dysfunction for professional learning teams because of the traditional nature of schools. In business, it is common for employees to work on various teams as a natural part of their normal work responsibilities. In schools, however, teachers have traditionally worked independently, especially when it comes to curricular and instructional decision making.

Being part of a PLC, however, is about committing to a common goal and working *interdependently*. Many teachers struggle to embrace the collective goals and decisions of their team, especially when those goals and decisions do not mesh with their individual opinions or practices. The danger is that a lack of commitment to shared goals can have a negative impact on team trust. As Cassandra Erkens (2008b) explains in *The Collaborative Teacher*, "Trust in a team is jeopardized when members hold fast to autonomy and self-select the responsibilities, conversations, or values to which they will commit. We *require* the participation and the expertise of the *entire team* when working collaboratively" (p. 14).

Lencioni argues that a team trying to overcome a lack of commitment should start by understanding that *always* striving for perfect consensus is impractical. Not everyone is going to agree 100 percent with every decision, and that is okay. Instead, teams should work to achieve buy-in when complete agreement is impossible (in other words, some people express reservations but are still willing to follow a decision), and at least make sure that everyone's ideas are solicited, heard, and considered.

Next, Lencioni suggests that teams recognize that a mediocre decision is often better than no decision at all. Some PLCs work themselves into a state of paralysis, trying to specify every detail of a work plan, goal, or new strategy before taking action. Teams have to give themselves permission to try and fail, and then to learn from their failures.

Lencioni also makes some nuts-and-bolts recommendations. At the end of each meeting, effective teams should formally review decisions that were made, make sure that everyone is clear on those decisions, and then record those decisions in sets of meeting notes that are widely available to all members. They should also establish specific deadlines for making decisions, rather than leaving timelines up in the air (for example, "We will have identified all of next semester's essential learning goals by next Thursday"). Finally, teams should use straightforward decisions to create early wins, building a sense of collaborative momentum and shared commitment. Back in chapter 4, "Supporting Team Development," the sixth-grade language arts/social studies teachers tried to develop a series of complicated student interventions when they would have been much more successful starting with a lower-risk decision, such as developing an initial common assessment.

Avoidance of Accountability

The next dysfunction that teams face is an avoidance of accountability. There are two sides to this dysfunction: on the one hand, individual members ignore their own responsibility for meeting team goals; on the other hand, team members fail to hold each other accountable by calling their peers on performance or behaviors that are hurting the work of their team.

Both of these elements of failed accountability are evident in the sixth-grade story. Jennifer failed to hold herself accountable for meeting team responsibilities, and no one on the team confronted her about her late work. In addition, neither Jennifer nor Karen called Michael and Sarah on the fact that they were dominating team discussions.

An avoidance of accountability is usually about maintaining relationships. Team members want to avoid uncomfortable conversations and the jeopardized team dynamics that can result. If, however, team members do not hold themselves and their peers accountable for meeting established standards for performance and behaviors, teams cannot become highly effective.

Lencioni makes recommendations on how to approach accountability in a systematic way. First, teams should set clear goals and norms, and review their performance on a regular basis. This could be anything from sharing basic feedback at the end of a meeting—for example, each member stating one positive thing that happened during the meeting and one area for improvement (often referred to as "plus/deltas")—to a quarterly review of team goals and action plans. Second, building leaders should support improved team accountability. When they visit learning team meetings, administrators can provide feedback to groups of teachers on their adherence to conversational norms and design reward systems that recognize team-based performance.

Inattention to Results

The final dysfunction Lencioni defines is an inattention to results. In many ways, this dysfunction is a challenge related to accountability avoidance, only at a deeper level. Teammates may be holding themselves accountable for sticking to work expectations and following team norms, but they are not holding each other accountable for improved student learning. In chapter 4, "Supporting Team Development," we noted that many teams find it difficult to shift from a focus on teaching to a focus on learning. Paying attention to results is what helps teams make this shift.

Lencioni explains this dysfunction as a problem of allegiance. In many professional learning teams, teachers work well with their teammates, but their true allegiance is to their own classrooms and students. This sounds sensible: teachers are ultimately accountable for the performance of the students assigned to them. After all, those are the standardized test scores that are reported at the end of the year!

However, on a high-performing professional learning team, *all* of the teachers on the team feel a sense of accountability for *all* of the students on the team. As DuFour, DuFour, Eaker, and Many (2006) argue, "We cannot meet the needs of our students unless we assume collective responsibility for their well-being" (p. 78). Such "collective responsibility" only happens when teams pay attention to the learning results of students across classrooms. It is not enough for the students in *my* classroom to reach the proficiency goal specified in our team action plan. In order for the team to be successful, the students in *all* of our classrooms need to reach the goal.

Lencioni recommends that, in order to overcome this dysfunction, teams make results public. Public disclosure can be difficult and painful for educators; in fact, most teachers shy away from openly comparing their students' performance to the performance of students in other classrooms. An attention to results, however, is not about comparing student performance. It is about analyzing student learning and working as a team to figure out how to improve that performance. In chapter 7, "Connecting Data Analysis and Instructional Improvement," we provide more specific advice on how teams can successfully analyze student learning data and use an attention to results to improve student performance.

Recommendations

As professional learning teams progress in their work, frustrations *will* develop and conflict *will* emerge. This is a natural and healthy development—teams cannot become high-performing teams until they learn how to capitalize on divergent opinions and ideas—but it is not easy. Tears may be shed, relationships may become strained, and talented professionals may feel like failures. Here are our recommendations for dealing with disagreement in a productive manner.

Don't Avoid Conflict, but Address It Constructively

In a professional learning team, conflict is going to take many forms. There will be passive-aggressive sniping, behind-the-back gossiping, and, as Jennifer and Michael discovered, all-out war. There will also be patient negotiations, honest discussions of differences, and carefully worded conversations.

The bottom line is that teams cannot become high performing unless they learn how to deal with conflict. When teams avoid conflict, they are playing nice at the expense of real progress. According to Pamela Grossman, Sam Wineburg, and Stephen Woolworth (2001):

> As community starts to form, individuals have a natural tendency to *play community*—to act as if they are already a community that shares values and

common beliefs. . . . This is called "pseudocommunity". . . . The maintenance of pseudocommunity pivots on the suppression of conflict. Groups regulate face-to-face interactions with the tacit understanding that it is "against the rules" to challenge others or press too hard for clarification. This understanding paves the way for the *illusion of consensus*. Because there is no genuine follow-up, conversation partners are able to speak at high levels of generality that allow each to impute his or her own meaning to the group's abstractions. For example, if notions of "critical thinking" or "interdisciplinary curriculum" are never defined, every discussion member can agree to this common cause without giving it so much as a second thought. (p. 955–956, italics in the original)

Therefore, the question for professional learning teams committed to real results is not, will conflict happen? The question is, how will your team deal with it?

Effective teams deal with conflict proactively and constructively. By using the strategies recommended in *Crucial Conversations* (Patterson, Grenny, McMillan, & Switzler, 2002) and *The Five Dysfunctions of a Team* (Lencioni, 2002), teachers on professional learning teams can reduce frustration and emotional discomfort. In fact, successfully dealing with conflict can create a positive snowball effect. Once teams handle a few tricky disagreements, they begin to realize, "Hey, this conflict thing isn't so bad—we can do this!" The next time conflict arises, the team approaches it with a sense of empowerment instead of dread.

To better manage the conflict that occurs on your learning team, consider using the Managing Team-Based Conflict guide (page 117) included at the end of this chapter to slow your decisions down and to properly structure a successful crucial conversation.

Work to Understand the Perspectives of Others

Much of the conflict in team-based situations is driven by a defensive closed-mindedness: I have my own ideas and my own opinions, and I don't need someone else trying to impose their ideas or opinions on me. Many teachers are used to doing things the way they do them. Their first impulse is to resist anything that might feel like a criticism or a call to change.

In many ways, this is an inherent part of human nature. In addition, a professional culture in which every school year brings a new fad breeds a hardened skepticism that can be difficult to break. Unfortunately, this can sometimes lead to seen-it-all veterans like Michael ignoring the less-experienced Jennifers and less-vocal Karens on their teams—and that can cause some pretty hard feelings.

When teachers work to understand their colleagues' perspectives, they break down defensive barriers. It is important to point out, however, that working to understand is not the same thing as always being agreeable. Listening to the perspectives of others is about collegial tone, not professional capitulation. A willingness to listen with an open mind helps to prevent the types of blowups that the sixth-grade team experienced. Active listening also comes into play as teams discuss deeper issues around teaching and learning, a concept discussed in more detail in chapter 8, "Building a Collective Intelligence."

For Administrators, Tread Cautiously Around Team Dynamics

When it comes to administrators and team conflict, our general advice is, "Stay out of it." The road to ruin is paved with the best of intentions, and administrators often do more damage than good when they wade into team disagreements. Administrators usually do not understand the subtle personal dynamics of individual teams, and any positive outcomes of administrator involvement in conflicts are often outweighed by negative unintended consequences.

When you do get pulled into team disagreements, concentrate on listening instead of acting. Oftentimes, frustrated teachers are only looking for an open ear as opposed to a recommended solution. If you feel the need to share some advice, focus on process over practice. In other words, share ideas for how a team might resolve a disagreement instead of suggesting a specific way out. This provides a fresh direction forward and empowers a struggling team to resolve a disagreement themselves.

There are times, however, when administrator involvement really is necessary to solve team-based conflict. In those cases, we recommend responding to firsthand evidence instead of hearsay. In addition, consider how any involvement might play out in terms of team dynamics. Will a public rebuke help bring a recalcitrant team player into line, or will it further alienate her? Will reassigning a hard-nosed veteran to a different grade level solve the problem, or just amount to shuffling deck chairs on the Titanic? Administrators are empowered by their position to employ a heavy-handedness unavailable to teachers, but it is a power that should be used prudently and only as a last resort.

The quick guide titled Administrator Roles in Team Conflicts (page 118) included at the end of this chapter can serve as a reminder of action steps that accomplished school leaders take to successfully navigate conflict on learning teams.

Team Agenda Template

While there is no one way to create an agenda for a team meeting, the most successful agendas include topics to be discussed, decisions to be made, actions to be taken, and reasons for celebration. Some agendas also include short reflection surveys designed to collect information about team meeting processes. The following is a sample agenda that your learning team might find valuable.

Date of Meeting: _____   Start Time: _____   End Time: _____

Members Present: _____

Topics to Be Discussed: Effective teams limit the focus of their meetings, resisting the temptation to tackle too many topics at once. As a result, we will focus our next meeting on the following three topics.		
Topic 1: _____	**Topic 2:** _____	**Topic 3:** _____
How does this topic connect to our school's mission and vision?	How does this topic connect to our school's mission and vision?	How does this topic connect to our school's mission and vision?
Where do we currently stand?	Where do we currently stand?	Where do we currently stand?
What do we need to do to move forward?	What do we need to do to move forward?	What do we need to do to move forward?

1 of 3

Who is responsible for leading this effort?	Who is responsible for leading this effort?	Who is responsible for leading this effort?
When will this work be finished?	When will this work be finished?	When will this work be finished?

Reasons for Celebration: Remaining motivated by collective work means that we must find reasons to celebrate the actions that we've taken together as a team. For each topic that we talk about in a learning team meeting, we will find one reason to celebrate our work.

Reason 1: _____	**Reason 1**: _____	**Reason 1**: _____
How did this action help us to meet our school's mission and vision?	How did this action help us to meet our school's mission and vision?	How did this action help us to meet our school's mission and vision?
What evidence do we have to prove that our work made a difference?	What evidence do we have to prove that our work made a difference?	What evidence do we have to prove that our work made a difference?

How can we share the results of our work beyond our team?	How can we share the results of our work beyond our team?	How can we share the results of our work beyond our team?
Who deserves extra recognition for their efforts on this project?	Who deserves extra recognition for their efforts on this project?	Who deserves extra recognition for their efforts on this project?

To monitor the effectiveness of our meeting practices, please complete the following short survey and leave your responses with our meeting facilitator.

1 = Disagree, 2 = Neutral, 3 = Agree

Our meeting remained focused.	1	2	3
I know what action steps our team is taking next as a result of today's meeting.	1	2	3
Today's meeting was a valuable use of my time.	1	2	3
Please add suggestions for improving our work in any indicator that you scored with a 1.			

Team Roles to Consider

Effective learning teams conduct efficient meetings—and efficient meetings sometimes depend on each member filling an assigned role. Things just run smoother when everyone is clear about what his or her contributions to meetings should look like. The following list of roles might be worth considering when structuring team participation.

El Capitán
El Capitán is our team's official leader—the "Big Cheese," or "Senorita Importante." El Capitán will design our meeting agenda—organizing the information that we need to consider—and then share the agenda with the rest of us at least two days before we gather. El Capitán will also guide us through our agenda, starting conversations and moving us to new bullet points. Because El Capitán's role depends on communicating with others beyond our team, this is a role that depends on consistency. Therefore, El Capitán will remain our fearless leader for at least a quarter at a time.

The Rounder
What do you hate the most about meetings in schools? It's the wandering off topic that drives most teachers crazy! Teams that start by talking about grading sometimes end up talking about complete goofiness—and who has time for goofiness when there are papers to grade? That's where *The Rounder* comes in. The Rounder is responsible for keeping us on time and on task. When our conversations become something other than productive—drifting from the agenda or focusing on something that we just can't change, The Rounder is going to *politely* redirect the work of our group. The Rounder is also going to make sure that our meetings start on time and end on time. For that, we should all be thankful!

The Voice of Reason
Another mistake that ambitious learning teams tend to make is designing projects that are just plain impossible to pull off. They start talking about something simple, but somehow end up adding two thousand twists to make it "bigger and better than ever." By the time they come up for air, they've got a project that is way too complicated to tackle. As a result, they end up equal parts frustrated and defeated. Avoiding this professional frenzy requires someone to step in and be our *Voice of Reason*. The Voice of Reason's job is to shout, "Stop!" every time we start designing something that stretches the boundaries of our ability. However you have to do it, get our attention—and get our attention quick! Ask a few pointed questions. Remind us of the seventeen other projects that we're already involved in. Think about what's possible, what's probable, and what just isn't going to happen, and then make us think about it, too. I promise we'll thank you for this later.

Johnny Notes
Did you ever think about how many decisions a professional learning team makes in a year? Between designing lessons, creating common assessments, answering questions asked by administrators or department chairs, reflecting on student learning results, deciding on materials to purchase, and rearranging class schedules to accommodate random assemblies, professional learning teams are decision-making machines!

As a result, we need someone to be our team's *Johnny Notes*. Johnny Notes is the meticulous sort who is good at keeping track of everything we decide. He (or she, as the case may be) needs to design a system for recording our decisions and then needs to be able to track down our results whenever we can't find them!

Johnny Notes is easily one of the most important roles in our group because not everyone is capable of staying organized—or of keeping the rest of us organized! As a result, Johnny Notes should probably be a permanent position.

Sister Sunshine

Have you figured out exactly how grueling being a part of a professional learning team really is yet? After all, professional learning teams work in new and interesting ways that most teachers just haven't mastered. Professional learning teams need to learn how to collaborate and to make collective decisions. They need to learn to collect and analyze data. They are determined to ensure that every child is successful—and that's a level of pressure that can be hard to support over long periods of time.

This is where *Sister Sunshine* comes in! Sister Sunshine's job is an easy one: Remind us—early and often—that we're good teachers who are working hard and doing the right thing. Smile at us once in awhile. If it looks like we're discouraged or frustrated, slip us a bit of unexpected cheer.

Staying positive is what Sister Sunshine is all about, and sometimes staying positive is hard for professional learning teams.

The Skeptic

Believe it or not, the strongest professional learning teams are *not* the ones in which everyone agrees with every decision all the time! While complete harmony feels really good, it can also mean that teams aren't considering the full range of viewpoints on any given issue. Overlooking viewpoints is a recipe for weak decisions and complete disaster.

This is why our team needs an official *Skeptic* willing to throw some disruptions on the table every now and then!

Now, being The Skeptic doesn't mean being a complete curmudgeon who criticizes with impunity! Instead, being The Skeptic means forcing our team to consider things that we haven't thought of yet. Being The Skeptic means slowing our team down when we're moving too fast. Being The Skeptic means asking the questions that no one seems willing to ask—and looking at things through something other than rose-colored glasses.

Skeptics can force us to think differently, and thinking differently will make our decisions stronger.

Clarified Butter

The cooks in any group know that clarified butter is simply the best. It's made by heating and then removing the sediment from good old fashioned cow-given goodness. The resulting product is literally pure and clear.

In a lot of ways, professional learning teams need a bit of *Clarified Butter*—someone willing to listen to complex conversations carefully, put a bit of heat to them, and remove any waste. Adding Clarified Butter to a professional learning team can ensure that team decisions are pure and clear, too.

Our team's Clarified Butter will concentrate—and help to summarize—our work whenever needed. They'll consider both points of view, identify stumbling blocks that can be easily removed, and bring closure to our decisions. No meeting will begin without hearing Clarified Butter's summary of where we've been; and no meeting will end without hearing Clarified Butter's summary of where we're going.

Fist-to-Five Ratings

Each time our team comes together to make important decisions, we will use fist-to-five ratings as a strategy to identify our levels of collective consensus. When deciding on the rating that you will give to each decision, consider the following descriptors.

Rating	Descriptor
5	**Why didn't we make this decision sooner?** This idea is great, and we've got the capacity to make it happen without investing a ton of new effort. I've fallen in love with this idea and I'm willing to lead any efforts to make it become reality.
4	**This is a decision that I completely support.** I really believe that it aligns well with our school's mission and just know it is going to help our students to succeed. I'm willing to move forward and am also willing to put some time, energy, and effort into helping to make this happen.
3	**I believe in this decision, but question our timing.** I think this is a great idea and definitely something worth pursuing, I'm just not sure that this is the right time to move forward. I'm excited to see where this decision goes, but I think we should set it aside for now. I won't be opposed if others invest energy into making this happen, but I can't promise that I'll help.
2	**You know, I'm not totally comfortable with this decision, but I can see it has merit.** I'm willing to move forward with the decision as it currently stands—and I won't put any barriers in our team's way as we work to make this happen—but I'm probably going to need some practical and philosophical support before I'll completely embrace this action.
1	**This is a decision that I have strong reservations about.** While I can see some potential in taking this action, there are several things that we need to consider before I can be comfortable with this. Can we do a bit more talking before moving forward, please?
Fist	**There is no way I could possibly support this decision.** In fact, I think that supporting this decision would be irresponsible because it doesn't align with our school's mission and may even harm our students. We shouldn't even consider this action.

What thoughts do you have about the decision we are making? Are there any key ideas that we are forgetting to consider? What steps are we going to have to take before we can move forward?

Managing Team-Based Conflict

While conflict can be inherently intimidating to teachers, it can also be a positive experience that builds individual and group confidence. According to the authors of *Crucial Conversations: Tools for Talking When Stakes Are High* (Patterson, Grenny, McMillan, & Switzler, 2002), the key to managing conflict is slowing your decisions down. Use the following chart, based on the strategies suggested in *Crucial Conversations*, to think through the next challenging situation that you face with a colleague.

Crucial Conversation Strategy	Your Response
Describe the situation: From your perspective, what has caused the conflict that you are currently experiencing?	
Identify your motive: What is the real issue that you want addressed? What are you hoping to get out of this conversation? Remember that being honest about your true feelings is the first step towards working this conflict to conclusion.	
Make it safe: How can you communicate a sense of mutual purpose to your colleague? What shared goals are you working towards together? Remember that colleagues are much more likely to resolve conflict when they know that you see them as valuable members of your team rather than enemies.	
Master your emotions: What stories are you using to explain your colleague's behavior and/or decisions? Remember that the stories you tell are not always accurate pictures of reality. Concentrating on facts guarantees that you are not unfairly or inaccurately judging your peers.	
Understand other perspectives: How do you think your colleague views the discontent between the two of you? Remember that successful conflict resolution depends on collaborative—instead of competitive—conversations. Where might there be overlap in your ideas that you can use as building blocks for agreement?	

Administrator Roles in Team Conflicts

While it is often best for administrators to remain on the sidelines during team conflicts because they do not always understand the subtle personal dynamics of individual teams, sometimes avoiding conflicts is impossible. When you do get pulled into team disagreements, use the following quick guide to determine your actions.

Administrator Action	Key Points to Remember
Listen without commitment.	• Never forget that listening doesn't require action. • Use cautious language that does not convey a sense of commitment. • Avoid innocent comments that can be easily misinterpreted.
Base crucial conversations on facts that you have witnessed.	• Never approach teachers about concerns based on hearsay. • Base crucial conversations on facts that you have observed. • Show up to team meetings unannounced to gain a true picture of a team's current reality.
Coach before commanding.	• Build crucial conversation skills in teachers. • Provide teachers with access to resources and research on conflict resolution. • Send key faculty members to training sessions on team facilitation. • Ensure that new teachers have knowledgeable mentors to guide them through early struggles.
Collect feedback to improve systems.	• Accept responsibility for crafting structures that encourage successful collaboration. • Collect detailed information on the struggles of learning teams. • Take action to improve the systems and processes in your building.
When all else fails, be flexible.	• Understand that some people just should not work together. • Understand that dysfunctional teams that cannot be repaired do not benefit teachers or students. • Be willing to restructure learning teams or to reassign teachers when necessary.

CHAPTER 6

EXPERIENCING FRUSTRATION

Steve, Central Middle's principal, collapsed into his chair. He had just returned from an eighth-grade mathematics professional learning team meeting, and it was clear that the eighth-grade team was becoming tired and frustrated.

Back in the fall, Steve had set a deadline for every professional learning team in the school: create at least one common assessment and administer it to all students by February 1. Every other team had already met this expectation, but eighth-grade math was struggling to get it done. Worse yet, they did not seem to respect or enjoy each other at all and were doing little to come to any kind of shared consensus around collective action.

They disagreed openly about the kinds of content that were important to cover for each unit and that would best measure student mastery. Some members of the team wanted to use multiple choice quizzes that would be quick and easy to grade to meet Steve's expectation, while others felt strongly that students should be able to apply mathematical concepts in real-world situations. Despite Steve's best efforts, they truly seemed unwilling to move forward together.

On top of this, Steve had asked one of his assistant principals to create a midyear survey to give to the staff to gauge the progress of different learning teams. He had spent the previous evening reading through the survey results, and they were not pretty. No, scratch that—they were pretty in some places, but ugly in others. While many teams indicated they were starting to work well together, and a few teams had even begun to analyze student learning data, the most frequent statement in the comments section of the survey was, "This is hard. Collaboration takes a lot of time, and we're tired."

"Amen to that," Steve thought.

He had known that building a professional learning community would be difficult. The excitement of the initial months had given way to the reality of working in a collaborative environment. It took longer to make decisions now, both at the administrative level and at the classroom level, and decision making involved a lot more emotional friction.

In some ways, Steve thought it was like opening Pandora's box. On the one hand, working as a PLC was starting to pay some real dividends in terms of teaching quality and student learning. Steve had seen a number of teachers integrate innovative instructional strategies that they never would have used without the support of colleagues. He had also heard glowing reports from scores of parents about their children's progress.

On the other hand, however, Steve and the teachers at Central Middle were dealing with a whole new set of issues and challenges that many of them had never encountered before. Steve knew it was worth it. Heck, he would not have put in all this time and energy if he did not believe it was worth it. But did it really have to be this difficult?

A tap at the door brought Steve out of his introspection. Sarah, one of the sixth-grade language arts/social studies teachers, was waiting to see him. "Yes, Sarah, what can I do for you?"

"Do you have a minute, Steve? I had something neat I wanted to tell you about."

"For you, Sarah, I have at least two minutes, especially if it's something neat. I could use something neat right about now."

"Well, at the last staff meeting you asked us to tell you about any effective practices that we use at our professional learning team meetings so that you could share them with the whole staff. We've just started trying something new in our sixth-grade language arts/social studies team, and I wanted to show it to you. Is your computer on?"

For the next five minutes, Sarah showed Steve a digital tool that the team had been using to share online information and resources. Called *Pageflakes*™, the free service allowed a team of people to share using something called an *RSS feed*. As soon as one person found a good online resource, they added it to Pageflakes, and it was immediately available to everyone else. Sarah's team had also added a discussion board to their shared *flake*, which allowed them to easily communicate with one another between scheduled meetings.

"What has been really great about this," said Sarah, "is that we can keep collaborating outside of school. So often in our meetings we'll start talking about a new resource or idea, and then time runs out. This allows us to keep the conversation going. Some of the people on our team who might not be as involved during team meetings, like Jennifer, have ended up being the most active people online. She says that she feels more comfortable sharing when she has time to think about what she's trying to say."

"This is great!" Steve pushed back from his laptop. "So, outside of this new practice, which I love, how is your team doing? Do you feel like things are going well?"

Sarah paused for a minute. "Honestly? It's really hard. Working in a team like this is so different. It feels like being a first-year teacher all over again. Everyone's tired, there's not enough time to do everything we want to do. And it's not easy emotionally, either—a while back, we had this huge blowup because people were agreeing with team decisions while secretly being really frustrated."

"Is there anything I can do to help?" Steve asked.

"No, I don't think there's anything you can do. Or rather, you're already doing it. You put the expectations in place, you've given us tools for working together, you give us feedback on how the team is doing—you even covered our classes to give us the chance to observe each other. Those things are all helpful, but it's really up to us to figure out how to solve our own problems as a team. It's just going to take some time."

"Yes, the ever-present problem of time," Steve said. "Well, thank you so much for showing me Pageflakes. I'm going to have to explore it a little more over the weekend; and, I would be very interested in having you share it at our next staff meeting."

"My pleasure. See you at lunch duty!"

After Sarah left his office, Steve thought for a bit. While he might not be able to solve everyone's problems, maybe there was something he could do to at least lighten the mood. Steve had wanted to organize a staff party before the winter holiday, but scheduling had not worked out. Valentine's Day was a couple weeks away. Maybe the PTA would be willing to sponsor a staff get-together after school one day. Cheesy, no doubt, but a little lighthearted socializing might be just the ticket to help cure the postvacation winter blues.

Steve chuckled to himself. "Now I've got one more thing to worry about—planning the perfect Valentine's Day party!"

Lessons From the Front Line

Make no mistake. Developing an effective professional learning community is hard work. In this chapter's story, Steve and Sarah were experiencing firsthand the frustrations that go along with creating a collaborative environment. They were tired, progress was ambiguous, and frictions were emerging as people worked in closer proximity than they were used to.

For teachers and school leaders interested in creating a PLC, it is important to understand that the process will not always be smiles and laughter—but it is worth it. Whenever professionals join together to take ownership of student learning, kids benefit, and the long-term professional satisfaction that accompanies success more than makes up for short-term struggles. Working in the face of new frustrations, however, can seem simply overwhelming at times.

What factors lead to these frustrations? Why is collaboration such a tricky thing, bringing out both the best and the worst in us? And, are there common patterns to the types of frustration that emerge in a PLC?

One of the main causes of frustration in a developing PLC has to do with the nature of schools as organizations. Schools have traditionally been places in which teachers act independently: deciding what to teach, how to teach it, and how to test it.

In a PLC, teachers are required to work together when making these kinds of decisions, and collaboration both slows the process down and takes away an expected degree of teacher autonomy. As the process of decision making slows, teachers often become discouraged, realizing that there just are not enough hours in the day. Collaboration also involves a lot of face-to-face contact that may be new to many teachers. Educators used to maintaining a professional arm's length are asked to negotiate curricular and instructional decisions with people who share different philosophies about teaching and learning.

Such powerful conversations can be uncomfortable, but the process is not all bleak. There are a variety of strategies that teachers and building leaders can use to decrease and eventually move beyond these growing pains. This chapter focuses on the frustrations that emerge as schools work to become active PLCs.

We begin by looking at the organizational structure of schools and how this structure makes a certain amount of tension an inevitable byproduct of collaboration. We then focus on specific areas in which frustrations emerge and discuss a number of recommendations to decrease the impact of frustration. We conclude with an extended discussion of the ways in which collaborative technologies can enhance and extend team work, building on the theories in Clay Shirky's (2008) book *Here Comes Everybody: The Power of Organizing Without Organizations.*

Tightening a Loosely Coupled System

For Steve, Central Middle School had reached a critical turning point. What began as a simple plan to bring teachers together in collaborative teams had spiraled into a collection of interpersonal conflicts and open disagreements. Tasks that Steve expected everyone to easily embrace—such as creating common assessments and identifying essential outcomes for instruction—had become roadblocks for many learning teams. Even the groups that seemed to have embraced collaboration were exhausted.

Steve wondered, "Does it really have to be this difficult?" However, a more important question would have been, "*Why* is this so difficult?"

One answer has to do with the way in which schools are organized. Traditionally, schools have been structured as loosely coupled systems. The term *loosely coupled* was first used by an organizational researcher named Karl Weick in the 1970s and describes the somewhat informal connections between subgroups and individuals within a school.

Weick and his collaborators (1976) introduced the concept of coupled systems in an article titled "Educational Organizations as Loosely Coupled Systems." According to Weick, schools are made up of multiple systems and subsystems, such as grade levels, departments, and even individual classrooms, some of which might be tightly coupled, or attached, to each other. For example, Steve is tightly coupled to his administrative team. Central Middle's assistant principals report directly to, and work closely with, Steve on a daily basis—and his directives have a considerable impact on their behaviors and job performance.

Most systems within a school, however, are loosely coupled. The electives teachers at Central Middle are only loosely coupled with grade-level teachers, in that the actions of electives teachers have very little impact on, or relationship to, the actions of grade level teachers. Sure, when the band teacher asks to have his students excused early one day to get ready for the spring concert, he must coordinate and cooperate with core teachers. On most days, however, the actions and decisions of elective teachers rarely overlap with the work of core teachers. Despite working in the same building, they operate primarily in separate systems from one another.

In most schools, this lack of overlap exists even between classrooms at the same grade level. Teachers' actions are mostly *independent* of each other: you teach the way you want, and I teach the way I want. You're responsible for *your* students, and I'm responsible for *my* students. Such classrooms, which represent the status quo in education, are considered, by Weick's definition, to be loosely coupled. One of the best descriptions of loosely coupled classrooms in action is shared by Richard DuFour (2008), who wrote about his early work as a U.S. history teacher:

> I never had to concern myself with what content others were teaching, because each of us was free to determine his or her own curriculum. There was no process, expectation or even encouragement for me to discuss with colleagues my curriculum pacing, my instructional strategies, the methods and rigor of my assessments, my homework policy, my grading practices, my response to students who struggled, or any other vital issues essential to effective teaching. The only thing my sections of our U.S. history course had in common with the sections taught by others in my department was the title. (p. 1)

DuFour's experiences are not the case in a truly collaborative environment. In fact, one of the key components of an effective professional learning team is *interdependence* (DuFour, DuFour, & Eaker, 2008; DuFour, DuFour, Eaker, & Many, 2006). That is, the members of a professional learning team rely on each other, making collaborative decisions that impact each of their peers. The eighth-grade teachers at Central Middle simply could not operate in stand-alone systems and still meet Steve's requirement of developing and delivering a common assessment. Interdependence was unavoidable.

What makes this work even more challenging is that PLCs attempt to systemically tighten what is traditionally the most loosely coupled piece of schools: curricular and instructional decision making. All of those key decisions that we used to make independently for our individual classrooms are made interdependently in learning communities. As anyone who has ever had braces can tell you, tightening a system can hurt. At the end of the process, everything fits together nicely and you have a winning smile. But, as Steve started to discover, there is some real pain involved in getting from point A to point B.

The concept of loosely coupled systems helps explain why building a PLC is so difficult. It does not, however, provide much direction for someone trying to tighten the system. In our story, Steve was actually implementing a number of effective practices, even if the process felt difficult and moved more slowly than he would have liked. Steve was using the following strategies to counteract the loosely coupled nature of schools:

- **Setting, and sticking to, specific expectations**—At the beginning of the story, Steve reflected on one of the expectations that he had set early in the year: that each team would create at least one common assessment and administer it by a set date. By creating a specific and measurable expectation, and sticking to that expectation, Steve had sent a clear message about his priorities (DuFour, DuFour, Eaker, & Many, 2006). At the same time, Steve didn't just create a task and then walk away from struggling teachers. He was spending time in the eighth-grade hallway, doing what he could to support the team in their efforts to meet his expectations.

- **Limiting efforts to what matters most**—When setting expectations, it can be tempting for principals to develop a full laundry list of everything that they would like teachers to do. One of the reasons that schools are loosely coupled is that, because of time constraints, classroom teachers, instructional coaches, and administrators alike can only attend to and effectively monitor a small number of expectations. That is why it is so important for school leaders to limit their efforts to what matters most. Steve focused on common assessments, and that was a good place to start. When teachers are required to develop common assessments, they are likely to align (in other words, tighten) their curricular and instructional practices because they are all now teaching to the same end point.

- **Building in feedback loops**—Even though Steve was slightly depressed by the results of the faculty surveys administered by his assistant principal, he should continue to build in this type of feedback. By regularly assessing a faculty's progress toward effective collaboration, a principal can tweak the strategies and approaches needed to meet the reality of the building's progress. Steve's conversation with Sarah produced equally valuable feedback. While surveys can provide a quantitative snapshot of an entire faculty, in-depth conversations can provide the kinds of detailed, qualitative information that can inform decision making.

- **Leveraging social relationships**—In chapter 3, "Creating Trust," we talked about the importance of trust and relationships in a PLC. When staff members have strong relationships and trust each other, it is easier for school leaders to tighten the system, because staff members have a stake in maintaining those positive relationships. At the end of the story, Steve began planning a Valentine's Day party. While staff social functions might seem inconsequential, they provide opportunities for relationship building that can grease the wheels of collaboration, increasing staff members' willingness to give up some of their individual curricular and instructional decision making. As Gayle Moller and Anita Pankake (2006) explain:

    > Every school has social events, such as holiday gatherings and begin-ning- and end-of-the-year socials. These occasions are rich oppor-tunities for building relationships . . . [bringing] together teachers who might otherwise not know that they share the same birthday month, that they were hired in the same year, or they have children graduating from high school at the same time. These social functions offer new possibilities for the social exchanges necessary in building relational trust. (p. 78)

- **Using mission, vision, and goals as the glue**—Underlying all of Steve's actions was an understanding that, at Central Middle, collaboration was simply the way business gets done. This is a key point: if staff members do not buy into a philosophy of collaboration, they are likely to strongly resist any attempts to tighten the system of curricular and instructional decision making. While Steve's eighth-grade math teachers may have been struggling with the development of their first real team-based assessment, they had something important in common: a vision for a collaborative schoolhouse crafted together early during the school year.

As Richard DuFour and Robert Eaker (1998) explain, "What separates a learning community from an ordinary school is its collective commitment to guiding principles that articulate what the people in the school believe and what they seek to create" (p. 25). If a faculty is actively resisting the tightening inherent in a PLC, it may be time, as a school, to revisit the organization's underlying commitment to a common mission, vision, and set of goals. Mike Schmoker (2006) agrees:

> One of the greatest dangers to a successful improvement effort is losing focus, which results from trying to take on more than we have the time and resources to realistically achieve. . . . Schools are under enormous pressure to respond to every concern their constituents raise. . . . Among the hardest decisions a school community must make is to decide democratically which goals reflect the school's highest priorities—and which it must pursue later. (p. 33)

Ultimately, tightening is about focus. Because schools are loosely coupled systems, building leaders only have so much leverage to drive improvement. By putting their time and effort into developing collaborative structures, administrators keep teachers focused on their most important job: working together to achieve ever-improving student learning.

Recognizing the Frustrations

As buildings work to tighten their systems and curricular and instructional decision making, frustration is bound to emerge. There is an unfortunate truism of developing a professional learning community: if you're not feeling any frustration, you're probably not accomplishing much. Even DuFour and Eaker (1998) recognize that the work of PLCs can be maddening and unpredictable at times:

> Members of a professional learning community must be prepared to slosh around together in the mess, to endure temporary discomfort, to accept uncertainty, to celebrate their discoveries, and to move quickly beyond their mistakes. . . . They must recognize that even with the most careful planning, misunderstandings will occur occasionally, uncertainty will prevail, people will resort to old habits, and things will go wrong. (p. 283)

While there is no way to fully avoid the difficulty and messiness of developing a PLC, recognizing those frustrations for what they are—common byproducts of the collaborative process—can lessen their impact. As they say, forewarned is forearmed. Teams that can define the common sources of frustration caused by collaboration are less inclined to give up and can actively seek solutions together. In general, the frustrations of developing a PLC tend to fall into three general categories: time, social and philosophical friction, and increased responsibility and accountability.

Time

Time is already one of the scarcest resources in a school, and in a collaborative environment time becomes even more precious. This can cause frustration in a variety of ways.

For the individual teacher, the challenge is straightforward: she is being asked to take on new duties, such as meeting regularly with teammates, without having any existing responsibilities taken away. In a PLC, teachers still have to plan lessons, grade papers, and make parent phone calls. Demands have increased, but the time available has not. This is one of the reasons why many professional learning teams gravitate toward common planning. By divvying up planning responsibilities, teachers begin to use collaboration to save themselves time.

Decision making also takes more time. Decisions that teachers were accustomed to making individually are now made collaboratively, slowing down the process. This can be especially frustrating for veteran teachers. At Central Middle School, the eighth-grade team, one of the most experienced groups in Steve's building, is the most resistant to developing common assessments together. They have each worked long enough to find a successful routine, so collectively revisiting decisions like sequencing curriculum or assessing student learning feels nonsensical.

The decision-making process also changes in PLCs. Grade levels and departments that traditionally used meetings to focus on administrative decisions—scheduling lunch duties, counting textbook orders—must now switch their meeting focus to curricular and instructional decision making. Administrative decisions, however, still have to be made. The solution that many teams choose is creating two meeting times, one for the curricular and instructional discussions and one for the nuts and bolts discussions, which takes even more time away from individual planning.

Highly functioning teams encounter a different type of time challenge: trying to do too much. Because they have become more proficient at creating common assessments and analyzing student data, they often attempt to quickly spread these practices to every subject area (at the elementary level) or to every instructional unit (at the middle and high school levels). Some teams temporarily burn themselves out by over-collaborating—taking on more than they can legitimately handle. This can become especially frustrating when some members of the team have less discretionary time due to family obligations or second jobs. As a result, an imbalance develops in the amount of work put in outside of school by colleagues.

While more effective decisions almost always result from a careful, collaborative process, effective deliberation can still lead to short-term frustration.

Social and Philosophical Friction

In a PLC, decisions tend to take time. They also tend to involve numerous people working closely with one another. This can be a recipe for misplaced agendas, miscommunication, and misunderstandings: in short, decision making in a PLC can lead to social friction and personal frustration.

In traditional schools, a teacher can bite her tongue when that grating colleague brings up his pet project for the thousandth time at the monthly grade-level or department meeting. After all, there is no need to worry about his plan to have every incoming student take the placement exam he designed years ago. It will never happen, right?

Teachers in PLCs, however, work in closer contact with peers and have to be more willing to accommodate different personalities than do teachers in more traditional schools. That grating colleague's pet idea may become the design for a series of common assessments at Central Middle, and the old social policy of smile, nod, and ignore no longer works when behaviors become interdependent.

This leads to a frustration that really operates at two levels: the frustration of social friction, and the frustration of philosophical friction. At the purely social level, some people just do not particularly enjoy each other's company. They find the personality habits of individual colleagues annoying, or they have a negative history together.

Social friction is often philosophical friction in disguise, and philosophical friction is more problematic. In a professional learning team, teachers have to come to consensus about common practices, especially around essential curriculum objectives and common assessments. When the teachers on a team have real philosophical differences over what content should be taught and how it should be assessed, it is not enough to simply smile, nod, and ignore.

Back in chapter 5, "Negotiating Personalities and Conflict," Sarah's team learned firsthand about the emotional costs of collaborative decision making. In an effort to avoid conflict, Jennifer agreed to decisions with which she was philosophically opposed, placing harmony before honesty. Unfortunately, that bottled-up frustration eventually came out in an emotional blowup. Now, philosophical friction over just what effective assessment looks like is preventing the eighth-grade teachers from meeting one of Steve's basic expectations.

This is the difficulty of philosophical friction. To move beyond it, teachers have to figure out how to disagree without being disagreeable, honestly recognizing philosophical differences while keeping them from becoming social frictions. As Austin Buffum, the former senior deputy superintendent of the Capistrano Unified School District in San Juan Capistrano, California, writes:

> Most successful relationships require productive conflict; however, in many work environments, conflict is seen as something to be avoided at all costs. . . . It's important to differentiate between conflict that centers on personalities and that which centers on ideas. (2008, p. 63)

Increased Responsibility and Accountability

In traditionally run, hierarchically structured schools, teachers often complain that they are not given enough decision-making authority. In PLCs, however, teachers are given considerably more power over team- and school-level decisions; but, with that additional authority comes increased responsibility and accountability.

While the distributed leadership practices in a PLC result in empowered teachers and better overall decisions, they also result in increased anxiety. Teachers accustomed to being told what to do and how to do it are suddenly asked, "What do you think?" As teachers realize that they are in the position to make decisions, they often wrestle with concerns about making the wrong decisions and having ownership of their mistakes.

Another frustration comes from the increased sense of responsibility for results that develops in a professional learning team. As teachers have opportunities to observe each other teaching, to work with teammates' students, and to see their colleagues' results on common assessments, teachers can become concerned about the quality of teaching and learning happening outside their classrooms.

In a traditional school, teachers tend to focus primarily on the success of their own students. Sure, a teacher has a sense that her colleague down the hall is not doing a particularly good job, but that is the administration's problem to deal with. In a collaborative environment, however, teachers feel an increased sense of responsibility and accountability for all the students on a team. Suddenly, that teacher down the hall whose incompetence was always ignored by her teammates becomes a real source of frustration.

In addition, teachers on a professional learning team come to rely on each other in a way that teachers in a traditionally structured school do not. In the earlier stages of team development, teachers often distribute lesson-planning responsibility. If one of the teachers consistently creates poor materials or is consistently late in getting work done, everyone is affected.

As teachers begin to see each other's strengths and weaknesses, as the sense of student ownership expands, and as teachers come to increasingly rely on the work and expertise of their teammates, many teachers wrestle with how to address the subpar performance of their colleagues. Should they go to administration? Should they confront their colleagues? Should they just suck it up and continually rewrite the shoddy work of their less-talented or less-experienced teammates? No matter the answer a team chooses, it is bound to cause anxiety and frustration.

This section might sound like an argument against the development of PLCs. Far from it. Even though decision making in a collaborative environment takes more time and can lead to frustration, the outcome is better results. While top-down decision making may feel more efficient, it is not particularly effective. Because schools are loosely coupled systems, many of the decisions made in the principal's office never actually get implemented in the classroom. Worse yet, as Megan Tschannen-Moran (2004) explains, top-down decision making can result in a culture of distrust:

> The classic authoritarian bureaucracy is based on the foundational assumption that teachers, like workers in general, are untrustworthy. . . . The role of the system is to ensure that potentially reluctant and irresponsible teachers do what is prescribed by the school organization. The behavior of the leader serves to reinforce the distrust embedded in the system. (p. 98)

This section is, instead, an argument in favor of awareness. School leaders and teachers, alike, must understand the kinds of frustrations that are a natural byproduct of collaboration and work to develop systems that can facilitate collective action. While abandoning professional collaborative work between colleagues is an easier first step to resolving friction, responsible schools focus attention on efforts to make efficient collaboration possible.

The bottom line is this: calling a school a PLC does not produce results. In order to realize actual improvements in teaching and learning, teachers and school leaders must commit themselves to the difficult and sometimes frustrating work of true collaboration. As Brian Rowan (1995) cautions, "It is not structural change per se that creates successful schools. Instead, structural changes succeed in improving school performance only if they are consistent with, and support changes in, work practices (e.g., authentic instruction), and only if they are undertaken by a committed work force of teachers" (p. 15).

As Central Middle School discovered, the kinds of collaborative processes that result in better decisions, better results, and reduced frustrations can be supported by digital tools.

Relevant Theory and Research

In his book *Here Comes Everybody: The Power of Organizing Without Organizations*, Clay Shirky (2008) describes the ways in which new web-based tools have transformed collaborative opportunities within, across, and beyond organizations. While schools and educators have historically been slow to adopt new technologies, Shirky's book provides insight into how teachers can use technology to enhance both the efficiency and the effectiveness of their collaborative efforts.

Shirky begins with a discussion of organizations in general: why they exist and how they function. He makes three important points that have real relevance for professional learning communities. First, the reason that we have organizations (such as schools) is that organizations are typically more efficient and effective than ad hoc arrangements of services. While individual families could go out and hire teachers or tutors directly for their children, it is more efficient and effective to organize teachers into schools serving large numbers of students.

Second, once groups of people are organized, their work has to be coordinated. This coordination involves certain inevitable costs, called *transaction costs*. Transaction costs refer to the time, attention, and/or money involved in coordinating the work of people in an organization. In a school, every staff meeting, email message, or lunch-duty shift represents time and attention not spent directly on teaching and learning. Similarly, every administrator, guidance counselor, and front office employee represents dollars not spent directly on teaching and learning. Organizations require coordination, coordination requires interactions, and interactions require extensive fiscal, physical, and psychological resources.

Third, as organizations become more collaborative, there is a trade-off between efficiency and effectiveness. Hierarchical organizations, in which a few people at the top make decisions that everyone else follows, are highly efficient because they have fewer transaction costs; but, they also allow little room for creativity and organizational learning. Collaborative organizations in which people work together to make decisions and learn from each other produce more effective decisions but are much less efficient because of the increased transaction costs carried by collective efforts.

Many professional learning teams, including the eighth-grade math team at Central Middle School, struggle with the increased transaction costs that come with shared effort. Group decisions become cumbersome and time-consuming, causing friction between members of collaborative teams. Teachers, like any professionals working in large organizations, weigh the perceived benefits of new interactions against the additional mental and physical demands of collaboration before changing their behaviors.

Shirky argues, however, that collaborative technologies lower transaction costs by reducing or eliminating the need for close coordination between colleagues. Such technologies allow people to work collaboratively *and* efficiently—mediating the inevitable frustrations felt by learning teams working together for the first time.

As an example, consider a common practice of school departments and teams: putting together a binder of ideas or resources that anyone can use. Sounds good in theory, right? Everyone benefits from the collective input of the team. But have you ever seen a binder of great resources that was actually used on a regular basis in your building? Probably not.

The reason this practice almost never works is that the time and energy required to create, maintain, and monitor additions to the shared collection is not worth the payout for participants. In order for such a system to work, each person has to write or print out ideas on a regular basis; organize those resources in some common space; and take the time to regularly look through every new contribution, hoping to find something relevant.

At any point, this attempt at collective action can break down. Teachers could simply forget to add their best lessons to the shared collection—or could add *every* lesson without any sense of intended direction or quality control. Materials might never be returned or reorganized. Sifting through piles of papers even once without success discourages continued use. The costs of coordination, the transaction costs, are just too high for team resource binders to be a successful collaborative strategy.

Now consider the online service Sarah mentioned in the story that began this chapter. Pageflakes is a web-based tool that allows teachers to share, catalog, and manage online resources in seconds. If Sarah found a great website on ancient Greece, she could click a button and instantly share that resource with everyone else on her team. The next time one of her colleagues logged on to Pageflakes, he or she would see the new resource automatically and could then either explore it or ignore it.

Pageflakes, like many other social networking applications, also allows users to create forums for digital discussion. So Sarah's team can not only instantly share resources, but members can also leave messages for one another, discussing instructional strategies and challenging thinking without being constrained by the barriers of time and place. By using digital tools, teachers can offer just-in-time, targeted support to their peers from their classrooms, their workrooms, or their living rooms. The costs of team coordination are reduced to just about zero.

Shirky (2008) goes on to argue that there are three levels of collaborative technologies: tools that help you share, tools that help you cooperate, and tools that help you take collective action. These three levels—sharing, cooperating, and taking collective action—bear a strong resemblance to the stages of professional learning team work outlined in chapter 4, "Supporting Team Development." As groups move through each new stage of development, digital tools can make different kinds of work more efficient.

Pageflakes is a tool for sharing resources. Teams at the next stage of development, cooperation, might employ a different tool. For example, shared lesson plans or assessments can be developed in a wiki. *Wikis* allow groups of people to create common online documents, adding to and editing each other's work. Over the course of a year, a learning team well versed in the use of wikis (which are surprisingly intuitive tools) could create a full instructional calendar, complete with discrete lesson plans, online resources, and common assessments. Because wikis have a simple editing functionality, teams could update these resources on an ongoing basis.

For organizations interested in using collaborative technology tools, Shirky gives some advice: the success of digital collaboration rests on establishing a promise, finding an effective tool, and creating an acceptable bargain. Shirky's advice easily translates into schools restructuring as learning communities.

Collaboration of any kind in a PLC will only work if professional learning teams have bought into the basic promise that teachers will work interdependently to ensure student learning. This promise can exist at multiple levels as teams go through different developmental stages. Teams at an earlier stage of development may buy into the promise that "if we share ideas, we can learn from each other." Teams at a later stage of development may buy into the promise that "if we create and use joint materials, they will represent the best of our collective thinking."

Collaboration is unlikely, however, until all members of a learning organization or developing social network clearly embrace the promise. To put it simply, new digital tools will not ensure collaboration. Shared values and goals between networks of likeminded individuals ensure collaboration—tools just make collaboration easier.

Different digital tools are appropriate depending on the developmental level of a team and the level of promise to which that team has committed. A team looking to share ideas will likely find Pageflakes to be valuable. A team that wants to create common materials might appreciate the functionality offered by a wiki. One important fact to remember: there are no digital tools that will meet a team's every need because different tools do different things well. Successful digital collaboration depends on selecting the right tool for the right task. We have listed a number of suggested tools aligned with specific learning team tasks at the end of this chapter in Tools for Twenty-First-Century Learning Teams (pages 135–143).

Finally, participating members of a social network have to strike a bargain with each other before collaborative technologies can bring results. For teams to benefit from a tool such as Pageflakes, members have to agree to share valuable resources as they find them. For teams to benefit from a wiki, members have to agree to give up individual control of curriculum and instruction to achieve higher overall student learning.

Striking a common bargain, however, does not mean that every team member must contribute equally in order to make the use of digital tools effective. In any social network or learning team, it is likely that one or two members will identify the bulk of the resources or post the bulk of the materials. This is a common pattern often called the 80/20 rule: 20 percent of the people typically contribute 80 percent of the content. As long as members of the team are comfortable with this pattern, and as long as everyone is contributing something on a semiregular basis, there is nothing wrong with following the 80/20 rule (Shirky, 2008).

Teams willing to experiment are realizing that the creative use of collaborative technologies can carry real benefits. Tools such as Pageflakes and wikis reduce the transaction costs of coordination, allowing teams to share more efficiently. Technology also allows for asynchronous participation. Team members usually need to be in the same place at the same time to collaborate, but new technologies allow interactions to happen on individual schedules, both inside and outside the school building.

Finally, technology allows less-vocal team members to contribute in a safe environment. Back in chapter 5, "Negotiating Personalities and Conflict," Jennifer felt too intimidated and overwhelmed to participate in team conversations, leading to frustration for her and for other team members. But in the story in this chapter, Sarah noted that Jennifer was much more active online than she was in face-to-face environments. By extending collaborative opportunities to digital spaces, teams can often draw out contributions from less confident participants.

Regardless of the stage of development, digital tools can help to ease frustrations and philosophical frictions for learning teams, an essential step toward ensuring the long-term success of collective action in your building.

Recommendations

As schools become heavily engaged in collaboration, exhaustion is inevitable. The loosely coupled nature of schools can lead to "tightening" pains as teachers align curricular and instructional decisions. In addition, certain frustrations, which are usually related to time, social and philosophical friction, and increased responsibility and accountability, are unavoidable byproducts of the collaborative process. Following are several suggestions for coping with collaboration fatigue.

Be Patient

This recommendation applies to everyone, from school leaders to classroom teachers. Learning how to work in a collaborative environment takes time and hard work, and it is important that staff members be patient with themselves and each other. There will be unkind words said in frustration, but the goal of improved teaching and learning is worth the effort.

Being patient, however, does not mean relaxing standards. This is a difficult balance to maintain, especially for building leaders. On one hand, unreasonable standards and expectations can push a staff to the breaking point. On the other hand, lax enforcement of expectations can keep progress from occurring. Steve, Central Middle School's principal, took some smart steps to maintain this balance. He used a survey like the one included at the end of this chapter (the Midyear PLC Survey on pages 144–147) to get feedback about team progress from the whole faculty. He also informally touched base with an influential teacher whom he trusted to give him honest feedback. We recommend that building leaders, including teachers working on learning teams, create as many feedback loops as possible to find the right balance between patience and urgency.

Tighten the Areas That Matter

Learning teams—like schools—are complicated organizations, and building leaders could pick any of dozens of processes or practices to tighten. According to DuFour and Eaker (1998):

> Some schools are vigilant in their efforts to monitor their teachers' use of the copier, the attractiveness of bulletin boards, or the adherence to dress codes. There is little to suggest that this kind of vigilance will enhance the effectiveness of those schools. What a school is monitoring is more important than if a school is monitoring. (p. 108)

So what should your learning teams monitor and tighten? First, work on the collaborative identification of essential curriculum: are teachers working together to decide what students should learn? Second, address the development of common assessments: are teachers creating assessments tied to the essential curriculum and, then, giving those assessments to all students? Third, monitor the use of student learning data: are teachers regularly sitting down and collectively examining the results of common assessments? Finally, look at the use of structured interventions and enrichment opportunities: are teachers using student learning data to create targeted instructional responses for the high achievers and struggling students that they serve?

Monitoring, however, also means that some initiatives, tasks, projects, and actions—including those mandated by school or district decision makers—should receive a greater amount of your learning team's time and attention. Consider using the What Is Our Team Monitoring? document (pages 148–149) included at the end of this chapter to systematically prioritize the work of your professional learning team.

Recognize the Additional Frustrations of Veteran Teachers

Often, beginning teachers are much bigger fans of collaboration than veteran teachers. For those newest to the profession, learning teams are a godsend: beginning teachers are supported through the planning process, they are often given fully developed lessons, and they have regular access to other teachers who can answer their questions. What's not to like? For more veteran teachers, like Sarah in our story, collaboration carries a unique set of frustrations. Well-worn units may end up being discarded, instructional decisions made years ago might be suddenly called into question, and fresh-faced young colleagues might constantly be in need of ideas and resources.

For those veteran teachers, it can be helpful to expand the way in which they think about their impact on students. By working in such close contact with less-experienced teachers, veterans are able to have a positive effect on students across an entire building, not just in their own rooms. For administrators, it is important to know that veteran teachers may need an especially large dose of positive reinforcement. This can be particularly true when multiple veterans with varying teaching philosophies are working on the same team. Sparks may sometimes fly, but it is important for administrators to listen with empathy while maintaining a discrete distance.

Use Technology Where Possible to Support and Extend Collaboration

While digital solutions can never supplant face-to-face team meetings in your learning community, technology *is* increasingly enhancing and expanding collaborative possibilities. Tools such as Pageflakes and wikis allow teachers to work together 24/7 and reduce the coordination costs of teamwork. Consider using the Tools for Twenty-First-Century Learning Teams: Planning Guide and Matrices (pages 135–143) included at the end of this chapter to find opportunities to leverage technology to enhance collective action on your learning team.

One of the challenges of technology, however, is technical skill. You cannot use a tool if you do not know it exists, and some people are far more digitally comfortable than others. It is important for school leaders to recognize that they do not have to be technology leaders. By identifying people in the building who are comfortable with new social networking applications and encouraging them to search for and share collaborative tools, administrators can leverage technology even if they lack digital skill.

For those teachers or administrators who are early adopters of collaborative tools, a word of caution: not everyone shares your expertise and enthusiasm. Rather than overwhelming colleagues, try picking one or two new resources, providing clear examples of how those resources can enhance collective action, and offering hands-on professional development. As less digitally experienced teachers see the value in collaborative technologies and develop the requisite expertise to use them, they will become increasingly receptive to additional possibilities.

Tools for Twenty-First-Century Learning Teams: Planning Guide

All kinds of organizations are beginning to recognize that the transaction costs of collaboration are getting smaller every day as new digital tools become available. Effective decision makers, however, understand that individual tools are tailored for specific tasks. Pairing the right tool with the right task is the first step toward ensuring that digital collaboration reduces frustration in your building. To begin your exploration of the potential in digital collaboration, select the collaborative tasks in the chart that your team is working to master. Then, use the matrices found on pages 137–143 to explore services available for supporting the desired work of learning teams and collaborative teachers.

Collaborative Task	Collaborative Behavior	Tool Suggestions
☐ Our team wants to share websites with one another easily.	Information Management	Social Bookmarking Tools (page 143)
☐ Our team wants to be able to read and annotate online articles about our subject area or instructional practices together.	Information Management	Social Bookmarking Tools (page 143)
☐ Our team wants to easily follow updates to websites related to our content area.	Information Management	Content Aggregation Tools (page 142)
☐ Our team wants to be able to share quick messages and resources with one another.	Communication	Instant Messaging Tools (pages 139–140)
☐ Our team wants to be able to see resources shared by teachers from around the globe.	Communication	Instant Messaging Tools (pages 139–140)
☐ Our team wants to be able to have ongoing discussions with one another about teaching and learning.	Communication	Asynchronous Discussion Tools (pages 137–138)
☐ Our team wants to be able to have ongoing conversations with other teachers who teach similar subjects and grade levels in different states and countries.	Communication	Asynchronous Discussion Tools (pages 137–138)
☐ Our team wants to be able to easily follow all of the updates to the digital conversations in which we participate.	Information Management	Content Aggregation Tools (page 142)
☐ Our team wants to be able to bring instructional experts into our team meetings.	Communication	Video Conferencing Tools (pages 138–139)

1 of 2

☐ Our team wants to create shared documents and lesson plans with one another.	Creation	Shared Document Creation Tools (pages 140–141)
☐ Our team wants to create digital warehouses of shared materials.	Creation and Communication	Asynchronous Discussion Tools (pages 137–138) Wiki Tools (page 141)
☐ Our team wants to create a website of resources for parents and students.	Creation	Wiki Tools (page 141)

Tools for Twenty-First-Century Learning Teams: Matrices

The following matrices can help school leaders identify tools that may support the work of their teams and teachers.

Tools for Communication: Teachers in professional learning communities must be skilled communicators. Schools once driven by individuals completing stand-alone tasks largely in isolation are now driven by human interactions. The challenge, however, is finding time for ongoing conversations among peers. What is more, the structure of face-to-face meetings can intimidate and/or silence marginalized members of some learning teams. Digital tools for communication can address both of these core frustrations.

Tool Type	Essential Features	Preferred Features	Suggested Services
Asynchronous Discussion Tools Many teachers need time to process core beliefs before feeling comfortable enough to add to team conversations. Asynchronous discussion forums allow participants to carefully polish their thinking before sharing it with peers. What is more, participation can happen any time, making communication easier to fit into personal schedules.	• Ability for participants to post anonymously • Ability for participants to receive email updates when new comments are added to the conversation • Ability to follow additions to conversations in feed readers or content aggregators	• Ability for conversations to be made open to a broader audience when appropriate (for example, for learning teams that consist of members across buildings or communities) • Ability for segments of conversations to be downloaded or exported into other formats or forums • Ability to add comments recorded from webcams and microphones	**Blackboard** http://blackboard.wcpss.net Advantages: Teachers have individual logins. Application can be scaled for student use. Disadvantages: Conversations are "closed," limiting participation to a single building. Conversations are limited to text-based stimuli. Service must be purchased. **Voicethread** http://voicethread.com Advantages: Service is free to educators. Application provides opportunities for participants to follow ongoing conversations via email or RSS feeds. Conversations can include text, audio, or video comments. Disadvantages: Not designed for creating warehouses of shared documents. Sole function is facilitating asynchronous conversations.

Tool Type	Essential Features	Preferred Features	Suggested Services
			Ning www.ning.com Advantages: Service is free to educators. Application provides opportunities for participants to follow ongoing conversations via email or RSS feeds. Individual participants can create their own profile pages to track conversations in which they are involved. Disadvantages: Conversations are limited to text-based stimuli. Difficult to build warehouses of documents. **Tapped In** http://tappedin.org/tappedin Advantages: Service is free to educators. Application provides opportunities for participants to follow conversations via email. Application includes built-in instant messaging client. Disadvantages: Conversations are limited to text-based stimuli. Presentation lacks polish.
Video Conferencing Tools Learning teams in rural communities or unique content areas can struggle to find partners to pair with. Video conferencing opens the door to collaboration for these teachers by allowing synchronous conversations with digital peers across the county, state, or globe.	• Ability to easily stream video without dropped connections • Ability for recording video conferences for later playback	• Ability for participants/ viewers to engage in instant message and back channel conversations during video conference • Ability for users to broadcast to a wider audience than just those involved in the immediate video conference	**Ustream** www.ustream.tv Advantages: Users can broadcast presentations and content to a larger audience. Presentations can be recorded for future archiving and playback. Participants can engage in instant message conversations during presentations. Disadvantages: Only one-way video and audio communication is supported. **Skype** www.skype.com Advantages: Two-way video and audio conferencing between users is enabled. Application allows for instant message communication between users during teleconferences.

Tool Type	Essential Features	Preferred Features	Suggested Services
		• Ability for easy file and resource sharing to occur during a live video conference • Ability for desktop sharing during a video conference, allowing users to access one another's computers from remote locations	Disadvantages: Does not allow for recording or broadcasting of videoconferences. Does not allow for desktop sharing during videoconferences. **Google Video Chat** http://mail.google.com/videochat Advantages: A part of the larger Google suite of tools, so the application can be accessed by any user with a Google account. Two-way video and audio conferencing between users is enabled. Application allows for instant message communication between users during teleconferences. Disadvantages: Does not allow for recording or broadcasting of videoconferences. Does not allow for desktop sharing during videoconferences.
Instant Messaging Tools One of the greatest frustrations for learning teams is finding answers to quick and simple questions. Tracking down peers is just plain inefficient, wasting already limited amounts of planning time. Instant messaging applications can connect teachers in real time.	• Ability for teachers to connect with peers across schools and communities. In-house instant messaging limits effectiveness—particularly for members of isolated learning teams. • Ability for teachers to receive a list of posted messages sent from colleagues for later review	• Ability for messages from user accounts to be accessed through an RSS feed reader • Ability for messages to be made public to all members of a school community or grade level, allowing for cross-communication that may not happen otherwise	**Google Talk** www.google.com/talk Advantages: A part of the larger Google suite of tools, so the application can be accessed by any user with a Google account. Disadvantages: Opportunities to review content posted over time are limited. No opportunities to track posts through RSS feeds or to make posting public.

Tool Type	Essential Features	Preferred Features	Suggested Services
		• Automatic limitation on the size of posted messages to ensure that instant messaging remains a source for just-in-time support and communication instead of becoming a source for deep reflection.	**Twitter** www.twitter.com Advantages: Application is an open instant messaging system that pairs colleagues from across the globe in ongoing conversations. Participants can follow conversations through RSS feeds. Disadvantages: Audience may be too removed from teams of teachers to offer relevant or helpful advice.

Tools for Collaboration: One of the greatest frustrations for teachers new to professional learning communities is finding the time to manage additional responsibilities and expectations. Traditional tasks (grading papers, writing plans, communicating with parents) are paired with new tasks (analyzing data, making shared decisions regarding curriculum, developing common assessments), leaving teachers completely exhausted. Tools that facilitate shared creation of instructional materials can create a bit of breathing room for overwhelmed learning teams.

Tool Type	Essential Features	Preferred Features	Suggested Services
Shared Document Creation Tools Teams of teachers are constantly creating written documents and presentations that support lesson plans or grade-level policies. Collaborative elements could easily be introduced to this	• Ability to track changes to shared documents easily • Ability to restore earlier versions of shared documents • Ability to jointly produce and export all common file formats: DOC, XCL, PPT, PDF	• Ability to follow revisions through RSS feed readers, enabling colleagues to monitor changes easily	**Google Docs** http://docs.google.com Advantages: A part of the larger suite of Google tools, so application can be accessed by any user with a Google account. Multiple users can work on the same document at the same time. Revisions can be followed through RSS feed readers. Disadvantages: A Google email account is required.

Tool Type	Essential Features	Preferred Features	Suggested Services
work using digital tools for shared document creation.	• Ability for multiple teachers to work on the same document at one time		**Writeboard** www.writeboard.com Advantages: Users are able to revert to earlier versions and track changes through RSS feeds. Does not require a user account or login. Disadvantages: Does not allow for the creation of commonly used file types. Does not allow multiple users to work on the same document at once.
Wiki Tools Perhaps the most approachable collaborative tool available to teams of teachers. Wikis are editable websites that allow colleagues to create content together. Because of their ease of use, wikis are often the first digital tool that teachers embrace.	• Multiple layers of password protection: viewing, editing, deleting/ creating pages, and so on • Ability to easily embed content from other services • Discussion boards that enable participants to comment on pages created by peers closed to outside users	• Ability to follow revisions through RSS feed readers, enabling team members to monitor changes easily • Ability to export pages in other file formats: DOC, PDF • Sufficient storage space on free accounts to allow teachers to upload images, documents, and other supplemental materials	**PBworks** www.pbworks.com Advantages: Application allows for multiple layers of password protection. Users are able to follow changes through RSS feed readers. Discussion boards are provided for each page. Disadvantages: Free versions provide limited storage space and features. **Wikispaces** www.wikispaces.com Advantages: Multiple layers of password protection are provided. Free accounts for educators include ample storage space. Disadvantages: Application is occasionally balky and often has unattractive workspaces.

Tools for Information Management: Perhaps the greatest challenge facing teachers working in learning communities is sifting through the amazing amount of content being created by their peers. Collaboration provides access to volumes of information that can be overwhelming, and valuable materials can be easily overlooked as teachers try to make sense of what their team has gathered. To reduce frustration, teachers must be able to quickly access content that may be of value to their work and judge the quality of the sources with which they have chosen to interact. Without these skills, teachers on learning teams will be inefficient and aggravated.

Tool Type	Essential Features	Preferred Features	Suggested Services
Content Aggregation Tools Arguably the most important information-management tools for learning teams. Also called *feed readers*. They allow users to monitor regular updates to web content from one central location. For teachers, this means being able to watch document revisions or wiki additions made by their peers immediately and easily. It also means gaining access to interesting and appropriate resources without having to rely on Google searches.	• Ability for individual users to have their own online accounts that can be accessed anywhere • Ability for feeds to be made public if and when necessary to enable sharing and monitoring • Ability for individual users to access a range of other tools from within their feed readers: to-do lists, grade trackers, calculators, note takers, and so on	• Ability to easily copy interesting feeds from one account to another	**Pageflakes for Teachers** http://teacher.pageflakes.com Advantages: Application is designed specifically for students and teachers. Interesting teaching and learning feeds can be easily copied to individual accounts. Feed pages can be set to public or private, making sharing of content possible.

Tool Type	Essential Features	Preferred Features	Suggested Services
Social Bookmarking Tools While social bookmarking has not yet become widely popular, it is a tool that has remarkable potential for the collaborative teacher. Social bookmarking accounts allow users to easily share web links of interest with one another and to tag those links by topic area. Social bookmarking sites make searching for information more targeted.	• Ability to tag web links by topic, content area, or grade level • Ability to quickly access sites tagged by other users • Ability to add to or access a user account from any computer	• Ability to follow user accounts through RSS feed readers, enabling teachers and students to monitor changes easily • Ability to create user groups that include discussion forums • Ability to annotate websites and to easily share annotations with other users	**Delicious** http://del.icio.us Advantages: Web links can be tagged and sorted by category. Users can follow additions by other users via RSS feed. Disadvantages: Users are required to add browser buttons to their Internet Explorer toolbar. Does not allow users to annotate websites or to share annotations. **Diigo** www.diigo.com Advantages: Web links can be tagged and sorted by category. Users can follow additions by other users via RSS feed. Users can create groups and profile pages that provide opportunities for ongoing dialogue around shared resources. Users can annotate websites and share annotations with one another, making shared reading possible. Disadvantages: A smaller number of users than Delicious means access to fewer shared links.

Midyear PLC Survey

This survey is intended to help us, as a school, learn more about the type of work that has occurred in PLC teams so far this year and how we can best plan our PLC work for the remainder of the year. The survey is divided into two sections: the ways in which your team has managed PLC meetings and the types of tasks on which your team has focused. Thank you for completing this survey in an honest and thoughtful manner.

Your grade level and primary subject area: _____

Team-Based Collaboration: Meeting Management

Please indicate the extent to which each of the statements below is true by circling one of the four numbers using the following scale:

1 = Very true   2 = True   3 = Somewhat true   4 = Not true

We have an agreed-upon set of meeting norms in our PLC team (for example, expectations for participant behaviors during meetings).	1	2	3	4
We follow our meeting norms consistently at PLC meetings.	1	2	3	4
Our norms help us to have productive, effective conversations.	1	2	3	4
We have clear tasks to perform at our PLC meetings.	1	2	3	4
Our tasks relate directly to student learning goals.	1	2	3	4
Our tasks are determined by consensus among our team members.	1	2	3	4
A large majority of our PLC time (80 percent or more) is spent on tasks related to student learning goals.	1	2	3	4
During PLC conversations, team members sometimes disagree about ideas or practices.	1	2	3	4
When team members disagree about ideas or practices, we tend to discuss those disagreements in depth.	1	2	3	4
When I disagree with something a member of my PLC has said, I almost always voice that disagreement.	1	2	3	4
Within PLC meetings, we try to avoid emotionally charged or difficult topics or conversations.	1	2	3	4
I feel a strong sense of attachment to my team.	1	2	3	4

If we were given the option of no longer meeting as a PLC, I would still want to continue the meetings.	1	2	3	4
I have improved as a classroom teacher as a result of the conversations and work we have done in our PLC.	1	2	3	4
I have made changes to my teaching practices as a result of the work that we have done as a PLC.	1	2	3	4

Comments:

Team-Based Collaboration: Teaching and Learning Tasks

Please indicate the extent to which each of the statements below is true by circling one of the four numbers using the following scale:

1 = Very true   2 = True   3 = Somewhat true   4 = Not true

My PLC team has worked to define the most important student learning goals in our content areas.	1	2	3	4
If you were to ask each of the members of my PLC team to list the most important student learning goals in our content areas independently, we would all come up with nearly identical lists.	1	2	3	4
I could explain to a parent, in simple language, the most important grade-level learning goals for his or her child in the content areas I teach.	1	2	3	4
In my PLC team, we regularly (at least monthly) administer common assessments to our students (in other words, all students complete the same assessment).	1	2	3	4
In my PLC team, we regularly use rubrics to score students' common assessments.	1	2	3	4
In my PLC team, we have developed our own rubrics to help us score students' common assessments.	1	2	3	4
As a PLC team, we regularly (at least monthly) assess student work samples as a team.	1	2	3	4
As a PLC team, we regularly (at least monthly) analyze data from students' common assessments.	1	2	3	4
I adjust the instructional practices in my classroom based on my students' performance on common assessments.	1	2	3	4
As a PLC team, we regularly (at least monthly) make adjustments to our instructional practices across all classrooms based on students' performance on common assessments.	1	2	3	4
Over the course of this year, I have implemented numerous academic interventions in my classroom for struggling students.	1	2	3	4
As an individual teacher, I regularly think about how my specific instructional practices affect student learning and how changes in my instructional practices might lead to changes in student learning.	1	2	3	4
As a PLC team, we regularly discuss how our specific instructional practices affect student learning and how changes in our instructional practices might lead to changes in student learning.	1	2	3	4

3 of 4

Comments:

Review the tasks in the following chart and list the percent of time your PLC team spent on each of these tasks during the past semester. (Your total should add up to 100 percent.)

Percent of Time Spent on Task at PLC Meetings	Task
	Analyzing, comparing, or scoring student work samples
	Developing common assessments
	Analyzing assessment data
	Discussing grade-level or school business priorities (for example, field trips, recess, scheduling, and so on)
	Analyzing instructional practices (for example, discussing videotaped lessons, critiquing an instructional strategy)
	Planning curriculum or instruction
	Other (please specify): _____

What Is Our Team Monitoring?

One of the first steps that effective learning teams take is systematically focusing their time and attention on the work that matters most. To help your team bring focus to your work, complete the following chart. In the first column, list every program, initiative action, school requirement, or team decision that is consuming your team's time and attention. Then, work through the subsequent columns to identify important projects and to prioritize your efforts.

Monitored Initiative	Category That Initiative Addresses	Time Required to Implement Initiative	Priority Placed on Initiative
Include every program, initiative action, school requirement, or team decision that is consuming your time and attention.	*Effective learning teams focus time and energy on the tasks listed below. Which task does this monitored initiative address?*	*Effective learning teams must honestly assess the time demands that each initiative places on their collective work. How would you describe the amount of time necessary to make this project work?*	*Effective learning teams make systematic decisions about each project that they pursue based on its connection to student learning, its alignment with the building's mission and vision, and school district mandates. Considering each of these factors, how would you prioritize this initiative?*
	☐ Identifying essential curriculum: deciding what students should learn ☐ Developing common assessments: measuring what students should learn ☐ Monitoring student learning data: evaluating what students have learned ☐ Providing remediation and/or enrichment: ensuring that every child learns ☐ This project doesn't clearly meet any of the above goals.	☐ Extensive amounts of time ☐ Moderate amounts of time ☐ Small amounts of time	☐ This task should be at the center of our attention. ☐ This task demands attention, but it isn't our first priority. ☐ This task should be set aside for now. ☐ This task should be eliminated or ignored.

	□ Identifying essential curriculum: deciding what students should learn □ Developing common assessments: measuring what students should learn □ Monitoring student learning data: evaluating what students have learned □ Providing remediation and/ or enrichment: ensuring that every child learns □ This project doesn't clearly meet any of the above goals.	□ Extensive amounts of time □ Moderate amounts of time □ Small amounts of time	□ This task should be at the center of our attention. □ This task demands attention, but it isn't our first priority. □ This task should be set aside for now. □ This task should be eliminated or ignored.
	□ Identifying essential curriculum: deciding what students should learn □ Developing common assessments: measuring what students should learn □ Monitoring student learning data: evaluating what students have learned □ Providing remediation and/ or enrichment: ensuring that every child learns □ This project doesn't clearly meet any of the above goals.	□ Extensive amounts of time □ Moderate amounts of time □ Small amounts of time	□ This task should be at the center of our attention. □ This task demands attention, but it isn't our first priority. □ This task should be set aside for now. □ This task should be eliminated or ignored.

SPRING: LOOKING FORWARD

CONNECTING DATA ANALYSIS AND INSTRUCTIONAL IMPROVEMENT

Karen remembered the professional learning team meeting back in early February, the one that she had walked out of in tears. Oh, what a difference two months can make!

The team had decided to create a comprehensive common assessment in language arts to measure student achievement for the entire second quarter, and the February meeting had been their first chance to start analyzing the data from the assessment. In hindsight, it seemed that just about everything that could have gone wrong did.

Tom, the assistant principal, had facilitated the meeting, and everyone had sent him their students' scores from the assessment beforehand. No one had been quite sure what to expect from the meeting. The team had been discussing student work samples for months and had done some simple data analysis from a few formative assessments. This, however, was the first time they sat down together as a team to really look at some hard numbers. Needless to say, everyone was a little nervous going into the meeting.

Tom began the meeting by distributing several handouts.

"Okay, everyone, as you can see on this first handout, I have created a chart showing each student's overall score on the assessment, arranged by class. At the bottom of each column you can see the average score for each class. The number on the far right shows the average score for the whole grade level. I also highlighted in red all of the individual students' scores that were below 70 percent. So, does anyone see anything interesting?"

"I see something interesting," said Sarah. "My class had the second highest score on the grade level. I guess I did a better job teaching the material this quarter than I thought! And look at your scores, Michael, you did a great job—it looks like you only had two kids score below a 70 percent! I guess that's what happens when you're teacher of the year, right?"

As Karen looked at her own scores in shock, she saw a sea of red. She counted eight students—over a quarter of her class!—that had scored below 70 percent, and her class average was the lowest on the grade level by a good three points. As she looked up, she thought she caught both Tom and Michael trying to look away from her. There it was, right in front of her, proof positive that she was the worst teacher on the grade level, and now everyone knew it.

Karen made an attempt at levity: "Well, Tom, with scores like this, do you want to fire me right now or wait until the end of the year, when I'm sure *all* of my students will be failing?"

Tom laughed embarrassedly. "Look, Karen, this isn't about comparing scores, or good or bad teaching. This is about us trying to be realistic about how all our students are doing so that we can improve."

"Well," Karen responded, "it sure looks like we're comparing scores to me. I mean, those are our averages, right? Clearly I'm not cutting it, or my students would be doing better. Isn't that what the numbers say?" As her eyes began to tear, Karen excused herself, got up, and retreated back to her own classroom. All of her worst professional fears—not measuring up, embarrassing herself in front of her colleagues, and letting her students down—had just been realized.

What had begun as personal dismay, however, gradually hardened into professional resolve. Over the course of the next two months, Karen and the rest of the team had turned that meeting into a positive learning experience, and the students benefited from their hard work. But it had not been easy.

That first night, Karen spent hours looking through the assessment data. Even though she taught language arts and social studies, Karen always had a knack for numbers, and going through the data with a fine-toothed comb was therapeutic. Plus, the more carefully she looked, the more she spotted patterns that seemed to tell an interesting story. By the end of the night, she was actually excited to speak with her colleagues about what she found.

Karen tracked down Sarah early the next morning before school began.

"Sarah, I wanted to apologize for the way I left the meeting yesterday. It wasn't very professional of me, and I'm sorry."

"Apology accepted. You know, Karen, after you left we decided that just throwing all our numbers out there probably wasn't a good idea. Anyone could have had the lowest scores, and I know I would have felt the same way if it had been me. We decided to table the whole data-analysis thing for a little while until we can figure out how to do it better."

"To be honest," Karen replied, "I think that would be a mistake. I spent some time last night going through the numbers, and I found some really interesting patterns. I realized that, if we are going to try to use data to help us improve, we have to be willing to accept the good and the bad, and separate out our egos from the process. We have to be willing to believe that data aren't about the person. Instead, they're about practices.

"If everyone else is willing, I was actually hoping we could get together again today to talk about it."

That afternoon, Karen shared what she found with the team.

As she had looked through the assessment data, Karen noticed that many of her students had scored especially low on essay-response questions and questions that required students to make complex inferences. In addition, these low-scoring students were the same ones that usually struggled academically in her class. Most interestingly, even though Karen's class had scored lower on average than the other classes, there was a consistency to the low scores that extended beyond her own class.

Looking across the grade level, each class contained students who struggled with the same types of questions on the assessment. However, because Karen was one of the most experienced teachers at the grade level, she had been given a disproportionately high number of struggling students at the beginning of the year.

In other words, the trend was not that *Karen's class* had underperformed: the trend was that struggling students *throughout the grade level* had underperformed on the same sections, and Karen had simply been assigned more struggling students back at the beginning of the year.

As the team discussed this trend, they began dissecting the assessment in detail, posing questions as they went. Sarah noted that several of her students who usually displayed sophisticated thinking in class discussions struggled with the assessment questions that required complex inferences. Did those students do poorly because they did not have good inference skills, or were they not able to adequately explain themselves through written essays because of underdeveloped writing skills?

Michael brought up the fact that, while almost all of his students had done well on the questions requiring complex inferences, he had also spent an entire week near the end of the quarter focusing on drawing conclusions based on evidence from a text using a new unit he had created over the winter holiday.

The discussion extended over the next two months. Several of the team members attended an all-day workshop on data analysis, bringing new ideas back to the team on how to look at assessment data more effectively. The team gave several more common assessments to their classes and used the data to pinpoint specific instructional practices (such as Michael's unit on drawing inferences) that might have led to unusually high scores.

Most importantly, the team began using assessment results to inform their common planning. Up to that point in the year, the majority of the team's meeting time had been spent talking about curriculum and instruction—what each person would teach and how they would teach it. As the team began to analyze common assessments, however, and as the assessments helped to isolate students' academic strengths and weaknesses, their meetings started to look different.

The team began to devote more time to discussions of student learning: what concepts students found difficult, why students struggled with certain learning objectives, and how well different types of instructional practices worked with different types of students. The team developed new units, or adapted existing lessons, to support struggling students and further challenge high achievers. This led to some cross-classroom student grouping and team-teaching activities, which further spread innovative teaching practices across the team.

So, in hindsight, Karen decided that her now legendary "February flame out" had been worth it. She could have done without the tears and self-doubt. But it was that fateful meeting that had helped to switch the team's focus from evaluating teacher success to looking at the details of student learning—and the successes since then made all the difficulties worthwhile.

Lessons From the Front Line

In the story, the sixth-grade team ultimately improved as a result of the data-analysis process, but not without experiencing some significant bumps in the road. Despite their positive personal relationships and the help of a facilitating administrator, the examination of the results from their common assessment quickly dissolved into an emotional outburst.

In chapter 4, "Supporting Team Development," we talked about the stages that professional learning teams go through in terms of their work focus. Professional learning teams commonly start out by focusing on teaching-related tasks, such as curricular and instructional planning. Gradually, however, high-functioning groups make a shift toward focusing on outcomes: asking whether students are learning what they should be and discussing how to respond when students need additional support or challenge. According to Richard DuFour, Rebecca DuFour, and Robert Eaker (2008):

> Schools will not know whether or not all students are learning unless educators are hungry for evidence that students are acquiring the knowledge, skills, and dispositions deemed most essential to their success. Schools must systematically monitor student learning on an ongoing basis and use evidence of results to respond immediately to students who experience difficulty, to inform individual and collective practice, and to fuel continuous improvement. (pp. 18–19)

Often, the catalyst for this shift is the shared analysis of common assessment results, similar to the activity undertaken by the sixth-grade teachers at Central Middle. Making this shift can be difficult, initially setting a collaborative group back in terms of team dynamics and cohesiveness.

How did the sixth-grade teachers get past that initial meeting, and how did they eventually come to use data effectively? Furthermore, what is it about the data-analysis process that is so important? Why is it that positive outcomes can occur when teachers take a collective approach to analyzing and acting on evidence of student learning?

The answer is about building shared understanding. After the sixth-grade team was able to put their egos on hold—separating practice from personality—and create new group protocols for discussing student data, they were able to accomplish two things. First, they used open conversations to figure out what student learning looked like in their classrooms. Second, they began to learn from each other as their conversations developed.

In this chapter, we look at specific strategies and discussion protocols that can help teams make data analysis less emotionally painful and more professionally productive. We also talk about the concept of shared understanding, which lies at the heart of a professional learning team's success. Finally, we discuss a concept called *positive deviancy*, which sheds light on the direct link between teacher collaboration and instructional improvement.

Analyzing Student Learning Data

Collaborative data analysis is not easy. On one hand, it requires a pretty sophisticated look at numbers—a skill that does not come naturally to a lot of people. On the other hand, it means exposing professional successes and perceived shortcomings to one's colleagues, and that is a difficult endeavor in even the safest environments. Mike Schmoker (1999) argues that we avoid data because we fear its "capacity to reveal strengths and weakness, failure and success. Education seems to maintain a tacit bargain among constituents at every level not to gather or use information that will reveal a clear need for improvement: where we need to do better, where we need to make changes" (p. 39).

What makes data analysis even more challenging is that teachers often struggle to find the time for meaningful data conversations. Caught in the rush of a typical school day in which teachers are buried under the weight of lesson planning and paper grading, teams jump to quick conclusions rather than wrestling with the deeper meaning in student achievement data. Finally, we are also frightened about finding the time to respond to results. "Data almost always point to action," writes Schmoker, "They are the enemy of comfortable routines. By ignoring data, we promote inaction and inefficiency" (1999, p. 39).

Think about the consequences a lack of time and sophistication had on the sixth-grade learning team: Sarah concluded that she did a good job teaching, while Karen struggled with feelings of embarrassment and failure in front of her peers. Emotions ran high, and teachers left defensive, discouraged, and defeated. Few meaningful questions were asked, and instruction remained unchanged.

But as the team examined the data in more depth, they found several actionable patterns. Karen noticed that a group of students struggled with questions that required inferences. Sarah then deepened that insight by suggesting that the real challenge might lie in an inability to translate inferences into written language.

In a word, the team began to make the student learning in their classrooms *transparent*. According to Michael Fullan (2008):

> By transparency I mean clear and continuous display of results, and clear and continuous access to practice (what is being done to get the results). Transparency can be abused, such as when results are used punitively, but there is no way that continuous improvement can occur without constant transparency fueled by good data. . . . When transparency is consistently evident, it creates an aura of "positive pressure"—pressure that is experienced as fair and reasonable, pressure that is actionable in that it points to solutions, and pressure that is ultimately inescapable. (p. 14)

Through persistence, Central Middle's sixth-grade teachers also learned a valuable lesson: successful teams use specific data-analysis strategies and collaborative discussion techniques to make the evaluation of common assessment results more productive and less stressful. In their initial inexperience, they had failed to establish a set of learning-related questions from the outset, jumped straight to judgmental interpretations, and never utilized effective discussion protocols. By using the strategies discussed in this chapter, you can avoid some of the difficulties the sixth-grade team experienced.

Data Analysis Strategies

There are a number of excellent articles and books that provide practical advice on analyzing educational data. Titles like *Data Wise: A Step-by-Step Guide to Using Assessment Results to Improve Teaching and Learning* (2005), edited by Kathryn Parker Boudett, Elizabeth City, and Richard Murnane, and *The Data Coach's Guide to Improving Learning for All Students: Unleashing the Power of Collaborative Inquiry* (2008), by Nancy Love, Katherine Stiles, Susan Mundry, and Kathy DiRanna, lay out detailed plans for schoolwide data programs that might be right for your building.

Rather than focusing on overly technical recommendations, our intent here is to provide a general framework for slowing down your conversations and digging deeper into the results of your common assessments. The following strategies can be particularly effective for educators with limited experience crunching numbers:

- **Start with learning-related questions**—In the story that begins the chapter, Tom started the meeting with an overly ambiguous question: "So, does anyone see anything interesting?" Rather than helping focus the group, this question did just the opposite: it opened the meeting up to any possible comment or thought. Like most teams wrestling with data for the first time, the sixth-grade teachers drew shallow comparisons with little reflection. Karen's lower average and sea of red scores on Tom's spreadsheet seemed like logical places to begin the conversation.

  Effective data-analysis meetings benefit from explicit, learning-related questions that keep a group focused. In the sixth-grade meeting, Tom could have asked, "Across the grade level, were there any specific objectives or tasks with which multiple students appeared to struggle?" Teachers might also have shared one or two concepts that the students in their individual classes appeared to have mastered and one or two concepts that their students appeared to struggle with the most. By starting with specific learning-centered questions, a team can move past superficial observations (such as who had the highest class average) and on to more productive analyses (such as which concepts were problematic for large groups of students).

- **Come with an open mind**—While Karen's teammates were unlikely to admit it, each had formed longstanding beliefs about one another based on nothing more than chance interactions. Michael was a master teacher who could do no wrong. Sarah struggled with classroom discipline and did not challenge her kids. Karen had been teaching too long and relied on out-of-date instructional practices. Karen's team members had unknowingly set themselves up for failure, allowing preexisting notions of peers to drive their conclusions rather than letting the data tell the story.

When discussing the results of common assessments, it is important to bring an open mind and a willingness to reflect openly on possible preconceptions. What beliefs do you hold about yourself, your students, your colleagues, and your instructional practices? In what ways might those beliefs skew the way you look at student learning data? By acknowledging existing preconceptions, a team is more likely to find patterns that reflect real trends in student learning as opposed to cherry-picking confirmations of personal beliefs.

- **Turn numbers into pictures**—One effective technique Tom employed in the story that began this chapter is using visual cues to simplify data. The red highlighting he used made it easier for the team to spot students with particularly low scores quickly. He had always had a knack for numbers, and by spending time beforehand organizing and highlighting data—turning the numbers into pictures—he was trying to improve both the efficiency and effectiveness of data analysis.

  Highlighting is one of the easiest data-manipulation strategies that teams can employ because it does not require extensive time or materials. Teachers simply set targets and work through data sets annotating scores. Two additional highlighting techniques are Christmas tree and stoplight highlighting. For the *Christmas tree method*, teachers highlight all scores above a certain value green and all the scores below a certain value red. For the *stoplight method*, teachers use two jointly determined cut values; for example, all the scores above 85 percent might be highlighted green, all the scores between 70 and 85 percent might be highlighted yellow, and all the scores below 70 percent might be highlighted red. Both strategies create simple visuals quickly.

  Tom's mistake, however, was failing to engage his teachers in the process of developing charts and graphs together. As Nancy Love, former director of the Using Data Project at TERC argues, the very act of manipulating assessment information and generating large visuals helps to make the numbers more approachable and impersonal. Teams graphing together are forced to think carefully about what, exactly, student results show. Once the appropriate graphs or highlighted data sets have been created, encourage teams and teachers to hang final copies away from the group. The physical act of removing data from team members reinforces the idea that conversations are not about any single person (Love, 2007).

- **Leave a meeting with questions as well as answers**—The primary purpose of data analysis is to inform the ongoing conversations in which professional learning teams engage. For highly accomplished teams, those conversations are as much about questions as they are about answers. So the data say that some students are struggling with multiplying fractions. Why? What aspect of multiplying fractions do they find difficult? If students in one class were particularly successful at multiplying fractions, what is it that led to higher rates of success?

For Karen's learning team, a focusing question at the end of their initial meeting might have been, in what ways might deficient writing skills be keeping some students from adequately demonstrating proficiency in other content areas? This question invites further data collection, analysis, and discussion.

Questions, unfortunately, are often wrongly pushed aside by teachers working in a culture that embraces answers. As Cassandra Erkens (2008a) notes:

> Today, schools are predicated on having the "right answers," from classroom to classroom and building to building. This approach to learning confines our thinking and erroneously sets us up to view mistakes as detrimental to learning. Our entire culture must shift from "What did you learn in school today?" to "What questions did you ask in school today?" (p. 46)

By allowing results to drive additional questions, teacher teams gain a deeper understanding of the learning happening in their classrooms and keep conversations about data focused on instructional practices as opposed to people.

Discussion Strategies

The strategies listed here should help teams deal with the technical challenges of data analysis. But an equally tricky aspect of data analysis is dealing with human emotions. Sometimes the data say things that we do not want to hear or show things to our colleagues that we do not want them to see. When emotions run high, as they did for Karen in the story that started this chapter, it is hard not to let our feelings interfere with our thinking.

The good news is that teams can take proactive steps to make discussions about data safe. While it is never easy to face the reality of results or open ourselves to the judgments of our colleagues, the following strategies can have a positive impact on data-based discussions:

- **Start by defining the language of discussion**—In their first conversations about common assessments, the sixth-grade team members at Central Middle School used a number of emotionally loaded words and phrases: "I did a better job than I thought," and "You did a great job." These words and phrases are especially problematic because they represent personal judgments. Hearing Sarah tell Michael that he did a *great* job, Karen quickly came to believe that she was a *bad* teacher. In order for data discussions to be safe, they need to be value free.

  One way to reduce the value statements in conversations about results is to make a list of banned words, such as *good* or *bad*. Teams can have the list hanging every time that they reflect on common assessments, and the use of banned words could be met with a barrage of colored beanbags or a collective groan to lighten the mood of a conversation. Teams should also practice judgment-free phrases. For example, rather than the loaded "You did a great job, Michael," Sarah could have made a neutral statement of fact: "Almost all of your students scored above 70 percent on the assessment." While this may seem like splitting hairs, value statements, no matter how inconsequential or unintentional, often lead to hurt feelings.

- **Remember to use agreed-upon discussion protocols**—Perhaps most surprising about the failed sixth-grade data conversation that started this chapter was that Tom, Central Middle's assistant principal, forgot to use agreed-upon discussion protocols when meeting with his learning team. As we learned while studying conflict in chapter 5, "Negotiating Personalities and Conflict," engaging teachers in delicate conversations, such as those that involve reflecting on results, requires structures that some teams overlook. The failed sixth-grade data conversation at Central Middle started in an unfocused, haphazard way when Tom asked, "So, does anyone see anything interesting?" While Tom got immediate feedback from both Michael and Sarah, there are several discussion protocols that he could have used to engage everyone thoughtfully in his developing conversation.

  For example, he could have begun the meeting by giving the team five minutes of quiet time to look through the data. Next, he could have asked each team member to use sticky notes to record up to five observations and up to five questions about the data. Initiating the conversation, Tom could have then asked each team member to share his or her observations and questions. After organizing the observations and questions into categories, the team could then have started an open discussion centered on those categories. By using simple discussion-management strategies, Tom could have maximized the input of ideas and perspectives, while minimizing the opportunities for hurt feelings.

- **Create specialized discussion roles**—The use of banned words lists and discussion protocols help to keep data conversations safe. At the same time, however, teams need to be able to talk about potentially controversial patterns in student learning data. Sometimes, in the interests of keeping discussions safe, team members shy away from the topics that most need to be discussed. Even though it was a touchy subject, the sixth-grade teachers at Central Middle needed to be able to explore the pattern of low-scoring students in Karen's class.

  One way to ensure that teams do not intentionally avoid contentious findings is to assign discussion roles specifically tailored for conversations about student learning data, such as a Devil's Advocate or Questioner. *Devil's Advocates* deliberately challenge widely held assumptions, while *Questioners* turn every interpretation into opportunities for continued reflection. For the sixth-grade language arts/social studies team, Sarah fills the unofficial role of Devil's Advocate, challenging the notion that low scores on inference questions automatically reflect poor inferring skills.

  By assigning specialized discussion roles in advance, teams accomplish two things. Perhaps most importantly, they reduce the tension associated with disagreements over data. Members understand that Devil's Advocates are not attempting to embarrass their colleagues or be difficult on purpose when they spotlight potentially controversial findings or challenge preconceived notions. Instead, they are doing an important job that is essential for team success. Second, assigning roles in advance ensures that all teachers have opportunities to practice skeptical perspectives to data analysis, reducing the likelihood that teams will jump to quick judgments about data in the future.

- **Work to separate personality from practice**—One of the hardest things to do when discussing student learning data is to remain objective. As educators, we are passionate about our work. Those numbers represent *our* students in *our* classroom, so it is almost impossible not to take the results personally. That is why Karen was heartbroken in the story that started this chapter. She believed that her students' low scores meant that she was a bad teacher, and she was hurt because she had invested all that she knew into her classroom. It is common for teachers to react this way when they see results that are less than positive.

Moving beyond this reaction requires a real shift in thinking. Rather than seeing student learning as indicative of a teacher's *personal* worth, it is helpful to see that learning as a result of certain teaching *practices*. While it is difficult to change who you are as a person, it is quite possible to change the instructional approaches that you use as a teacher. By seeing student data as a result of specific teaching strategies, team members can take a more active ownership of their students' results. Rather than considering herself a bad teacher, Karen could say to herself, "Maybe some of the lessons I have been using have not been as effective as they should be. I will work on first identifying and then changing those practices."

More importantly, shifting attention from personality to practice is an incredibly empowering step for learning teams. It acknowledges the capacity of the group to identify solutions for student learning challenges and encourages a collective approach to instructional troubleshooting that has long been missing from traditional school buildings. Susan Huff, principal of Santaquin Elementary in Santaquin, Utah, notes:

> Collaborative data analysis is not about pointing fingers at teachers with nonproficient students. It is about trusting in the collective wisdom of the team to collaboratively bring about high levels of learning for all students. (Huff, 2008, p. 209)

Encouraging the use of formal data conversation templates like the one included at the end of this chapter (see the Structuring Data Conversations handout on pages 172–174) can help to ensure that the learning teams in your building think systematically about data analysis and discussion strategies while working through focused studies of student learning results.

Building Shared Understanding

It is common for the nature of teacher conversations to change over the course of a year, especially once teams begin the data-analysis process. Before data analysis really begins, team conversations often focus on planning, with very few questions asked. In fact, meetings for novice teams tend to be very efficient checklist affairs. Who is planning the reading lessons next week? Check. When are we giving that assessment? Check. Who has lunch duty tomorrow? Check.

As teams dive into the data-analysis process, however, the number of checks decreases, and the number of questions increases. Initially, there will likely be frustration that teams are not accomplishing as much work as they were previously. Some teams may even revert to storming behavior at this point, much like Central Middle's sixth-grade language arts/social studies teachers did. This is one of the reasons why the "planning, planning, planning" stage is so attractive to teachers and so difficult to leave behind. Who wouldn't be excited to have fewer lessons to develop—and end up discouraged when all of that distributed planning is replaced by other activities?

The real power of professional learning teams is not in common planning; it is in building shared understanding—the ideas, perspectives, and insights that result from collaborative dialogue about teaching and learning. According to Schmoker (2005), "Teachers do not learn best from outside experts or by attending conferences or implementing 'programs' installed by outsiders. Teachers learn best from other teachers, in settings where they literally teach each other the art of teaching" (p. 141).

For example, in our story, the sixth-grade team developed a shared understanding around student proficiency in making inferences. No one person arrived at this understanding on his or her own. Instead, it took the combined questions, thoughts, and reflections of the whole team.

So, how can teams develop shared understanding? What does it take to move from checklists to real professional learning opportunities for teachers?

As is true of most things in life, it takes some balance. On one hand, teams need to structure their shared dialogue in ways that encourage knowledge and insight development. When running a whole-class discussion in their own classrooms, teachers know to use a variety of facilitation techniques to keep collaborative conversations productive. Think-pair-shares, brainstorming, sticky note taking, and thumbs up/thumbs down surveys are all simple techniques to make sure that every student has a chance to participate and invest cognitive energy into considering the conversation topics.

The same approach works in professional learning team meetings. In any team discussion, some members are likely to contribute more and some are likely to contribute less. By using specific discussion and facilitation protocols, teams can ensure that everyone gets a chance to be heard and that every idea gets a chance to be considered. According to Susan Sparks, the executive director of the Front Range Board of Cooperative Educational Services for Teacher Leadership in Denver, Colorado:

> Complex systems such as collaborative teams need collective commitments to be productive. Your team will be more honest and achieve more clarity when members do not worry about "stepping on" each other or become confused about how to participate. Protocols provide consistent structure to conversations and

create a sense of safety around expressing opinions. They invite deep think-ing and reflection, allowing team members to say what is truly on their minds. The steps will slow the conversation down and stop others from interrupting before their turn. Each team member knows he or she will have an opportunity to speak, thus members stop their inner self-talk and listen to each other more. (Sparks, 2008, p. 50)

For a team that has never used discussion protocols or conversation templates before, these strategies can make meetings feel somewhat stilted and artificial. Previously free-flowing dialogue is replaced by more formalized, business-like interactions. Unstructured conversations on novice professional learning teams, however, generally become one-sided affairs, where many teachers fail to make any contributions, allowing one or two members to do all of the heavy lifting. Discussion protocols and conversation templates ensure that all members of a learning team have opportunities to be heard and that critical issues are given more than just a cursory glance.

There are numerous discussion protocols that can be effective in structuring team conversations. As was described earlier, sticky notes can be used to record questions or observations about student data and then shared in a round-robin fashion after individual members have had the opportunity to reflect. Teams interested in capturing multiple ideas and insights can use *everything-goes brainstorming*, a form of *affinity diagramming* in which a facilitator records everything said by a learning team in a ten-minute period without edits. Next, team members sort contributions into logical categories, creating a visual representation of a group's collective thinking. Because the emphasis in everything-goes brainstorming is on generating ideas, rather than judging them, creative solutions are often elicited easily.

Final word is another simple protocol that can work well. In final word, an initial par-ticipant has sixty seconds to share a thought or insight. Then, each team member takes up to thirty seconds to respond to that insight. After everyone has had a chance to com-ment, the initial thinker has another thirty seconds to respond to what he or she has heard from the other members of the group. Final word forces teams to slow down and reflect as they work through conversations with one another. What is more, members are likely to have their thinking about an issue challenged by peers, leading to natural revisions that improve final decisions.

Effective teams also develop action plans at the beginning of every school year as a way of focusing ongoing work around a specific set of measurable goals drawn from a careful analysis of student achievement data. Team action plans become objective standards for collaborative decision making. Conflicts over joint actions are minimized when members can refer back to a collective direction set early in a school year. We have included the Team Action Planning Template at the end of this chapter to give you an idea of what this might look like (see page 175).

While structure is one part of the balance necessary for moving teams from superficial meetings to powerful professional learning centered on student outcomes, teams must be careful not to allow structure to stifle open-minded inquiry. In the story that started this chapter, the sixth-grade team was not able to move forward until they started asking questions and allowed themselves to walk together in a new direction: What patterns existed in student performance? What range of explanations might explain those patterns? Which instructional practices appeared to be most effective? What about those practices might have led to their effectiveness?

Shared understanding happens when teams avoid assumptions about their students and themselves and instead focus on asking questions regardless of where the answers lead. Confident teams plan initial routes, while remaining flexible and ready to embrace unexpected results. In the process, team members uncover differences in understanding and develop deeper levels of professional knowledge together.

Novice learning teams tend to hold on to the belief that initial decisions are inevitably correct as long as they are made collectively. "Without error," the thinking goes, "we can identify essential learning outcomes, develop effective lessons, and create high-quality assessments for each new group of students that walks through the classroom door—regardless of how complex those decisions are!"

One of the unspoken truths in many learning communities, however, is that some teams are making it up as they go along—uncertain about the effectiveness of their curricular and instructional choices but refusing to veer from a course set months ago. An over-reliance on structures ends up leading to the same troubling inconsistencies between teaching and learning commonly found in traditional schools.

As inquiry-oriented professional learning teams engage in increasingly sophisticated conversations, those uncertainties and inconsistencies are uncovered: "Wait a minute, we thought that our students would know how to make conversions to the metric system, but they're completely clueless. We're going to have to change our plans quickly!" "Are you still teaching mixed fractions? I think my students are ready to move on to probability." "I taught all of the lessons we developed on word choice and author's purpose, but half of my students still failed the assessment! Maybe our strategies weren't as good as we thought they were."

The key is to make sure that when inconsistencies are uncovered they are not viewed as failures, but instead become conversations focused on clarifying and exploring assumptions about curriculum, assessment, and instruction. When that happens—when teachers discuss student notions, talk about curricular sequencing, and take a detailed look at results—they are creating shared understanding. As Susan Huff (2008) explains:

> When teachers have opportunities to reflect on their practice and dialogue with their collaborative team, they are able to make the connections they need to improve instructional practice in the future. Reflective dialogue helps teachers build on each other's ideas and expand their own learning in ways that they cannot do alone. (p. 209)

Relevant Theory and Research

One of the most important outcomes of professional learning team work is the individual learning that takes place for teachers. In the United States, school systems spend literally billions of dollars each year on professional development, and yet some of the most powerful professional learning occurs when teacher teams simply sit down together and have collaborative conversations. In Richard DuFour's words, "The best staff development happens in the workplace rather than in a workshop" (DuFour, 2004b, p. 63).

How is that? How is it that teachers can improve just by talking to their colleagues? What sorts of conditions are necessary to make sure those conversations become effective professional learning opportunities?

One answer to these questions comes from Vietnam. In the early 1990s, Jerry Sternin and Robert Choo, both with Save the Children, were attempting to address high levels of malnutrition among children in Vietnam. Rather than bringing in a prefabricated program or solution, Sternin and Choo (2000) started looking for examples of Vietnamese families who bucked the trend. In other words, they tried to identify families who lived in villages with high levels of malnutrition, but whose children were not malnourished themselves.

Sociologists call these people who do not fall in line with the common trends *positive deviants*. In an interview with Dennis Sparks (2004), Jerry Sternin defined positive deviants as "people whose behavior and practices produce solutions to problems that others in the group who have access to exactly the same resources have not been able to solve" (p. 46). In other words, within just about any setting, whether it be a village, a business, or a school, there will be individuals who outperform others in identical settings. What Sternin and Choo (2000) wanted to do was identify those families whose children were not malnourished and figure out what they had done to get superior results.

What they found was that successful Vietnamese families (the positive deviants) were supplementing their diets with a variety of foods, such as shrimps, crabs, and sweet potato greens that were easily and freely found in the local rice paddies. While these were not foods typically fed to children, Sternin and Choo latched onto these successful practices, and they were able to create opportunities for the successful families to spread these practices throughout their villages.

Sternin and Choo are not the only ones to study positive deviancy. In the book *Influencer: The Power to Change Anything* (2008), Kerry Patterson, Joseph Grenny, David Maxfield, Ron McMillan, and Al Switzler describe the role that positive deviancy played in helping a regional medical center improve its level of service to patients.

According to Patterson, this medical center had seen its service quality scores decrease for over a year, indicating that patients and their families did not think that they were being treated respectfully by center employees. As the center's executive team investigated the problem, they found that some employees had consistently higher satisfaction ratings. In other words, the research team found some positive deviants.

After identifying these positive deviants, the team studied what it was that those individuals did differently that led to such high results. The team found that it was a combination of five simple behaviors: smiling, making eye contact with patients, identifying themselves, explaining what they were doing and why, and consistently asking patients if there was anything else that they needed.

It does not seem like rocket science: exhibit behaviors that people think of as "friendly" (smiling, making eye contact, and so on), and people will think of you as friendly. Clearly, however, a large number of employees at the center were not exhibiting those behaviors, and that accounted for the center's low scores.

Once the center was able to identify the positive deviants, it put together a program to help spread their unique behaviors throughout the organization. As everyone began smiling, making eye contact, and exhibiting the other friendly behaviors, the center's service quality scores began to rise. Problem solved.

This approach, identifying positive deviants and then attempting to spread their practices, is one of the key components of successful student data analysis. As teachers in a professional learning team look at the results of common assessments, they will naturally identify trends. Sometimes those trends exist across classrooms, just as the sixth-grade team found a trend of low-achieving students across all of their classrooms. Sometimes the trend will reflect a pattern predicted by teams in their initial action plans. Other times, however, those trends will differ from one classroom to the next, or point teams in unexpected directions. Unexpected findings almost always indicate a positive deviant who has discovered how to take available resources and produce extraordinary results—like Michael, whose sixth-grade students scored noticeably higher than the other classes at Central Middle on questions requiring inferences.

One of the purposes of student data analysis is to identify the areas in which students need extra support and in which students are ready for additional challenge. Another purpose is to spread especially successful practices across an entire building. As inquiry-oriented teams identify classrooms in which students appear to be achieving at higher-than-average levels (just as researchers identified Vietnamese villagers who were not malnourished and medical center executives identified employees with high service quality scores), they can use questioning and structured conversations to develop a shared understanding about the teaching strategies that might have led to higher achievement.

It is important to emphasize, however, that simply spotting successful instructional practices is not the end goal of learning communities. In Vietnam and at the medical center, it was not enough for researchers or executives to identify positive deviants. What was critically important was to figure out *which practices made a difference* and then *to spread those positive practices* to others. As the researchers and center executives found, other Vietnamese families and medical center employees initially resisted adopting these new practices.

This is where structured conversations, trust, and shared understanding become so important in a professional learning team. Teams need structured conversations to tease out the underlying practices that might have led to superior results. Trust is critical to ensure that teachers feel comfortable sharing their own data and remain open to the possibility of learning from the successes of their peers. Shared understanding is necessary to ensure that everyone on a team understands the practices that led to superior results and commits to bringing those successful practices back to their own classrooms.

Positive deviancy, therefore, is one of the key concepts at the heart of PLC success. As teams become proficient with data analysis, they are able to develop a shared understanding of the strategies that result in student progress. By identifying the positive deviants within a team—the teachers who implemented especially successful practices during a curricular unit—a learning team can spread high-quality instructional approaches across classrooms, benefiting every child.

Recommendations

The analysis of student data and the conversations that result from that analysis are critical components in the development of highly functioning professional learning teams. It is at this point that professional learning teams make the switch from focusing on teaching to focusing on learning. Following are several suggestions for making this essential transition successful.

Make Team-Based Data Analysis Happen

Most of this chapter focused on the details of student data analysis at the teacher and team level, but we have an important recommendation for school leaders: regardless of what role you fill in your professional learning community—building principal, instructional coach, teacher leader—it is up to you to ensure that team-based data analysis happens. It is just too important to leave to chance. As Rick Stiggins (2005) argues, "To the extent that we team to (1) analyze, understand, and deconstruct standards, (2) transform them into high-quality classroom assessments, and (3) share and interpret results together, we benefit from the union of our wisdom about how to help our students continue to grow as learners" (p. 82). In the story that began this chapter, Tom, the assistant principal, made a mess of things, but at least he facilitated movement toward making data analysis a priority.

Most teachers will not make the decision to collectively analyze student learning data without the prodding of school leaders simply because data are just plain difficult. Therefore, school leaders must make it an explicit expectation that teams take on the task of collaborating to analyze data. This can be accomplished in a variety of ways: incorporating data analysis into team action plans (see the Team Action Planning Template on page 175), systematically tracking the impact that key practices have on student achievement (see the Evidence of Practice in Action handout on page 176), scheduling schoolwide "data crunches" on early-release or teacher work days, and gently encouraging colleagues to embrace data analysis in formal and informal conversations.

Model an Open Approach to Data

Requiring that data analysis be a part of the actions of every learning team is the easy part. It is also incumbent on leaders to model an open approach to data analysis. For teacher leaders, modeling an openness to data is easy: bring a set of results from a recent assessment to your next team meeting and ask your peers to help you spot trends in student learning. Nothing sends a more powerful message about the important role that data can play in personal and professional development than when influential teachers enthusiastically open their practice to critique and review. Then, ask for help brainstorming a set of simple action steps to address the outcomes of your team's review, implement the suggestions offered, and return to the group with a new set of findings. By doing so, you will not only model openness to data, you will also model a cycle of responsible reflection.

For those working beyond the classroom, modeling an open approach to data means collecting and then sharing school data reflecting your work—such as teacher or parent surveys—in public forums. Dedicate faculty meetings to a review of critical numbers reflecting on the decisions made by school-based educational professionals working beyond the classroom. Open conversations designed to identify positive deviants in the administrative team or supporting staff should become a regular part of your school's culture. By modeling a results-oriented approach, formal leaders send the message that data analysis is about improving practices for everyone, not just classroom teachers, and that careful reflection does not have to threaten personalities or lead to judgments about individual performance.

Be Prepared to Offer Technical and Emotional Support to Teachers and Teams

As we mentioned in chapter 4, "Supporting Team Development," accomplished administrators recognize that learning teams beginning to analyze data together are going to need both technical and emotional support. To ensure that your teachers embrace a results-oriented approach to their collective actions, start by providing access to timely, appropriate, and easy-to-interpret sets of results generated by professionals working beyond the classroom. Nothing can frustrate a team's desire to embrace data more than complicated reports or cumbersome collection efforts.

You should also be prepared to increase data capacity in your building either by repurposing positions to create schoolwide data experts or providing additional professional development to interested members of each learning team. Finally, remember to emphasize time and again that data analysis is about identifying accomplished practices, not accomplished practitioners. By doing so, you create the kinds of safe environments that allow results to take center stage in instructional decision making.

Administer Regular Data Literacy Surveys

As with every aspect of PLC development, learning teams demonstrate different levels of data mastery at different times. Some write effective common assessments from day one, while others struggle to agree on the content that should be tested. Some teams naturally trust one another, independently engaging in deep and meaningful conversations, while others need ongoing facilitation from unbiased outsiders.

For school administrators, this means that effective technical and emotional support for teams working with data needs to be differentiated. You can identify the strengths and weaknesses of each of the teams in your building by administering regular data-literacy surveys like the one included at the end of this chapter (see the Professional Learning Team Data-Literacy Survey on pages 177–179). By collecting information from learning teams at several points during the course of a school year, you will be better able to customize the support you offer to the teachers of your building, ensuring that data use is efficient and purposeful.

Identify and Encourage Your Positive Deviants

Every school has them: teachers who are able to achieve high results regardless of circumstances. In order to identify these positive deviants, administrators should use objective evidence. Positive deviants are not necessarily the most popular teachers, the ones with the most graduate degrees, or the ones with dozens of flattering letters from parents (although they can be). Positive deviants are the teachers whose students consistently overperform on common assessments. Positive deviancy can also come in specialized areas. Is there one teacher whose special education inclusion students always seem to excel or whose English as a second language students are consistently successful? Is there someone whose high-achieving students show exceptional growth?

For Lillie Jessie, principal of Elizabeth Vaughan Elementary School in Woodbridge, Virginia, identifying positive deviants is a key element in her efforts to improve teaching and learning:

> In my responsibilities as a principal, I am tight on looking at teachers who have mastered the objectives at high levels instead of focusing all of my energy on teachers whose students are performing poorly. My goal is to reinforce the interdependence that comes with the collaborative process of a PLC. The conversation is not about why one person did so poorly, but rather, what is the high-performing teacher doing that can be shared? (Jessie, 2008, p. 115)

You can share the practices of positive deviants both formally and informally. Formally, school leaders must consistently emphasize the expectation that professional learning teams will use data analysis to identify effective practices. Begin by encouraging teams to create a "Best Practices Hall of Fame," where positive deviants document instructional approaches that worked.

Consider asking a tech-savvy parent volunteer or part-time office assistant to help with organizing an online forum spotlighting effective instruction. Short video interviews of teachers and students describing high-quality learning experiences can be embedded into blogs or wikis and paired with instructional materials and evidence of student outcomes in an online warehouse systematically documenting the characteristics of effective instruction in your building. As an increasingly broad range of skills are reviewed and assessed, it is likely that every teacher on your faculty will see his or her practices publicly recognized.

Informally, school leaders should engage positive deviants in ongoing conversations, encouraging them to share their expertise. Working in the egalitarian culture of education, where individual educators rarely question the practice of their peers, highly accomplished teachers are often embarrassed to see their work celebrated. Successful principals reframe this type of knowledge transfer: sharing effective practices is not about being the best; rather, it is about helping every adult and every child to be as successful as possible.

Emphasize Long-Term Process Over Short-Term Results

As educators, we work in a high-stakes/high-accountability environment defined by tremendous pressure to achieve constantly improving results. Many educational leaders view professional learning communities through that lens: a means to the end of improved test scores. But the paradox of the PLC model is that, in order for it to truly have an impact on student learning and achievement, school leaders must have patience and emphasize long-term processes over short-term results.

Nowhere is this truer than in data analysis. As professional learning teams begin to score and analyze the results of common assessments, school leaders can become antsy to see improvements: "Well, your classrooms had a 75 percent average on the first common assessment, so surely we can raise the average to 80 percent on the next one." In order for professional learning teams to develop the trust and experience necessary to move toward shared understanding, they need some time and space. For this reason, school leaders initially need to focus on the success of the process, rather than immediate improvements in results.

What does a successful process look like? It looks like teams sharing data from across their classrooms, having structured and open-minded conversations about the data, asking insightful questions, and identifying successful strategies. When school leaders see these types of activities happening on a regular basis in team meetings, they can rest easy knowing that improved student learning and achievement are just around the corner.

Structuring Data Conversations

Unstructured conversations around student learning results can often end in emotional disasters. As a result, effective learning teams carefully structure data conversations. Use the following template to provide focus to your team's next attempt at studying learning outcomes.

Date: _____

Common Assessment to Be Reviewed: _____

Teachers Present: _____

Step 1: Prepare Your Mind

The most effective learning teams recognize that successful data conversations start slowly, with teachers collectively reflecting on intended outcomes and preconceived notions. Use the following reflection tasks to prepare your mind for today's data conversation.

Reflection Task	Examples	Responses
Start With Learning-Centered Questions By starting with specific learning-centered questions, a team can move past superficial observations and on to more productive analyses.	• Across the grade level, were there any specific objectives or tasks with which multiple students appeared to struggle?	
Identify Preconceptions What beliefs do you hold about yourself, your students, your colleagues, and your instructional practices? In what ways might those beliefs skew the way you look at student learning data?	• Michael is a master teacher who can do no wrong. • Sarah struggles with classroom discipline and does not challenge her kids. • This year's students are completely irresponsible. • The lessons we taught were some of the best we've taught in years. • The test we gave was poorly written.	

Step 2: Prepare Your Data Set

The most effective learning teams recognize that successful data conversations depend on approachable data sets that have been carefully prepared to spotlight trends and patterns in student learning. Use one of the following strategies to prepare the results of the common assessment that your team is studying today.

Christmas Tree Highlighting	Stoplight Highlighting
Collectively decide on a score that represents passing performance on today's assessment. Highlight all scores in today's data set that are at or above this passing indicator in green and all the scores below this passing indicator in red.	Use two jointly determined cut values to highlight today's data set; for example, all the scores above 85 percent might be highlighted green, all the scores between 70 and 85 percent might be highlighted yellow, and all the scores below 70 percent might be highlighted red.

Step 3: Prepare Your Findings

Now that your team has carefully set initial questions, brainstormed potential preconceptions, and prepared your data set, it is finally time to begin looking at your results. Use one of the following strategies to draw some conclusions about what it is that you've learned.

Sticky Notetaking	Final Word
Use self-stick notes to record up to five observations and up to five questions about today's data set. After organizing the observations and questions into categories, start an open discussion centered on those categories.	Give one participant 60 seconds to share a thought or insight about today's data set. Then, each team member takes up to 30 seconds to respond to that insight. After everyone has had a chance to comment, the participant gets 30 seconds to respond to what he or she has heard from the other members of the group.

Step 4: Prepare Your Next Steps

The most effective learning teams recognize that successful data conversations end in actions that are designed to improve student learning across entire grade levels and departments. Use the following questions to plan next steps.

Conversation Task	Examples	Responses
Interpret Results It's time to dig into your results! Begin discussing the patterns that you see in student performance. Brainstorm a list of three to five specific result statements on which your team can take action. Remember to avoid emotionally loaded words and phrases. What patterns do you see in student performance?	• Almost all of our students scored above 70 percent on the assessment. • The active boys in our classrooms all seemed to struggle with the questions at the end of the assessment. • Question 4 was missed by almost 80 percent of the students in our advanced classrooms.	

| **Leave With Questions as Well as Answers**

 For highly accomplished learning teams, data conversations are as much about questions as they are about answers. Never leave a data conversation without new questions to pursue. | • The data say that some students are struggling with multiplying fractions. Why?

 • What aspect of multiplying fractions do they find difficult?

 • Why were the students in first block more successful at multiplying fractions than the students in second block? | |

Step 5: Write a Set of Summary Statements

The most effective learning teams end data conversations with a set of short statements summarizing the outcomes of this powerful professional learning experience. Use the following sentence starters to craft summary statements for today's data conversation.

Prompt	Response
The finding that surprised us the most in today's data conversation was . . .	
Today's data conversation has left us convinced that . . .	
Today's data conversation has us continuing to wonder whether or not . . .	
To act on today's data conversation, we plan to . . .	

Building a PLC at Work™ © 2010 Solution Tree Press • solution-tree.com
 Visit **go.solution-tree.com/PLCbooks** to download this page.

Team Action Planning Template

For novice learning teams, the decision to collectively analyze student learning data does not come naturally. To ensure that your team incorporates the analysis of student learning data into its work, include explicit references to data in any team action planning documents. By doing so, you will constantly reinforce the message that data are important. Use the sample action planning template below as a guide.

Your Team: _____

1. What is your area of focus? Please identify both general content area and specific curricular objectives, and any appropriate student subgroups.

2. Why did you pick this area of focus? What data did you use in making your decision?

3. What is your SMART goal for this area of focus?

4. How will you regularly assess progress toward this goal? How will you respond to the results of these assessments? In your answer, please include the following elements:
   - Use of common assessments
   - Plans for analyzing data from common assessments
   - Plans for making team-based instructional adjustments based on assessment data
   - Clear timelines

5. What additional skills might your team need to accomplish the goal? What professional learning opportunities or resources would help your team acquire these skills?

Evidence of Practice in Action

On highly functioning learning teams, data—instead of personal preferences—are used to evaluate the impact of every instructional practice. Use this worksheet to track the impact that the key practices embraced by your learning team are having on student achievement.

Key Instructional Practice	Evidence of Impact	Next Steps
Write a short description of each of the key instructional practices that are implemented in the classrooms of your learning team.	*Describe the steps that you have taken to document the effectiveness of each key instructional practice and the conclusions you have drawn from team data sets.*	*Indicate the action your team plans to take based on your findings.*
Example: Our team has students annotate selections of text while reading, hoping that by slowing the reading process down, student comprehension will increase.	On the last two reading comprehension quizzes, students were required to annotate before answering any questions. The average score on these assessments increased by 4 points.	☐ Practice has proven to be successful and should be replicated. ☐ Practice needs continued study because the data collected point to inconsistent conclusions. ☐ Practice has no impact on student growth and should be eliminated.
		☐ Practice has proven to be successful and should be replicated. ☐ Practice needs continued study because the data collected point to inconsistent conclusions. ☐ Practice has no impact on student growth and should be eliminated.
		☐ Practice has proven to be successful and should be replicated. ☐ Practice needs continued study because the data collected point to inconsistent conclusions. ☐ Practice has no impact on student growth and should be eliminated.

Professional Learning Team Data-Literacy Survey

Because professional learning communities focus on results and make every effort to ensure that all students are successful, effective manipulation of data is essential. This survey is intended to help us, as a school, learn more about our levels of data literacy. The results of this survey will help us target our professional development in the next year, and we thank you in advance for answering in an honest and thoughtful manner.

Your Team: _____

Please indicate the extent to which each of the statements below is true by circling one of the four numbers using the following scale:

1 = Very true   2 = True   3 = Somewhat true   4 = Not true

Data-Literacy Statement	Rating			
Our team has regular conversations about what student mastery looks like.	1	2	3	4
Our team has agreed-upon expectations for mastery on most assignments.	1	2	3	4
Our team has measurable instructional goals for all common lessons.	1	2	3	4
Our team has developed our own set of common assessments that we use regularly (at least monthly).	1	2	3	4
I believe that our common assessments are tied to state standards and are reliable measures of what students should know and be able to do.	1	2	3	4
Our team has developed our own set of common rubrics we can use to score performance-related tasks.	1	2	3	4
I believe that our common rubrics are tied to state standards and are reliable measures of what students should know and be able to do.	1	2	3	4
Our team has established an effective system for recording results from our common assessments.	1	2	3	4
Our team has an effective process for looking at the results of common assessments together.	1	2	3	4
Our team is able to discuss common assessment results in a positive and constructive way.	1	2	3	4
Our team uses graphs and charts to make student achievement trends visible in our conversations about results.	1	2	3	4

Our team makes predictions about student learning based on common assessment results.	1	2	3	4
Our team considers multiple hypotheses and looks for multiple sources of verification before drawing conclusions from common assessment results.	1	2	3	4
Our team changes our instructional practices based on common assessment results.	1	2	3	4
Our team provides remediation and enrichment to students based on common assessment results.	1	2	3	4
Our team celebrates achievements that are highlighted in the results of our common assessments.	1	2	3	4
I feel safe when revealing my common assessment data in front of my peers.	1	2	3	4
Our team uses data as a tool for identifying effective practices rather than as a tool for identifying effective people.	1	2	3	4
Our team has a sense of shared responsibility for the success of all our students.	1	2	3	4
Our team has the skills necessary to collect and manipulate data effectively.	1	2	3	4
I know the difference between and understand when to use aggregated and disaggregated data.	1	2	3	4
I know the difference between and understand when to use formative and summative assessments.	1	2	3	4
Our team respects the confidentiality of students and teachers when looking at data.	1	2	3	4
Our team has looked at our students' standardized exam results.	1	2	3	4
Our team is aware of all of the varied populations we serve and looks at results for each of these populations individually.	1	2	3	4
Our team refers to reliable research when we are testing a prediction we have made about student learning.	1	2	3	4
Our team has created systems for engaging students in data collection for self-assessment.	1	2	3	4

Please take a few moments to share any final thoughts about the use of data on your learning team. What are you most proud of? What are you the most concerned about? What kinds of support would you like from administration to continue your work next year? What are the most significant barriers preventing your team from using data more effectively? What kinds of resolutions can you imagine for those barriers?

CHAPTER 8

BUILDING A COLLECTIVE INTELLIGENCE

Sarah leaned forward and pushed the play button. Slightly apprehensive, she sat back in her chair and looked at the television monitor.

It was near the end of the year and the sixth-grade language arts/social studies teachers were trying something new. Sarah had videotaped herself teaching a lesson, and her colleagues then gathered to watch and discuss the video together. Michael had read an article earlier in the year about the lesson study process, and the team agreed to give it a shot. Sarah volunteered to be the first guinea pig.

The lesson focused on a whole-class discussion of the book *Number the Stars* by Lois Lowry, which chronicles the fictional experiences of a young Danish girl during World War II. The team had devised an innovative activity to help students reflect on the challenges faced by citizens in an occupied country. In the activity, students had to decide whether or not they would have participated in the Danish underground, a militant group that actively opposed the Nazi occupiers.

For the activity, Sarah arranged the classroom's seats into five clusters. At one end was cluster 1, reserved for students who held the position that they would have actively and violently participated in the Danish resistance. At the other end was cluster 5 for students who believed they would have tried to go about their normal lives during the occupation, staying far away from the resistance efforts. There were three other clusters in between, reflecting the spectrum of possible positions.

Throughout the conversation, students were allowed to get up and move to different clusters as their opinions changed. Sarah moderated an organic discussion, posing questions and challenging students on their positions.

As the taped lesson progressed, Sarah's peers made positive comments about what they were seeing.

"Wow, Sarah, this is really a neat lesson!" noted Karen. "The students seem to really be enjoying it."

Michael chimed in: "Remember, it's great to note the positive things that we see happening in the lesson, but the real purpose of lesson study is to focus in on the patterns of student learning behavior that we see."

"Alright," said Jennifer, "I see a pattern. Notice how the kids seem to move in small packs when they switch from one cluster to another. It never seems like one kid moves at a time. As soon as one student changes his or her position, a couple of more do, too. I wonder if they feel some social pressure to follow their friends. That's something I always forget in class—a lot of the kids' behavior isn't dependent on me, it's dependent on how they think their peers will react to what they say and do."

The group watched for several more minutes in silence. One of the children in the class, a boy named Trevor, made an especially insightful comment. Karen noted to herself that it was the third or fourth time Trevor had said something impressive. She turned toward Michael and said, "I'm guessing Trevor got an A on the unit test!"

Sarah leaned forward and hit the pause button on the VCR. "Karen, would you mind saying that again?"

Karen responded, "Oh, I was just saying to Michael that that boy—I think his name is Trevor—must have gotten a good grade on the unit test. It seems like that's the third or fourth time he's said something insightful. He had a really sophisticated understanding of the book, didn't he?"

Sarah paused for a moment. "You know what's funny? I think he got a pretty low grade, something like a C or a C+. If I remember correctly, his essays on the test were nowhere near as in-depth as the things he said in the classroom discussion. I didn't think about that fact until just now."

Michael jumped into the discussion, noting that the pattern in Trevor's performance actually mirrored a trend the team had been studying for the past several months. In nearly every unit it seemed that students mastered content at a deep level in classroom activities and conversations, but they failed to show the same levels of sophistication on written assignments. Trevor was, in a way, the perfect poster boy for the sixth-grade language arts/social studies teachers. It was pretty clear from his comments in Sarah's videotaped lesson that he understood many of the most important themes and issues in the novel the team was studying, but he could not express that understanding in written form.

"So should we be testing kids through classroom discussions, rather than essays?" asked Jennifer. "If a student has mastered the standard, does it really matter whether he shows that mastery through writing or through oral discussion?"

The team thought for a moment, remembering that some of their required standards were very clearly connected to written expression, while others were not so clear. Together, they decided that unless a standard specifically stated that students demonstrate understanding through writing, it would be legitimate to grade them on participation in an oral discussion. Excitement rippled through the room!

"So how would we do that?" asked Sarah. "Does that mean we have to make a rubric for oral expression, and videotape our class discussions? Do we give students a choice: you can either take the written test or accept a grade from class discussion?"

"Good questions," said Michael. "If our goal is to collect evidence that shows whether or not a student has mastered a standard, well, this seems to be clear evidence that

Trevor mastered the standard. But to be honest, the real question for me is, How do we help our students to effectively demonstrate their thinking through writing? The state still has a writing test for students; and, let's face it, these kids are going to be graded in high school based on their ability to articulate thoughts in research papers and essays. It's one thing for us to accept oral representations of knowledge when the standard allows it, but that isn't helping these students become better writers."

"You know what we need to do," said Karen. "We need to design a comprehensive writing assessment to give to all our students within the first couple weeks of school next year, and create a series of focused writing lessons targeted at different levels of writers."

"That's an excellent idea," noted Jennifer. "I have a bunch of students this year who I feel really haven't progressed that much in writing, and it frustrates me."

"So what would that look like?" asked Michael.

Sarah suggested that the team develop a common writing prompt with a scoring rubric that every student would respond to and that they could score together as a team. Using the results of this new shared assessment, students would be grouped into similar achievement categories. They could carve out time over the course of the year to work with students across the grade level in writing groups, and use periodic assessments to monitor students' ongoing progress. Confidence in Sarah's plan was high across the team because it resembled an instructional model they had used the month before to teach students a unit on drama.

"You know what, this is an awesome idea!" noted Karen. "I would be happy to spend some time working on this and fleshing it out over the summer. Is anyone else free?"

"I've already locked myself into a summer gig designing professional development workshops for central office," said Michael. "I might be able to steal a little time, but I don't think I could spare much." Sarah and Jennifer were already committed for the summer, too. Both had plans to see family throughout most of July and then to work part-time jobs as caterers for Sarah's husband.

"No problem," responded Karen. "I have more free time during the summer than you all do. I'll see if I can put together a rough draft of a plan and post it online. If you can try to check in every now and then over the summer and leave me comments, I can continue to revise it so that we have something to start with in the fall. I'll keep in touch by email. If anyone finds some time to meet, let me know. I'm excited!"

Lessons From the Front Line

The sixth-grade language arts/social studies team has clearly come a long way. Back in the winter, they were tired and frustrated, struggling to figure out how to work consistently well together. As recently as three months ago, their first attempt at collaborative data analysis resulted in tears and hurt feelings.

But in this story, the team had a sophisticated conversation that led to some important insights. Furthermore, the team left the meeting with a possible plan of action: for the following year, they intended to assess incoming students' writing abilities and create targeted, team-based interventions to address areas of weakness.

What made this conversation so successful? How was the sixth-grade team able to reach this level of sophistication in their discussion, allowing them to produce new insights together? What about their planned intervention strategy: how do team-based interventions differ from standard interventions administered in the traditional schoolhouse?

The sixth-grade teachers had reached a point in their collective development at which they were ready to take on challenging topics together. They had achieved a high level of interpersonal trust. Sarah even felt comfortable enough to have the team dissect one of her taped lessons. The team had also learned how to use questions and in-depth discussion to develop a sort of group wisdom.

Better yet, they became action-oriented, a trait defining the best professional learning teams. As Richard DuFour, Rebecca DuFour, and Robert Eaker (2008) note:

> Members of PLCs are action-oriented: They move quickly to turn aspirations into action and visions into reality. They understand that the most powerful learning always occurs in a context of taking action, and they value engagement and experience as the most effective teachers. . . . Furthermore, educators in PLCs recognize that until members of the organization "do" differently, there is no reason to anticipate different results. They avoid paralysis by analysis and overcome inertia with action. (p. 16)

Most importantly, however, the sixth-grade team took collective responsibility for learning, responding as a cohesive unit to address a potential area of student weakness. Accomplished professional learning teams put formal intervention strategies in place to support struggling students and challenge more advanced students, differentiating their curricular approach to meet identified needs.

This final chapter focuses on advanced practices in the areas of team-based reflection. Specifically, we discuss how lesson study and action research can lead teams to new insights and innovations. Next, we examine the range of enrichment and remediation alternatives commonly found in schools and make an argument for the implementation of targeted team-based interventions. Finally, we discuss a concept that is at the heart of advanced teams' successes: the development of collective intelligence.

Implementing Team-Based Reflective Initiatives

At a certain point in the story that started this chapter, the sixth-grade team achieved what could almost be described as an "a-ha!" moment: some students have a deeper understanding of class content than they are able to demonstrate through their writing, and these students would likely benefit from intensive support designed to improve their writing skills.

If sometime during the next school year, one of their Central Middle School colleagues were to ask members of the sixth-grade team how they came up with the idea for implementing targeted writing interventions for their students, the answer would probably be,

"Well, we had this really great meeting at the end of last year where we all came to this sudden realization that our students were struggling with writing, and we decided that we needed to do something about it."

The interesting thing is that this answer would not be correct. In fact, the team's realization about Trevor and his inability to express his thoughts through writing was the result of months of individual thought and team dialogue. Way back in February, the team began to notice some important disparities in student writing abilities, and they had been informally talking and thinking about this issue for a while.

In his book *Group Genius: The Creative Power of Collaboration* (2007), Keith Sawyer explores the process that collaborative teams go through in achieving important insights. Sawyer dispels the notion that "a-ha!" moments result from lightning-quick sparks of inspiration. Instead, Sawyer shows how insight is largely the result of two things: ongoing collaboration and patience.

Take, for example, the invention of the telegraph, which Sawyer describes in detail in his book. In 1832, Samuel Morse (the creator of Morse code) was on a boat sailing from Europe back to the United States. While en route, he overheard one passenger talking about electricity, explaining that scientists at the time believed that electrical charges could pass instantaneously down any length of wire. Morse was a tinkerer and amateur inventor, and he was struck by the notion that electricity could be used to send messages at quick rates of speed. Cue the invention of the telegraph, right?

Wrong. The idea of using electricity to send messages over long distances had actually been proposed almost eighty years earlier, and multiple scientists had made headway over the intervening decades on methods to turn this idea into a reality. While he did not realize it at the time, Morse would need twelve long years to produce the first working telegraph. Along the way, he hit many dead ends, implemented solutions that did not solve anything, and became frustrated and despondent as his "a-ha!" idea failed to be realized.

But Morse had two things going for him: collaborative partners and patience. A number of different individuals worked with Morse to solve the intermediate problems he encountered, and he kept at it. Then, in 1844, he sent his first long-distance message from Washington, DC, to Baltimore. By 1861, just seventeen years later, the first transcontinental telegraph put the Pony Express out of business.

What lessons can professional learning teams take from Morse's experiences? First, collaborative teams are smarter and more innovative than any single individual. Morse would never have arrived at a working telegraph without the input and collaboration of a collection of scientists and inventors. Similarly, in this chapter's story, Karen would likely not have come up with the idea of a common writing assessment and differentiated writing interventions on her own. In the words of Conzemius and O'Neill (2002), "Teams . . . serve a unique purpose and when they are performing at high levels, they are generative—they create new knowledge, stimulate energy, and promote improvement in ways that individuals acting in isolation could not achieve" (p. 12).

Second, insight takes time. It took Morse twelve years to go from his initial idea of a telegraph to a working model. For the sixth-grade language arts/social studies teachers at Central Middle, insight about student writing weaknesses was the result of months of individual and collective thought—and the patience to keep returning to the same unresolved topic. Chances are the team's first attempts at creating and implementing a program of writing interventions will require considerable revision and additional time before members get it right.

Sawyer (2007) suggests several strategies to help collaborative teams get to moments of insight and inspiration. One suggestion is to practice what he calls *deep listening*. This means that group members consciously and attentively focus on listening to what other members have to say. In many group conversations, individuals spend more cognitive energy thinking about what they would like to say, rather than listening to the thoughts of others. When this happens, it is next to impossible for insights to emerge because the conversation does not build: rather than team members expanding upon existing thoughts, they just stack their preconceived ideas next to each other.

The importance of deep listening is echoed by Mike Schmoker, who emphasizes the connection between the quality of teacher conversations and the quality of student learning. According to Schmoker (2006):

> To take full advantage of the collective expertise of the team, we can listen carefully—and nonjudgmentally—to each other's best ideas. . . . Listening helps to ensure that we select the best of several alternatives. The collective wisdom of the team can then inform the all-important direction the team will take. This kind of thoughtful approach will have a high payoff in student learning. (pp. 16–17)

Another one of Sawyer's (2007) strategies is to think of team dialogue as improvisation. Checklist meetings, in which a team sticks tightly to an agenda and allows little time for organic conversation, are scripted. There is no room for deviation from the script, which rules out the opportunity for novel thinking and original insights. While agendas nurture the work of novice learning teams, they can also restrict the work of creative professionals.

The sixth-grade team at Central Middle did not set out to address students' writing in the story that started this chapter. They agreed, instead, to engage in a reflective activity and then let the conversation go where it may. Many times, threads in organic conversations will not go anywhere. In fact, during the team's conversation, Jennifer notices a pattern of student behavior based on social inclinations, yet no one expands on this observation. But sometimes, when teams patiently pursue an important topic and listen deeply to each other, improvisational conversations can lead to inspiration.

The bottom line is that the more time a team puts into reflective processes—and the more open a team is to improvisational conversation—the more likely members are to arrive at important insights that can lead to new, innovative practices. So what types of reflective processes can teams use to do this? Two examples are lesson study, which the sixth-grade team uses in the story, and action research.

Lesson Study

In their article "A Deeper Look at Lesson Study," Catherine Lewis, Rebecca Perry, and Jacqueline Hurd (2004) describe the ways in which the lesson study process can lead to instructional improvements. Originally developed in Japan, lesson study involves a team of teachers developing a lesson, observing its implementation, and then collaboratively analyzing its effectiveness. One of the advantages of lesson study is that it offers a ready-made reflective framework that professional learning teams can use to deepen their conversations about teaching and learning.

In the lesson study process, a team first develops a common lesson centered on the required curriculum that is built from research and reflects current understandings of best practice. One of the teachers then implements the lesson with her students. The rest of the team members either observe its implementation in the classroom or the original teacher videotapes the lesson and the team watches the videotape together (the choice of the sixth-grade team at Central Middle). Finally, the team analyzes the success of the lesson, focusing on the extent to which it helps students to master targeted objectives.

What makes lesson study a valuable strategy for learning teams is that it inherently separates personality from practice, an important step toward building team safety discussed in chapter 7, "Connecting Data Analysis and Instructional Improvement." Shared lesson planning ensures that no one person's work is being judged. Instead, teams are evaluating the pedagogical knowledge of the group. Skilled lesson study facilitators, a role being filled by Michael in the story that started this chapter, consistently remind colleagues to focus on student responses to instruction instead of the individual decisions made by teachers. This targeted work builds trust and makes collective reflection a risk-free situation for teams.

According to Lewis, Perry, and Hurd (2004), lesson study can also lead to:

- **Increased knowledge of subject matter**—As teachers initially develop a lesson, they engage in discussions of how best to help students master the targeted curriculum objectives. This type of conversation can lead to an in-depth examination of content standards and the academic skills involved in mastering those standards.

- **Increased knowledge of content-specific pedagogy**—In the process of developing a lesson and discussing its effectiveness, teachers can critically reflect on the effectiveness of different instructional approaches such as whole-group discussions, cooperative learning, project-based work, and so on. This enhances teachers' knowledge of various instructional strategies.

- **Increased ability to observe students**—Because lesson study involves a group of teachers observing a lesson, teams have the opportunity to focus in on student behavior during the teaching and learning process. Student thinking, and the connections between various instructional approaches and student academic behavior, can be explored together.

- **Stronger connection of daily practice to long-term goals**—When implemented effectively, lesson study ties the objectives of individual lessons to overarching goals. For example, the sixth-grade team might decide early in the next school year to study a lesson addressing students' deficient writing skills. In this way, they could analyze how their micropractices (in other words, daily classroom lessons and activities) are connecting to their macrogoals (such as improving student writing skills overall).

For teacher teams or school leaders interested in implementing the lesson study process, we have included a list of recommended readings at the end of this chapter (see page 200).

Action Research

Action research has been around for decades. Professional learning community advocates sometimes point to the collective inquiry inherent in action research as a way for professional learning teams to reflect on their practices. According to Robert Eaker (Eaker, DuFour, & DuFour, 2002):

> In a professional learning community we use collaborative teams to engage in collective inquiry and action research. Perhaps the best way to think of collective inquiry is to think of it in these terms: we expect collaborative teams to seek out best practice. We have a tendency in more traditional schools to have teachers collaborate and essentially average their opinions about what they think about a particular problem or issue. . . . But in a professional learning community, we do the opposite. We expect collaborative teams and teachers to seek out best practice. (p. 91)

So what is action research, and how can professional learning teams use it to "seek out best practice"? According to Jean McNiff (2003), an expert on action research in education, *action research* is a structured approach to reflecting on and evaluating our own practices. Whereas traditional research is usually conducted by a third party attempting to study and publish findings for a larger audience, action research is about self-examination for the purpose of improving one's own actions.

In the context of a professional learning team, action research follows a basic process (McNiff, 2003):

- The team identifies an issue to investigate.
- The team discusses a possible solution to the issue.
- The team implements the proposed solution.
- The team evaluates the solution.
- Team members change their practices in light of the evaluation.

If the sixth-grade team wished to conduct action research on students' writing, they would begin by identifying a key issue to investigate and formulating the issue as a research question. For example, "How can we help struggling writers to improve?" or "What specific instructional strategies can best help students to articulate complex thought in writing?" The next step would be to research and discuss possible solutions. In the case of the sixth-grade team, members would likely spend time developing and delivering a collection of minilessons centered on the most promising practices.

In the story that started this chapter, the team had already come to this step, working to develop a writing assessment, scoring rubric, and system of interventions to be implemented during the upcoming school year. What makes action research especially effective, however, is that the process does not stop at implementation. After implementing the interventions, the sixth-grade team would then ask, did it work? In other words, they would evaluate the intervention.

Efforts to evaluate interventions, argues learning community expert Cassandra Erkens, are the central difference between reflective *people* and reflective *practitioners*. As she explains (2008b):

> Reflective practitioners have a strong sense of their personal strengths and learning curves, but they take it one step further and seek confirmation of their strengths in student results. They set aside personal defensiveness regarding past efforts and preconceived notions of what may or may not work regarding future efforts. A reflective person might spend considerable time pondering her effectiveness, but a reflective *practitioner* seeks answers outside of herself and takes action to address gaps. (p. 22)

So how could the sixth-grade teachers seek answers about their writing interventions outside of themselves? They could simply give a follow-up assessment and see if students showed improvement in their writing. They could identify or develop a collection of anchor papers to quickly and easily compare student performances with agreed-upon levels of mastery. If the team wanted to be really sophisticated, it could assign only half of the struggling writers to participate in extra writing sessions and then, after a month of interventions, see if there were any differences in performance between the students who received interventions and those who did not.

The key point is that in action research, a team follows up to evaluate the effectiveness of its initiatives, and then acts on the results of that evaluation. If the sixth-grade team determines that the writing interventions are successful, they could continue to refine those interventions. If the team determines that the writing interventions have not had a positive impact on student achievement, then they could go back to the drawing board knowing that they did not waste extra months of time on an unsuccessful instructional strategy.

Often, the greatest challenge for teachers engaged in action research ends up being the personal value they attach to their favorite teaching practices. Teams that are true to themselves and dedicated to identifying effective strategies must set their long-held biases aside and be prepared for the possibility that their best lessons may not survive under scrutiny. As we discussed in chapter 7, philosophical differences around curriculum, instruction, and assessment can lead to conflict within professional learning teams. Action research can help to overcome these philosophical conflicts by focusing on measurable results. Without a commitment to objectivity, however, action research is unlikely to drive measurable change on our teams and in our schools.

We have included a list of recommended readings (see page 200) that provide more how-to details at the end of this chapter for teacher teams or school leaders interested in implementing the action study process.

Adding Team-Based Interventions

At the end of the story that opened this chapter, the sixth-grade team discussed a plan to create targeted writing interventions based on student formative writing assessments. Pretty good stuff for a team tired after a full year of teaching!

It is precisely this type of team-based intervention that is one of the most important, practical outcomes of the collaboration between members of professional learning teams. But interventions in and of themselves are nothing new. They happen all the time in traditionally organized schools. What is it that makes team-based interventions different from more traditional attempts at remediation and/or enrichment, and why are they such an important outcome of professional learning teams?

Before answering these questions, we would first like to discuss interventions in general and describe the range of interventions commonly found in schools. The word *intervention* can mean a lot of different things to different people. For us, an *intervention* is a targeted response to an identified area of student strength or weakness, as determined by a specific assessment or set of criteria. In addition, we believe that:

- Interventions do not have to be academic in nature—for example, behavioral interventions are common in schools.

- True interventions are systematic, instead of ad hoc. As an example, a teacher may be concerned that a student is struggling in math and recommend that his parents hire a tutor outside of school. This is an ad hoc response: the teacher has no specific criteria to determine which students need tutors, just a general concern about this individual student's progress. What is more, there are no guarantees that this intervention will actually occur! While this child's parents are likely to be well intentioned, they may not be able to identify or afford a tutor for their son.

  In contrast, an example of a systematic intervention would be a schoolwide expectation that all students receiving a C or lower on their report cards will participate in an organized, school-based tutoring program for the following quarter. According to DuFour, DuFour, and Eaker (2008), "There are schools at all grade levels that do not leave learning to chance. These schools have created coordinated plans to ensure any student who struggles in core classes receives additional time and support for learning in a directive, timely, and systematic way" (p. 246).

- Interventions are not just remedial. While interventions are typically targeted at struggling students, a student who leaves the classroom once a week to participate in academically gifted (AG) activities would also be participating in an intervention—just one that was focused on enrichment, as opposed to remediation.

We have found two criteria particularly useful in thinking about interventions: the frequency of the intervention and the adult(s) responsible for implementing the intervention. For example, students participating in a weekly, school-based tutoring program would be receiving an intermittent intervention provided by a specialist (which could be anyone from a classroom teacher to a volunteer parent or a high-achieving peer). The following descriptions provide more detail about each of the common interventions implemented in schools.

Specialist Interventions

These are some of the most common types of interventions found in a traditionally organized school. A student or group of students leaves the classroom to work with someone other than the classroom teacher on either an intermittent basis (no more frequently than once a week) or an ongoing basis (daily to biweekly). A range of assessments or criteria might be used to identify students for this type of intervention: reading scores (for example, DIBELS or Running Records), IQ scores, a specific medical diagnosis (for example, ADHD), limited English proficiency status, standardized testing results, social skills indices, grades on report cards, and so on. Examples of these specialist interventions include:

- Leaving class once a week (intermittent) for an extra dose of guided reading by a reading specialist or spending fifteen minutes each day (ongoing) with a reading specialist for targeted phonics work

- Working intermittently with a speech pathologist as part of an individualized education plan (IEP) or working on a daily basis with a special education teacher to meet IEP goals

- Meeting once a week with an academically gifted teacher for accelerated work (intermittent) or meeting with an English as a second language (ESL) teacher three times a week to work on English language skills (ongoing)

- Meeting bimonthly in a small group with a guidance counselor to address social skills

Classroom Teacher Team Interventions

In classroom teacher team interventions, a student or group of students remains in the classroom and works either with the classroom teacher or another member of the classroom team (teacher assistant) to focus on work developed by members of the team. Participation in these types of interventions can be based on a wide variety of assessments or criteria: reading scores, scores on formative assessments, IQ scores, frequency of homework completion, and other such measures of "performance." Examples of this type of intervention include the following:

- Meeting in a classroom-based guided reading group on either an intermittent or ongoing basis

- Working one on one or in a small group with a classroom teacher assistant

- Spending lunch once a week in the classroom to complete missing homework assignments

- Participating in curriculum compacting designed by the classroom teacher or a specialist (For example, a student might score highly on a unit pretest and test out of parts of the unit, and then complete enrichment assignments instead.)

- Completing differentiated projects based on identified student skill sets
- Working with a specialist (for example, an ESL teacher or special education teacher) who "pushes into" the regular education classroom to work with individual students or small groups on an intermittent or ongoing basis

Professional Learning Team Interventions

The writing intervention discussed by the sixth-grade team in the story that opened this chapter is an example of a team-based intervention. In this type of intervention, a student or group of students works with the classroom teacher, with another member of the professional learning team, or with a designated specialist on either an intermittent or ongoing basis. The intervention itself (the curriculum or strategy being employed) is a product of the learning team's collaborative work. Typically, team-developed common assessments are used to identify students for these types of interventions. Examples include the following:

- Using common assessment data to regroup students across a grade level to work on differentiated assignments on an intermittent or ongoing basis
- Working with a specialist (such as an ESL teacher or AG teacher) in a small group on a learning-team-designed assignment or activity
- Working with the classroom teacher in a small group on a learning-team-designed assignment or activity
- Using common assessment data to identify students eligible for curriculum compacting, and introducing a team-designed compacted curriculum

A Range of Interventions

When considering the range of interventions available, it is important to note that no one type of intervention is superior to another. In fact, interventions from any one of the categories can be hugely successful. At the same time, schools that limit their range of interventions are not fully meeting student needs.

In traditional schools, classroom teachers are often individually responsible for initiating the intervention process. The final decision to intervene is frequently based on the results of a standardized evaluation tool, such as an IQ test or standardized test of English proficiency. These evaluation tools result in categorical interventions—in other words, they group students into clear categories (such as special education, limited English proficient [LEP], or academically gifted) for which there are prescribed criteria, curricula, and corresponding staff specialists.

These categories, the curricular programs that accompany them, and the specialists who are responsible for delivering them, can serve some children well. But what about the students who do not fall into these clearly outlined categories? Is it possible that students that do not meet the criteria for special education, LEP, or AG, may require—or benefit from—interventions at some point during each school year?

Of course it is possible. In traditional schools, again, it is individual teachers who are responsible for identifying students in need of interventions beyond the categorical varieties. Those same teachers are then individually responsible for putting interventions into place. According to DuFour, DuFour, and Eaker (2008):

> In most schools, what happens when students experience difficulty in learning will almost invariably depend on the teacher to whom they are assigned. . . . This lack of a coordinated response when some students do not learn ranks near the top of the list of the many illogical and incomprehensible practices that occur in schooling. (pp. 244–245)

Now, this is not to say that individual teachers are not capable of identifying student needs and providing targeted, effective interventions. Thousands of teachers do this every day through differentiation. But, is the first-year teacher who is just trying to stay one day ahead in her lesson book really capable of designing and implementing the same quality of interventions that are second nature to the twenty-year veteran next door? Would the students in that first-year teacher's class not benefit from the kinds of remediation or enrichment opportunities that their neighbors are getting?

In contrast to the traditional model, in which interventions are almost entirely the responsibility of individual teachers, professional learning team–based interventions involve collective ownership and are the product of collaborative thought. Geri Parscale, the director of professional development and instruction for Fort Leavenworth Unified School District 207 in Leavenworth, Kansas, describes the differences between intervention decisions in traditional schools and PLCs in this way:

> In a traditional school, interventions occur when the teacher feels help is needed. Teachers are on their own in deciding the appropriate response to the student, and they respond in very different ways. . . . In a professional learning community, interventions occur in response to student performance on common assessments. There is a systematic, directed, timely response for all students in the school, and each teacher knows all the interventions. It is not left to the individual teacher to "supply" a way to help this child. The system has a plan, and all are required to use it. (2008, p. 182)

This is a major change in the thinking around interventions in schools. Professional learning communities *never* require individual teachers to be the sole people responsible for intervention decisions. Instead, interventions become the responsibility of the entire team or, quite often, a schoolwide system of intervention that goes beyond the team. This means that the students in classrooms with first-year teachers *do* get to benefit from the high-quality extensions developed next door because PLCs embrace the idea that collaborative teams are smarter and more innovative than individuals and that schools working systematically can ensure that every child has opportunities to master required content.

The story at the beginning of this chapter is a good example of this change in action: it is unlikely that all the members of the sixth-grade team would have individually developed targeted interventions to help the full range of their students in writing. In fact, it may be unlikely that *any* of them would have done so alone. By working together as a team—by creating and administering common assessments, analyzing common assessment data, and then engaging in open-ended, reflective conversations—they were able to arrive at a collective insight that will result in concrete changes in every classroom.

Those concrete changes represent important outcomes. According to DuFour, DuFour, Eaker, and Many (2006), when teams develop interventions collaboratively, they are likely to change their collective teaching practices in ways that result in improved learning experiences for students. Students that need extra support in targeted areas receive it. Students that are ready for an additional challenge to build on grade-level expectations also receive it.

When looking at the range of possible interventions in a school, it is important to remember that team-based interventions do not replace specialist and classroom-based interventions—they supplement them. If your team is considering how to put professional learning team-level interventions in place, we make the following recommendations:

- **Use data to determine student needs**—We strongly recommend that teams use student learning data from common assessments, not just intuition, when identifying students' academic strengths and areas of weakness. (For help in this area, refer to the data-analysis strategies discussed in chapter 7, "Connecting Data Analysis and Instructional Improvement.)

- **Do not allow tiered interventions to turn into tracking**—*Tiered interventions* are a form of performance-based grouping that separates students into small groups based on common assessment results and provides targeted instruction to those groups based on identified needs. Unfortunately, flexible intervention groups can sometimes solidify into permanent tracks. Professional learning teams must be careful to assign students to intervention groups based on assessment results and reassess regularly.

- **Start small and build upon successes**—Effective learning teams first dip their feet in the water, rather than diving head-first into the deep end, to avoid becoming overwhelmed. Consider working as a team to develop a one-hour, differentiated block of intervention time after implementing a common assessment, regrouping students throughout the grade level or subject area. See how it goes, work out the kinks, and then try it again.

- **Innovate**—There is no rule that all subject areas or grade levels must implement the same program of tiered interventions. Effective teams try a wide range of approaches to see what works. Effective school leaders encourage innovation, and then figure out ways to "cross pollinate" those initiatives that demonstrate success.

- **Do not just assess students; assess the intervention**—Some teams fall into the trap of assessing, intervening, and then moving on. But how do they know if the intervention was successful? The most accomplished teams use common assessments both before and after implementation, and then analyze the results to determine the effectiveness of the *intervention*.

Parscale (2008) reminds us that assessing interventions must always begin and end with an analysis of the impact the intervention has on student learning:

> As you help your staff in identifying strengths and weaknesses of an intervention, keep the focus on the student . . . what strengths are there for the student? What specific assistance does the child receive from this intervention? The same is true with weaknesses. Ask, Why doesn't this intervention help the child? . . . Stress that the teacher implementing the intervention is not being judged; the success or failure of the intervention does not imply that the teacher is good or bad. The quality of an intervention is determined solely by its results for the child. (p. 191)

Regardless of the step you choose to take first, take it with the kind of resolve emergency medical technicians demonstrate in the critical situations that are a part of their everyday work lives. Parscale (2008) argues, "When someone collapses in the presence of one of these trained professionals, immediate action is taken to avoid permanent damage. Similarly, when children are dying academically, we must approach them with the same sense of urgency" (p. 188).

Relevant Theory and Research

Throughout this chapter, we have talked about how smart groups can be: how they are more likely to achieve insight or inspiration than people working alone, and how they are better at developing effective interventions than are individual teachers. But is this true? Are teams really smarter than individual people? What about the old phrase "death by committee"? Isn't group decision making supposed to be *less* effective because it is more cumbersome and bureaucratic?

In his bestselling book *The Wisdom of Crowds*, James Surowiecki (2004) argues that teams really can be smarter than their smartest members, but they can also be remarkably dumb. A team's intelligence—its *collective intelligence*—depends on the makeup of the team and the way the team does its work. Surowiecki believes that in order for a group of people to be smart, three conditions have to be in place: diversity, independence, and a certain kind of decentralization.

According to Surowiecki (2004), the more diverse the participants in a team and the more diverse the ideas that they bring to the table, the greater the chance that something successful will emerge from their shared work. In fact, a lack of diversity—when everyone on a team has similar backgrounds and thinks pretty much the same way—is one of the conditions that can make teams unsuccessful. Homogeneous teams can get caught in narrow ways of thinking, only seeing situations or challenges through a limited perspective. It is kind of like the old saying, "When the only tool you have is a hammer, all of your problems start to look like nails." However, when team members bring different backgrounds, perspectives, and ideas to the group, the team has a broader set of mental tools at its disposal.

The concept of diversity as a prerequisite for successful teams has significant implications for professional learning communities. Perhaps most importantly, Surowiecki's emphasis on diversity suggests that school leaders and existing team members interviewing potential new hires should look to add people with diverse experiences and backgrounds. While it is clearly easier from a group dynamics standpoint to work with people who think similarly, a collection of diverse opinions, experiences, and views can lead to higher collective intelligence.

On the sixth-grade language arts/social studies team at Central Middle, there were less-experienced teachers and more-experienced teachers, teachers who were more innovative in their instructional approaches, and teachers who were more conservative. From a diversity standpoint, this combination of experiences and approaches was a good thing. What they shared, however, was a core commitment to the school's central mission of ensuring student learning, even while they believed there were different strategies to achieve that desired reality. Diversity of commitment to a building's mission can cause learning communities to collapse.

Surowiecki's (2004) next condition for group intelligence is independence. In the context of a professional learning team, independence means that each member of the team experiences a relative amount of freedom from the influence of other team members.

In chapter 4, "Supporting Team Development," we talked about the *norming* stage of team development, and the *planning, planning, planning* stage of task development. There is a strong tendency in teams to create intrateam harmony—to accept unwelcome compromises so that everyone can get along. There can also be social pressure within teams for members to change their classroom practices to be more like each other in an attempt to standardize what happens across classrooms. While this trend may initially have positive outcomes such as less-experienced teachers changing their practices to resemble those of more-experienced teachers and teams having positive "everyone's getting along" meetings, teams have to push past this point to become truly high performing.

Successful teams do need to incorporate a certain amount of standardization and interdependence: agreeing to the same set of curriculum standards, creating common assessments for use in all classes, and collaboratively analyzing student data. In high-performing teams, however, individual members still feel comfortable expressing independent, even contrary, ideas and opinions and leveraging diversity of thinking to approach challenges, such as students' inability to express their thoughts through writing, from a variety of perspectives.

The data-analysis process is especially helpful in maintaining independence. When teams use the strategies suggested in chapter 7, "Connecting Data Analysis and Instructional Improvement," to allow student learning data to drive instructional decision making, they are less likely to fall into potentially ineffective "follow the herd" practices. For example, at the end of this chapter's story, the sixth-grade team was gung-ho to implement a set of targeted interventions. By creating, implementing, and analyzing a set of writing assessments, however, the team might find that some of their assumptions about student writing were incorrect. If the team members are able to think and speak independently, they will be able to revise their intervention approach and match it to student needs.

Surowiecki's (2004) final condition for group intelligence is a certain level of decentralization. This is a condition that school leaders must attend to, and it can represent a difficult balancing act.

On one hand, professional learning teams must have a high degree of autonomy and decision-making authority in order to develop a high group IQ. If teams are not given the flexibility to define the scope of their work, and are not invested with the power to implement shared decisions, the divergent, organic thinking that drives true innovation is stifled. For example, if Steve, the principal of Central Middle, were to step in and tell the sixth-grade team that the school was purchasing a schoolwide writing program and that they needed to scrap their plans for developing writing interventions, he would severely undermine the sixth-grade team's development as a high-performing group.

On the other hand, teams benefit from a certain amount of structure earlier in their development, and schools as organizations benefit from some level of coordination across multiple teams. There is no way that the sixth-grade team could have had the conversation that took place at the start of this chapter back in August without some level of coordination at the school level. They required a certain amount of guidance and support from administration to get from where they were at the beginning of the school year to where they are now. In addition, other teams throughout the building would likely benefit from the insights and strategies that the sixth-grade team developed. It is up to school leaders to ensure that the cross-fertilization of ideas happens throughout a school.

In summary, Surowiecki's theory of collective intelligence adds a whole new dimension to the concept of a professional learning team. A professional learning team is not just a setting in which individual teachers come together, learn from each other, and then return to their individual classrooms. A professional learning team is a collective entity that takes responsibility for a large group of students and, through a variety of structured processes (such as developing common assessments, analyzing student data, and reflective conversations), is constantly evolving, developing a collective intelligence about practice. Individual teachers maintain their independence while becoming extensions of the professional learning team, which is in a constant cycle of growth and improvement. By working together, the members of a professional learning team are able to create something greater than themselves: a collective, organic vehicle that is more than simply the sum of the parts.

Recommendations

When teams develop a collective intelligence and use that intelligence to implement highly successful practices such as team-based interventions, they can achieve a level of performance that is astonishing. The following are our recommendations for helping teams to take this final step in their development.

Encourage and Support Innovative Practices

One of the truths of innovation is that when teachers and teams go out on a limb to attempt new practices and approaches, sometimes they fail. Successful teams and supportive school leaders accept failure as part of the process of innovation.

Accepting that failure is a part of innovation does not mean that teachers and school leaders maintain ineffective innovations. High-performing teams identify and eliminate poor innovations quickly, but they view those failures as learning opportunities instead of setbacks. While the sixth-grade team may struggle initially in implementing a writing intervention, members can learn from their mistakes and improve their practices to create a revised plan that *will* lead to better student writing.

There is also an important difference between accepting that it is okay for *innovations* to fail and accepting that it is okay for *students* to fail. In a professional learning community, student failure is unacceptable. Effective school leaders have to be willing to allow teachers to fail in terms of innovative practices (for example, the creative lesson that bombs and the initial writing intervention that does not pan out)—and effective members of learning teams have to be willing to allow themselves to try new things and fail—in order to create an environment that encourages and supports the exploration of new practices.

Emphasize Process Over Product With Dialogue in High-Functioning Teams

In chapter 4, "Supporting Team Development," we stressed that teams in early stages of development need specific tasks on which to focus their energies, such as developing common assessments or creating action plans. Novice teams have yet to develop the intrateam dynamics necessary for effective improvisational dialogue, and the creation of products successfully narrows the focus of a team's conversations.

As teams become high functioning, however, process becomes more important than product because the kind of deep collective reflection that leads to transformational insights about teaching and learning cannot emerge in narrowed conversations. School leaders supporting independent teams that have reached the *performing* stage of growth should, therefore, place less emphasis on the development of products and instead judge team success by the emergence of reflective practices.

By that definition, the outcome worth celebrating in the story that started this chapter is less about the specific writing intervention strategy that the sixth-grade team developed. Instead, the outcome worth celebrating is the recognition on the part of a group of interconnected teachers that interventions are necessary and the belief that they have the capacity to design meaningful solutions together. Process mattered more than product.

Engage Teams in Conversation About Their Team-Based Interventions

Administrators never make an appearance in the sixth-grade team's conversation at the start of this chapter, and that is to be expected. Most of the work and the dialogue that happens in professional learning teams occur without administrator participation.

This does not mean, however, that once teams become high functioning, school leaders can or should completely disengage. In fact, just the opposite is true.

As teams take on increasingly sophisticated opportunities for reflection, school leaders should continue to engage those teachers in conversations about their practices. This strategy can pay a number of dividends. First, school leaders bring an outside perspective to a team conversation that can help add to the creative process. By staying in touch with intervention-based conversations throughout a school, school leaders can also cross-pollinate ideas. It may be that the eighth-grade language arts team is struggling with some of the same questions as the sixth-grade team. Because administrators and instructional coaches have the opportunity to sit in on meetings throughout a PLC, they can serve as the "glue" in a school, connecting individuals, teams, and ideas across subject areas and grade levels. The handout at the end of this chapter (Tracking the Interventions in Your Building, page 201) might help you track the team-based interventions that are developing in your building.

It is important to note that "engaging teams in conversation" does not mean telling teams what they should do. The most important role an administrator can play at this stage in team development is that of questioner. By asking teams about their intervention practices—Why did you implement this strategy? What data did you use in making that decision? What outcomes are you hoping to achieve?—administrators can help professional learning teams clarify their thinking. For those teams that have not yet made a decision to implement team-based interventions, a pointed question from administration can help jump-start the process.

Stress Collective Intelligence Over Individual Intelligence

In their book *Reframing Organizations: Artistry, Choice, and Leadership*, Lee Bolman and Terrence Deal (2003) talk about the symbolic power of leaders to shape and define an organization's culture and practices. In what they say and do not say, in what they do and do not do, school leaders send messages to their colleagues about their beliefs and priorities. One of the symbolic shifts that is critically important in a PLC occurs when school leaders—principals, instructional coaches, and classroom teachers—begin to talk about and emphasize the collective over the individual.

School leaders can accomplish this in a variety of ways. When speaking with teachers, remember to focus all conversations on collective, rather than individual efforts. What has the *team* identified as its areas of focus for the semester? How are students performing throughout the *team*? What challenges is the *team* experiencing? What one or two *team-based* practices have been most successful this year?

Also consider rewarding collective effort. Many schools recognize an employee of the month. What about a team of the month? Taking it a step further, at staff meetings, ask teams to present on their efforts and successful initiatives. By using your symbolic power to emphasize collaborative efforts, rather than individual ones, you can send a powerful message that collective intelligence is a prized commodity.

Recommended Resources for More Information on Lesson Study

- The Lesson Study Research Group at Teachers College, Columbia University, has a number of practical resources. You can find it online at www.tc.edu/lessonstudy/lessonstudy.html.

- An online article by Sonal Chokshi and Clea Fernandez in *The Professional Journal for Education* from Phi Delta Kappa explores challenges to the use of the Japanese Lesson Study model. You can find the article online at www.pdkintl.org/kappan/k0403cho.htm.

- The Lesson Study Group at Mills College lists a number of articles and resources that explain lesson study and provide recommendations on its implementation. You can find it online at www.lessonresearch.net.

Recommended Resources for More Information on Action Research

- Jean McNiff's action-research booklet can be found online at www.jeanmcniff.com/booklet1.html.

- An article by Emily Calhoun in *Educational Leadership* provides a case study of how to implement action research in a school. You can find it online at www.wethersfield.k12.ct.us/Curriculum/action_research.pdf.

- For nearly twenty years, Marian Mohr has been writing about the work of teacher researchers. She has published countless articles and books about the action-research process on behalf of the National Writing Project. Her 2008 article provides a complete chronology of her publications and includes direct links to many pieces available online. You can access the article at www.nwp.org/cs/public/print/resource/2508.

- The Graduate School of Education at George Mason University has assembled an impressive collection of resources for teachers interested in beginning action-research projects that covers topics ranging from collecting data to publishing findings. You can find it online at http://gse.gmu.edu/research/tr/tr_action/.

- Richard Sagor's *Guiding School Improvement with Action Research* (2000) is a classic title that provides readers with a foundational understanding of the connections between action research and improved teaching and learning as well as a detailed overview of the action-research process.

- Wikipedia provides a general overview of action research, along with suggested readings and resource links. You can find that listing online at http://en.wikipedia.org/wiki/Action_research.

Tracking the Interventions in Your Building

School leaders can often best support efforts at intervention by documenting and cross-pollinating effective strategies across their buildings. Use this handout to track the work being done by the diverse teams in your school and to identify potential overlaps that can strengthen the collective intelligence of your teachers.

Intervention Effort	Evidence of Effectiveness	Required Resources	Key Players/Who to Approach
In a few short sentences, describe this team-based intervention effort. Include the name of the team involved and the reason the intervention was initially designed.	How do you know that this intervention was effective? What evidence has the team collected to show that the intervention has impacted *students* in a positive way?	What resources were necessary to ensure effective implementation of this intervention? Include consumable physical supplies as well as professional development, additional time, or additional faculty members. Can your school support the expansion of this intervention strategy?	What teams could benefit from learning more about this intervention? Which faculty members were essential to the success of this intervention? Who are they connected to in your building? How can you use their relationships to spread this intervention?

EQUAL PARTS LOOKING BACK AND LOOKING FORWARD

Steve loved the last day of school. He loved shaking the hands of all the eighth graders as they walked across the stage at the end-of-year ceremony. He loved the video montage that the PTA parents put together, ending with Sarah McLachlan's song "I Will Remember You." He loved waving goodbye to the buses as they pulled out of the parking lot, full for the last time that year.

But most of all, he loved the quiet of the building after everyone else had left. The bittersweet sense of finality and emptiness in the silent halls spoke to him—halls that only hours earlier had been filled with laughing students. It was like freezing time, and it only happened once a year.

This year, however, felt different. This year, the last day of school felt less like an ending and more like a momentary pause in an ongoing cycle. After all, Steve knew that many of the professional learning teams in the school were planning to meet over the summer to build on the structures and processes they had collectively developed this year. Even though the kids were gone, Steve was feeling a sense of urgency and anticipation that did not usually set in until August.

"I guess PLCs really do change everything," Steve thought to himself, smiling at his sentimental mood. The phone rang, breaking his spell of introspection. Steve recognized the superintendent's phone number.

"Dr. Tines, how are you?"

"I'm doing well, Steve. The real question is, How are you? Has your first year at Central Middle been everything you hoped it would be?"

"You asked the question I was just thinking about. The simple answer is 'Yes,' but the longer answer is more complicated. I thought I knew what to expect when you first offered me the position, but I think it's a classic case of not knowing what you don't know. It has been a great year, but I think I learned more than anyone else in the building."

Dr. Tines chuckled to herself. She loved Steve's honesty and practice of open reflection—it was one of the reasons she had chosen him to lead Central Middle School. She had known that Steve would exemplify and model the "learning" in "professional learning community."

"I know we'll talk about this in much more detail during your performance review in a couple weeks, but give me the elevator pitch, Steve: what did you learn this year, and what are you doing to get ready for next year?"

Steve grinned; leave it to Pat Tines to ask the million dollar questions. To be honest, he hadn't yet taken much time to think about next steps for the following year. He had planned a two-day offsite meeting in August with his core team, and he was hoping that much of next year's focus would come out through those conversations. He had also given a PLC survey to his staff several weeks before the end of school, focusing on how teams managed their PLC meetings and the types of tasks on which they focused their time. Steve had not yet done a careful analysis of the results, but his back-of-the-envelope calculations suggested that different teams were in very different stages of development.

"The elevator pitch, huh? I would say I learned that the biggest challenges of school leadership—managing and navigating the different personalities of your staff, keeping your school focused on what's most important, making effective decisions that impact numerous people—are exponentially more challenging in a PLC. But at the same time, the rewards of our profession—uniting as colleagues, learning and improving every day, and seeing student success really happen, one kid at a time—are exponentially more gratifying in a PLC."

"Beautifully said, Steve. But I noticed that you avoided the more difficult half of my question: what about next year?"

"Well, I was hoping my poetic language would distract you." In actuality, Steve thought that the next year might be even more challenging than this one. He knew that several influential members of his staff had never really bought into the PLC concept, but had held their tongues as they waited to get the feel of their new principal. Steve guessed that their opposition would likely be more vocal this coming year.

In addition, Central Middle's growing student population and the retirement of several staff members meant that Steve had multiple staff positions to fill next year. While this represented a great opportunity to bring talented new people on board, it also represented a challenge. How would new personalities change the character of the learning teams they joined? Would teams be willing to revisit their norms and action plans, or would they expect new members to simply go along with premade decisions?

Finally, Steve had seen divisions begin to develop within his core team. He was hoping that the two-day retreat would help to address these divisions, but Steve knew that there was an equally likely chance that two days of face-to-face interaction could end up adding fuel to the fire.

The main divisive issue involved the use of different practices at different grade levels. For example, sixth-grade teams had made the decision not to count homework in student grades this past year, and several seventh-grade teachers were beginning to voice their opposition to this plan. If seventh graders would still be expected to complete homework for a grade, wasn't the sixth-grade practice setting students up for later failure, and setting seventh-grade teachers up for encounters with unhappy parents?

Steve had allowed teams and grade levels wide latitude this past year in devising their own practices. As long as teams could show that they had achieved defensible consensus, he was willing to empower teams to make their own decisions. But in several cases, those decisions had become mutually exclusive, and now core members were butting heads as they defended their own practices and attacked the practices of others. Steve had urged teams to use the school's mission as a litmus test for making decisions, but what happens when two teams have equally compelling arguments for practices that are at odds with each other?

As Steve explained these challenges to Superintendent Tines, she voiced her agreement. "No one can convince me that we should return to the days of teacher isolation," she responded, "but that doesn't mean that collaboration is easy. If there is anything that I can do to support you and your school, just let me know. You've done a heck of a good job this year!"

Steve thanked his boss and hung up the phone. He looked down at the pile of résumés sitting on his desk and decided they could wait until Monday. Besides, Michael and Karen would be in next week to help him sort through them.

Walking out of his office, Steve hesitated for one last moment before turning out the light. It had been one of the most challenging years of his professional career, but it had also been one of the most rewarding. His phone call with Superintendent Tines had reminded him of their conversation from a year ago, when she had offered him the job as Central Middle's principal. If he had know then what he knew now, would he still have accepted her offer? *Absolutely!*

Steve turned out the light, locked the door, and broke into a big smile as he walked to his car, the last one sitting in the lot.

Lessons From the Front Line

We would love to tell you how Central Middle School's story ends, but you know as well as we do that the hard work of dedicated educators never stops.

Steve has good reason to be confident, though. Like the leaders of the most accomplished learning communities, Steve and his teachers have laid a foundation for future success that Central Middle can build on for years to come. A strong mission now drives decisions at Central Middle—decisions from which teachers will be hired to how the budget will be spent. Instructional decisions across classrooms are more naturally aligned because teams remain committed to one another and to a common vision. Opportunities for remediation and enrichment are in place, collective reflection is more common, innovative practices are encouraged, productive conflict is understood, and continuous improvement has become something more than a cliché.

Will Central Middle be confronted with unexpected barriers to overcome in the next few years? Definitely. As Steve explained in his conversation with Superintendent Tines, next year may end up being more challenging than the last.

Regardless of what the future may hold, however, Steve knows only too well that a focus on collaboration and a commitment to meeting the needs of every student must remain a constant. To put it simply, everyone at Central Middle must walk forward together and remain willing to hold one another accountable for *ensuring student success.* In the words of Richard DuFour, Rebecca DuFour, and Robert Eaker (2008):

> When confronted with difficulty and uncertainty, it is natural for people to seek the security and comfort of the status quo. It will always be more comfortable, and easier, to focus on teaching rather than learning, to work in isolation rather than collaboratively, to use summative rather than formative assessments, to leave the question of responding to student difficulties to the discretion of each teacher rather than create a systematic response, to assign responsibility for results to others rather than ourselves, to care only about what happens in our room or our school rather than concern ourselves with the success and well-being of others, to cling to our assumptions and practices rather than examine them. It will always be easier to quit and return to the familiar than to persevere in the face of challenges, reversals, and disappointments. Therefore, the key to success in implementing PLC concepts is demonstrating the discipline to endure at the hard work of change rather than retreating to the comfort of traditional practices. (pp. 421–422)

By writing this book—by engaging you in stories capturing the realities, struggles, and achievements of day-to-day life in a developing PLC; by offering insights and lessons that we have learned from our experiences working in schools at various stages of PLC development; and by providing practical advice and resources that you can use to improve professional learning in your building—our goal has been to help you to walk forward with the same confidence as Steve and his Central Middle School colleagues simply because confidence inspires action. As DuFour, DuFour, Eaker, and Many (2006) explain:

> When people begin to act, people begin to hope. When people begin to gain hope, they begin to behave differently. When people behave differently, they experience success. When people experience success, their attitudes change. When a person's attitude changes, it affects other people. This is the essence of reculturing schools into professional learning communities. (p. 6)

While the challenges of reculturing schools into professional learning communities are great, the rewards—successful, empowered practitioners and students who are learning regardless of circumstance—are worth the effort!

REFERENCES

Achinstein, B. (2002). Conflict amid community: The micropolitics of teacher collaboration. *Teachers College Record, 104*(3), 421–455.

Alleman, G. B. (2004). *Forming, storming, norming, performing and adjourning.* Accessed at www.niwotridge.com/PDFs/FormStormNormPerform.pdf on August 14, 2009.

Ball, P. (2004). *Critical mass: How one thing leads to another.* New York: Farrar, Straus, and Giroux.

Barth, R. (2006). Improving relationships within the schoolhouse. *Educational Leadership, 63*(6), 8–13.

Block, P. (2003). *The answer to how? is yes: Acting on what matters.* San Francisco: Berrett-Koehler.

Bolman, L. G., & Deal, T. E. (2003). *Reframing organizations: Artistry, choice, and leadership.* Hoboken, NJ: Jossey-Bass.

Boudett, K. P., City, E. A., & Murnane, R. J. (Eds.). (2005). *Data wise: A step-by-step guide to using assessment results to improve teaching and learning.* Cambridge, MA: Harvard Education Publishing Group.

Bryk, A. S., & Schneider, B. (2002). *Trust in schools: A core resource for improvement.* New York: Russell Sage Foundation.

Buffum, A. (2008). Trust: The secret ingredient to successful shared leadership. In *The collaborative administrator: Working together as a professional learning community* (pp. 55–71). Bloomington, IN: Solution Tree Press.

Collins, J. (2001). *Good to great: Why some companies make the leap . . . and others don't.* New York: HarperCollins.

Conzemius, A., & O'Neill, J. (2002). *The handbook for SMART school teams.* Bloomington, IN: Solution Tree Press.

DuFour, R. (2004a). What is a "professional learning community"? *Educational Leadership, 61*(8), 6–11.

DuFour, R. (2004b, Spring). Leading edge: The best staff development is in the workplace, not in a workshop. *Journal of Staff Development, 25*(2). Accessed at www.nsdc.org/library/publications/jsd/dufour252.cfm on April 4, 2004.

DuFour, R. (2008). Introduction. In *The collaborative teacher: Working together as a professional learning community* (pp. 1–8). Bloomington, IN: Solution Tree Press.

DuFour, R., DuFour, R., & Eaker, R. (2008). *Revisiting professional learning communities at work: New insights for improving schools.* Bloomington, IN: Solution Tree Press.

DuFour, R., DuFour, R., Eaker, R., & Many, T. (2006). *Learning by doing: A handbook for professional learning communities at work.* Bloomington, IN: Solution Tree Press.

DuFour, R., & Eaker, R. (1998). *Professional learning communities at work: Best practices for enhancing student achievement.* Bloomington, IN: Solution Tree Press.

Eaker, R., DuFour, R., & DuFour, R. (2002). *Getting started: Reculturing schools to become professional learning communities.* Bloomington, IN: Solution Tree Press.

Erkens, C. (2008a). Growing teacher leadership. In *The collaborative administrator: Working together as a professional learning community* (pp. 39–53). Bloomington, IN: Solution Tree Press.

Erkens, C. (2008b). The new teacher leader: Transforming education from inside the classroom. In *The collaborative teacher: Working together as a professional learning community* (pp. 11–28). Bloomington, IN: Solution Tree Press.

Ferriter, W. (2009). Yes, I can. Responsible assessment in an era of accountability. In *The teacher as assessment leader* (pp. 55–86). Bloomington, IN: Solution Tree Press.

Fullan, M. (2008). *The six secrets of change: What the best leaders do to help their organizations survive and thrive.* San Francisco: Jossey-Bass.

Gladwell, M. (2002). *The tipping point: How little things can make a big difference.* Boston: Little, Brown.

Grinder, M. (1997). *The science of nonverbal communication.* Battle Ground, WA: Michael Grinder & Associates.

Grossman, P., Wineburg, S., & Woolworth, S. (2001). Toward a theory of teacher community. *Teachers College Record, 103,* 942–1012.

Hord, S. M. (1997). Professional learning communities: What are they and why are they important? *Issues About Change, 6*(1). Accessed at www.sedl.org/change/issues/issues61.html on August 14, 2009.

Huff, S. (2008). Digging deep into data. In *The collaborative administrator: Working together as a professional learning community* (pp. 197–215). Bloomington, IN: Solution Tree Press.

Jessie, L. G. (2008). The principal's principles of leadership in a professional learning community. In *The collaborative administrator: Working together as a professional learning community* (pp. 109–124). Bloomington, IN: Solution Tree Press.

Kain, D. L. (2003). *Camel-makers: Building effective teacher teams together.* Westerville, OH: National Middle School Association.

Kotter, J. (1996). *Leading change.* Boston: Harvard Business School.

Kouzes, J., & Posner, B. (1999). *Encouraging the heart: A leader's guide to rewarding and recognizing others.* San Francisco: Jossey-Bass.

Lencioni, P. (2002). *The five dysfunctions of a team.* San Francisco: Jossey-Bass.

Levine, M. D. (2002). *The myth of laziness.* New York: Simon & Schuster.

Lewis, C., Perry, R., & Hurd, J. (2004). A deeper look at lesson study. *Educational Leadership, 61*(5), 18–22.

Love, N. (2007, July). *Using data and getting results: Improving student achievement through collaborative inquiry.* Session presented at the National Staff Development Council (NSDC) Summer Conference on Teacher Leadership, Denver, CO.

Love, N., Stiles, K. E., Mundry, S., & DiRanna, K. (2008). *The data coach's guide to improving learning for all students: Unleashing the power of collaborative inquiry.* Thousand Oaks, CA: Corwin Press.

Martin, T. L. (2008). Professional learning in a professional learning community. In *The collaborative administrator: Working together as a professional learning community* (pp. 143–157). Bloomington, IN: Solution Tree Press.

McNiff, J. (2003). *Action research for professional development.* Accessed at www.jeanmcniff.com/booklet1.html on August 14, 2009.

Moller, G., & Pankake, A. (2006). *Lead with me: A principal's guide to teacher leadership.* Larchmont, NY: Eye on Education.

Muhammad, A. (2009). *Transforming school culture: How to overcome staff division.* Bloomington, IN: Solution Tree Press.

Noonan, P. (2008). Breaking through the barriers of time: How to find time to support struggling students. In *The collaborative administrator: Working together as a professional learning community* (pp. 159–178). Bloomington, IN: Solution Tree Press.

Owens, R. G., & Valesky, T. C. (2007). *Organizational behavior in education: Adaptive leadership and school reform.* Boston: Pearson Education.

Parscale, G. (2008). Building a pyramid of interventions. In *The collaborative administrator: Working together as a professional learning community* (pp. 181–195). Bloomington, IN: Solution Tree Press.

Patterson, K., Grenny, J., Maxfield, D., McMillan, R., & Switzler, A. (2008). *Influencer: The power to change anything.* New York: McGraw-Hill.

Patterson, K., Grenny, J., McMillan, R., & Switzler, A. (2002). *Crucial conversations: Tools for talking when stakes are high.* New York: McGraw-Hill.

Perlstein, L. (2007). *Tested: One American school struggles to make the grade.* New York: Henry Holt and Company.

Rowan, B. (1995, Fall). Focusing reform: How the Lee, Smith and Croninger report can enhance school restructuring. *Issues in restructuring schools, 9,* 14–16.

Sawyer, R. K. (2007). *Group genius: The creative power of collaboration.* New York: Basic Books.

Schmoker, M. (1999). *Results: The key to continuous school improvement* (2nd ed.). Alexandria, VA: Association for Supervision and Curriculum Development.

Schmoker, M. (2005). No turning back: The ironclad case for professional learning communities. In R. DuFour, R. Eaker, & R. DuFour (Eds.), *On common ground: The power of professional learning communities* (pp. 135–153). Bloomington, IN: Solution Tree Press.

Schmoker, M. J. (2006). *Results now: How we can achieve unprecedented improvements in teaching and learning.* Alexandria, VA: Association for Supervision and Curriculum Development.

Shirky, C. (2008). *Here comes everybody: The power of organizing without organizations.* New York: Penguin.

Sparks, D. (2004). From hunger aid to school reform: An interview with Jerry Sternin. *Journal of Staff Development, 25*(1), 46–51. Accessed at www.nsdc.org/news/getDocument. cfm?articleID=456 on August 14, 2009.

Sparks, S. K. (2008). Creating intentional collaboration. In *The collaborative teacher: Working together as a professional learning community* (pp. 31–55). Bloomington, IN: Solution Tree Press.

Sternin, J., & Choo, R. (2000, January-February). The power of positive deviance. *Harvard Business Review,* 14–15.

Stiggins, R. (2005). Assessment FOR learning: Building a culture of confident learners. In R. DuFour, R. Eaker, & R. DuFour (Eds.), *On common ground: The power of professional learning communities* (pp. 65–84). Bloomington, IN: Solution Tree Press.

Surowiecki, J. (2004). *The wisdom of crowds: Why the many are smarter than the few and how collective wisdom shapes business, economies, societies and nations.* New York: Random House.

Tschannen-Moran, M. (2004). *Trust matters: Leadership for successful schools.* San Francisco: Jossey-Bass.

Tuckman, B. (1965). Developmental sequence in small groups. *Psychological Bulletin, 63,* 384–399.

Vygotsky, L. S., & Cole, M. (1978). *Mind in society: The development of higher psychological processes.* Cambridge: Harvard University Press.

Weick, K. E. (1976, March). Educational organizations as loosely coupled systems. *Administrative Science Quarterly, 21*(1), 1–19.

Wheatley, M. J. (1999). *Leadership and the new science* (2nd ed.). San Francisco: Berrett-Koehler.

Willingham, D. T. (2009). *Why don't students like school? A cognitive scientist answers questions about how the mind works and what it means for the classroom.* San Francisco: Jossey-Bass.

INDEX

Revisiting Professional Learning Communities at Work™: New Insights for Improving Schools
Richard DuFour, Rebecca DuFour, and Robert Eaker
This 10th anniversary sequel to *Professional Learning Communities at Work™* offers advanced insights on deep implementation, the commitment/ consensus issue, and the human side of PLC. **BKF252**

Raising the Bar and Closing the Gap Whatever It Takes
Richard DuFour, Rebecca DuFour, Robert Eaker, and Gayle Karhanek
This sequel to the best-selling *Whatever It Takes: How Professional Learning Communities Respond When Kids Don't Learn* expands on original ideas and presses further with new insights. Foundational concepts combine with real-life examples of schools throughout North America that have gone from traditional cultures to PLCs. **BKF378**

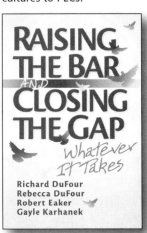

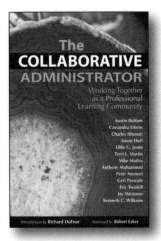

The Collaborative Administrator: Working Together as a Professional Learning Community
Austin Buffum, Cassandra Erkens, Charles Hinman, Susan Huff, Lillie G. Jessie, Terri L. Martin, Mike Mattos, Anthony Muhammad, Peter Noonan, Geri Parscale, Eric Twadell, Jay Westover, and Kenneth C. Williams
Foreword by Robert Eaker
In a culture of shared leadership, the administrator's role is more important than ever. This book addresses your toughest challenges with practical strategies and inspiring insight. **BKF256**

The Principal as Assessment Leader
Edited by Thomas R. Guskey
Expert practitioners address the role of school leaders to model and spark positive change and ignite a shift toward assessments that drive instruction. **BK344**

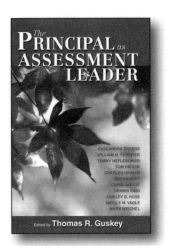

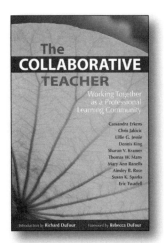

The Collaborative Teacher: Working Together as a Professional Learning Community
Cassandra Erkens, Chris Jakicic, Lillie G. Jessie, Dennis King, Sharon V. Kramer, Thomas W. Many, Mary Ann Ranells, Ainsley B. Rose, Susan K. Sparks, and Eric Twadell
Foreword by Rebecca DuFour
Introduction by Richard DuFour
Transform education from inside the classroom with this accessible anthology. Specific techniques, supporting research, and real classroom stories illustrate how to work together to create a guaranteed and viable curriculum and use data to inform instruction. **BKF257**

The Teacher as Assessment Leader
Edited by Thomas R. Guskey
Packed with practical strategies for designing, analyzing, and using assessments, this book shows how to turn best practices into usable solutions. **BKF345**